The Monuments of Civilisation

Text by
GILDO FOSSATI

Translated by
BRUCE PENMAN

Foreword by
ANTHONY BURGESS

CHINA

New English Library

Frontispiece
The Liaodi Ta, or Pagoda for Controlling the
Enemy, at Dingxian, Hebei. The pagoda was
built as part of the Kaiyuan, or Temple of
Beginning of the Principle, near the south
gate of the city of Dingxian. The temple itself
has been destroyed and only the pagoda
remains. Construction of the pagoda began in
AD 1001, on the instructions of the Emperor
Zhen Zhong, of the Northern Song dynasty
(AD 960–1126). Completed in 1055, it was
designed to overlook and control the enemy –
that is to say, the army of the Liao dynasty. Of
brick construction and about 70 metres (230
feet) in height, it has eleven storeys and is an
example of the 'louge' (tower of pavilions)
style. Each storey has an arched doorway and
four square windows. The building is
octagonal in plan.

Editor-in-chief MARIELLA DE BATTISTI

Compilation DONATELLA VOLPI

Page make-up GIANCARLO LACCHINI

Design ENRICO SEGRÈ

Copyright © 1982 by Arnoldo Mondadori
Editore S.p.A. Milan – Kodansha Ltd,
Tokyo
Illustrations Copyright © 1982 by
Kodansha Ltd
Text Copyright © 1982 by Arnoldo
Mondadori S.p.A. Milan – Kodansha Ltd,
Tokyo
English translation Copyright © 1983 by
Arnoldo Mondadori S.p.A. Milan

Italian edition first published 1982 by
Arnoldo Mondadori Editore

This edition first published in 1983 by
New English Library, Mill Road, Dunton
Green, Sevenoaks, Kent.
Editorial office: 47 Bedford Square,
London WC1B 3DP

Photoset in Great Britain by
Rowland Phototypesetting Ltd,
Bury St Edmunds, Suffolk
Printed in Italy by Arnoldo Mondadori

British Library Cataloguing in Publication
Data

Fossati, Gildo
   China. – (Monuments of civilisation)
   1. China – Civilisation
   I. Title   II. Series
   951   DS721

ISBN: 0 450 06048 9

Contents

China: A Foreword

THE GATEWAY to China, ancient or modern, is the Chinese language. My own contacts with the country have been more linguistic than geographic. When I lived in Malaysia, which has a large Chinese population, I regarded it as my secondary duty to try to learn Chinese – my primary duty being, of course, to learn Malay. Naturally, being in daily contact with Chinese coolies, policemen, shopkeepers, schoolmasters and government officials, I could not fail to become acquainted with China's exported culture – its religions, philosophies, cuisines, folklore, even its architecture. But, so long as personal contacts were made and sustained in the lingua franca of Malaysia – English – I could not hope to know how the Chinese mentality worked and what was the nature of the civilisation built on that mentality. So I settled, in my spare time, to the study of the major dialect of modern China – *Kuo-yü*, or the National Language – and, for a long time, considered my task hopeless. For the official language of China, like any other official language, is a sort of abstraction. The Malaysian Chinese who spoke Cantonese or Hakka often had little acquaintance with *Kuo-yü*, though their children learned it at school. But I refer to the spoken language: many Chinese whose spoken dialects differ from each other as Rumanian differs from Spanish are able to meet on the common ground of the written or printed script. Here is a situation which does not apply in Europe, where we expect a script to be a representation of the sounds we utter in our languages. The Chinese language is two things: a system of sounds and structures, but also a script whose study forms a quite different discipline. The Chinese utter meaningful sounds, like the rest of us, but they write a script which attempts to symbolise the ideas which lie behind the sounds.

But learning to speak Chinese, without reference to the script, involved a reorientation of thinking, phonating, articulating and intoning quite different from anything I had known with other languages – even including Malay, which is a thoroughly Oriental tongue and refuses to behave like Italian or English. Chinese do not think in terms of words but in terms of syllables which are the bricks of the building we call an utterance. There seem to be about four hundred of these basic bricks, and they can consist of (a) a single vowel or diphthong, (b) a vowel or diphthong preceded by a consonant, followed by a consonant, or both preceded and followed by a consonant. Typical Chinese bricks are: *a, ai, ang, cha, chang, chiang, ch'iao.* Each of these is a free morpheme, or word, but they are placed together to form bigger words. The sounds of these words resemble those of our own Western languages, but one does not have to go far in the language to discover that the resemblances are very superficial. Thus, we oppose voiced sounds like *b* and *d* and *q* to their unvoiced equivalents *p* and *t* and *k*, but the Chinese opposition is between unvoiced consonants that are aspirated and those that are not aspirated. Such a pattern is very difficult for the Westerner to learn.

Now, if you consider that the pattern of a Chinese morpheme, or minimal meaningful structure, is limited to a vowel, a vowel and a consonant, or a vowel and two consonants, it is clear that there are just not enough of these little structures to provide a sufficient vocabulary for a civilised language. So Chinese introduces a modifying device to vary the meanings of a morpheme – a way of intoning the vowel which gives the language its distinctive singing quality. Learning Chinese, my first difficulty appeared when I had to distinguish between the words for *buy* and *sell*. Both are *mai*, but when *mai* means *buy* it has tone 3, and when it means *sell* it has tone 4. There are four tones in what we call Modern Standard Chinese (some dialects have more), and they may roughly be described as follows: tone 1 is a high level contour of pitch; tone 2 has a rising pitch; tone 3 dips in the middle; tone 4 is a falling pitch contour. But, in rapid speech, one tone tends to influence another, and the ear of the learner must learn an unwonted acuity. In saying *I want to buy* (*wo yao mai*) I had to drop my voice in the middle of the *mai*; in saying *I want to sell* (*wo yao mai*) I had to maintain a pattern of descent. To be on the safe side, I had to memorise the written forms of the two words which, as they represent different ideas, are very different in form:

buy   sell

If you want the Chinese word for *business*, which is a matter of buying and selling, you put the two symbols together and say *mai3-mai4*.

It is a highly logical language and it despises grammar – which, we must admit, is more decorative than useful. If I say *der Volk* instead of *das Volk*, I will be clearly understood by a German, but I will be despised as one who has failed in linguistic etiquette. Chinese has no articles, no verb endings and no noun inflections. And it reserves etiquette to verbal formulae which bespeak the graciousness of an ancient civilisation. If Mr Li, calling on someone, is asked by a servant, '*Hsien sheng kuei hsing*' ('What is your name, sir?'), he will reply: '*Pu kan tang*' ('I am unworthy of such an honorific as *sir*') and follow with '*Wo chien hsing Li*': 'I humble name Li.' Ask someone how many children he has, and you will convert the children into 'noble princes'. You will hear in reply: 'I have six little puppy dogs.' When my teacher called on me he would ask politely if I had yet partaken of food. I would reply that I had and ask if he himself had eaten. He would say: '*P'ien kuo la*', which carries the flavour of 'I have deprived you of your share' or 'I have acted in a selfish and improper manner.' This excessive politeness is the sign of a nation that has learned, over thousands of years, that civilisation is built on formal self-effacement.

It is possible, in time, to distinguish between these monosyllables that sound so alike at first and to ring the changes on the tones. But to master the reading or writing of Chinese script is an arduous task that requires a particular kind of visual memory. True, some symbols are easy, like the following:

one   man   table   cliff   mouth

but we can end up with symbols which contain anything from fourteen to seventeen strokes of the pen and seem excessively complex for the thing described:

鼻   龠   齒

nose   teeth   flute, pipe

True, you can see a few fangs in that second ideogram, but where is the flute or the flautist in the third? And does the *nose* ideogram represent complicated layers of olfactory sensation?

Generally, even with the most abstract words you can see the ghost of an original pictorial image – hence the term pictogram. The word for *brightness* presents the sun and the moon together, and *pu*, meaning *not*, seems to show a plant trying to grow with a preventive bar on top – a metaphor of opposition to a living process. But this is mere palaeography: no living Chinese sees the original images any more than Europeans see the hieroglyph of an ox in the capital A of the Roman alphabet. The Chinese symbols stand for morphemes and their configurations are taken in unanalytically.

Clearly, such a complex system of writing could only be developed by a leisured class of priests and scholars. The ideogram stands for an ancient inequality and perhaps, as with the Egyptian 'holy writing' which was democratised into the Phoenician syllabary, a desire to mystify the common people. Only in this century has the notion of democracy taken root, and democracy has demanded – as commerce too has demanded – a simpler system of verbal notation. The impulse towards phonetic representation of words came with the Phoenicians because they were a commercial people, not a democratic one (though trade, creating new hierarchies not based on noble blood, is a powerfully democratising force). The Chinese have developed their own Romanising technique, making it possible to set down any morpheme in phonetic symbols with diacritics indicating tone (a superscript line for tone 1, an acute accent for tone 2, a circumflex inverted for tone 3, and a grave accent for tone 4), but the Chinese generally have been slow to accept that the body of a word (meaning its sounds) has a superior validity to its soul or meaning. To jettison a writing system that has millennia of authority behind it, linking it with ancient poets and philosophers, is an act of filial impiety, and even modern industrial Communist China remains loyal to the scriptural tradition of the tyrannical emperors.

This conservatism in the field of language is, as we know, an aspect of a deeper conservatism. Attempts to apply revolutionary principles to the logical limit – as with the so-called 'cultural revolution' – never succeed in China. The living weight of the past rests, like the weight of the air they breathe, on its citizens – not only the pragmatic philosophy of Confucius but also the Taoist opposition of *yin* and *yang* which sustains the universe. There is also what may be termed a higher common sense, not necessarily cognate with what we of the West would regard as such, which has been bred out of centuries of not asking too much from the world: the Chinese have never had enough to eat, and they have never had enough justice. Their cuisine can be exquisite, but it is made out of the immediately feasible, not the grandiose dreams of French chefs. The Chinese elegance, which not even utilitarianism of the Marxist brand can extirpate, is an elegance of extreme economy – the thin-toned flute and the single flower in a vase.

Finally, the cult of economy and the sense of the immense antiquity of the Middle Kingdom combine in the language itself, which, I repeat, is the gateway to an understanding of the people. The incrustations of a past which stretches, without interruption, to remote beginnings hardly conceivable in the West, are embodied in the system of writing. But the spoken language seems based on the principle of making much out of very little. There is an immense elegance in the manner with which a structure of monosyllables and tones can be made to serve the subtlest discourse, without the elaborate luggage of grammatical terminations and agglutinative sesquipedalia. Such a language does not take kindly to evasive political pronouncements or orotund slogans. If we are told that the

Peking street in which the Russian embassy is located is called 'The Street of Struggle Against Revisionism', we smile at the pomposity. Call the street *Fan xiu lù* and the pomposity is at once deflated. For *lù* means a road or avenue, *fan* means to turn over (as a piece of paper) and *xiu* is to build or repair: you *xiu* (repair) a watch or *xiu* (trim) your nails. So you turn over or change a building process and you leave to the languages of the West the bloating of the image into the humourless terminology of the *apparatchik*. To gain our picture of modern China out of inept translation is a sure way to falsification, and the same is as true of the ancient country whose character and achievements, as well as struggles and sufferings, this volume memorialises.

Anthony Burgess

14   CHINA

The Land

CHINA LIES in the east of Asia, and covers some 9,600,000 square kilometres (3,700,000 square miles). It measures 5,000 kilometres (3,000 miles) from east to west, so that when the first rays of the sun begin to lighten the sky in Shandong, it is still dark night in the Tarim valley and on the Pamirs. From north to south it is 5,500 kilometres (3,400 miles) long, encompassing 49 degrees of latitude, ranging from the temperate zone of the north to the tropical climate of the south. Thus while the end of winter work is beginning in the fields of the south, in the north snow is still falling. The natural boundaries of the land are formed by the Gobi desert to the north, the Tibetan massif to the west and south-west, the foothills of the Himalayan chain, the Song koi or Red River plain, and the Pacific Ocean, or South China Sea, to the south, and to the east the Pacific Ocean once again, here known as the Bohai Sea, the Yellow Sea, or the East China Sea. Some five thousand islands dot these seas, the most outstanding being the chain of large islands in the South China Sea including Hainan, Taiwan, Benghu, and Ihoushan, which form a kind of maritime 'great wall' guarding the mainland.

The geographical position of China thus effectively cut it off to the west, south-west, and east, leaving open only the north, and a small area in the south. Here the settled populations of Burmese, Thais, Khmer, Yao (in Laos), and Yfueh (in Vietnam) occupied the mountainous or jungly, marshy and subtropical zones of South Asia lying between China and the sea, establishing kingdoms and developing distinct civilisations and cultures according to their own genius, at different periods, and much later than the birth and spread of Chinese culture. In investigating the development of Chinese culture the peoples of South-East Asia may thus safely be ignored.

It was the north which was the great door for the nomadic populations who attempted on several occasions to break into China, forcing the Chinese to erect against them the famous bulwark of the Great Wall. This did not, however, prevent Turks, Mongols, and Manchus from breaking through and remaining in China for many centuries; but being culturally considerably more backward than the Chinese, these peoples adopted the manners of their subjects and became sinocised.

The geographical position of China thus not only affected Chinese culture but gave it its distinctive character, since it came into contact only with less developed peoples, and never with other higher civilisations.

There was one break in the ring isolating the country, and this was the opening in the north-west between the northern slopes of the Nanshan and the desert, in the Lopnor region. Through this ran the Silk Road which crossed central Asia to reach the eastern shores of the Mediterranean. This was the route by which Buddhism reached China, along with the merchants' caravans, and with it the art of Gandhara and Bamiyan, and by which China received the influence of Iran, India, and the Muslim world, and even distant echoes from the Roman empire.

Bronze vase of the 'tsun' type, shaped like an owl – late Shang period (eleventh century BC). These ritual vessels were often in the shape of birds or animals – owls, tigers, rhinoceroses or elephants – and were used to hold rice wine. They were in very common use in the late Shang period and the Zhou period. Cooked foods were also offered in the sacrificial rites, and Shang bronzes occur in many different shapes, often closely modelled on items of ordinary domestic earthenware. Careful study of these shapes makes it possible to establish their original use, and to separate them into cooking vessels, serving vessels and storage vessels.

Prehistoric China

SOME FIVE hundred thousand years ago the north-east of China was inhabited by an erect hominid, standing about 1.57 metres (5 feet 1 inch) in height. These creatures lived by gathering and hunting, perhaps even eating human flesh, and had discovered fire. In 1918 the Swedish anthropologist J. G. Andersson discovered a cave near Khon kon dian, twenty-five kilometres (fifteen miles) from Peking, which had been inhabited during the middle Pleistocene. Excavations under the Swede Birger Bohlni carried out some years later, between 1927 and 1939, brought to light fragments of skeletons of some forty individuals of a type which was given the name *Sinanthropus pekinensis*; these were able to make crude stone tools typical of the lower Palaeolithic Age. Following these discoveries excavations were carried out with great vigour in various different regions of China, in the search for remains by which to establish definite types and dates within the Pleistocene for Palaeolithic, Mesolithic, and even Neolithic man. As far as tracing the development of *Sinanthropus pekinensis* was concerned, the results proved disappointing, notwithstanding the interesting facts which they uncovered.

In 1930 new deposits were discovered in the Upper Cave of Zhou kou dian, dating from twenty-five million years ago, and thus from the upper Palaeolithic and the threshold of the Mesolithic. Between 1956 and 1957

Vase with painted decoration, from the Neolithic period of Yangshao in the province of Gansu (2500–1000 BC). The shape and the nature of the ornament show that this vase belongs to the Banshan culture. The clay is of a very fine texture, and the smooth profile shows that a potter's wheel has been used. From its narrow base, the vase swells out in the middle region, and then narrows and lengthens to form a neck, on which a handle is mounted. The dentate spiral decoration may indicate a funerary use.

Xian, Shânxi. A view of the Neolithic village of Banpo, near Xian (5000–3000 BC). First excavated in 1954, the settlement occupies a 200 metre (220 yard) square area, which contains the remains of round or square dwellings, about 5 metres (16½ feet) across, and communal buildings of larger size. All the buildings were partly underground, and were roofed with leaves. The whole village was surrounded by a ditch, the depth of which was 5–6 metres (16½–19½ feet), and it served both for defence and for the irrigation of the fields. Tombs were sited outside the ditch. The many utensils and other artefacts found at Banpo provide evidence of an industrious farming community that was also widely concerned with hunting and fishing. Especially interesting is the earthenware, both because of the quality of the clay and because of the variety of the decoration.

further excavations were carried out in Shanxi and the southern province of Guangxi.

The Jesuit priests Lincent and Teilhard de Chardin had discovered deposits of the Palaeolithic period dating from fifty million years ago on the borders of China, in the village of Shui dong kou, not far from Ningxia, in the Ordos region.

There is a great hiatus between the remains of the Palaeolithic and the late Neolithic period of the third millenium BC. We do not know what occurred during the twenty thousand years which separate the upper Palaeolithic and late Neolithic periods in China. This may well have been the period during which the loess stratum was laid down fastest in the valley of the Huang He, the Yellow River, and this, together with the other natural upheavals which accompanied it, may have been responsible for the poor survival of remains. What is certain is that the late Neolithic period springs to light fully evolved and with a high degree of refinement, with all the signs of the existence of a stable culture.

The Late Neolithic Period: Yangshao and Lungshan
Three distinct Neolithic cultures developed successively after the middle of the third millennium BC in the Huang He valley, along the northern border of China, where the loess stratum was laid down like a great mantle. Excavations carried out in an area known as Hongang in northern Henan have revealed that the three cultures lie above one another in quite distinct strata. The lowest of these, and thus the earliest in time, is the Yangshao culture. The middle stratum is the Lungshan, whilst the third and topmost stratum contains a rough, grey ware of inferior quality, suggesting the intrusion of a culture foreign to China towards the end of the Neolithic. The Yangshao culture developed on the plateau in the centre west of northern China, and is characterised by its red ware. The name Yangshao comes from the first deposit of this type of ware discovered by Andersson in 1921 in the village of Yangshao in the province of Henan, whilst other examples of the same culture and ware have been found in the provinces of Shanxi and Shânxi, at Banpo on the banks of the River Wei, in Banshan and Xin dian, along the valley of the River Tao in Gansu, and at Machang in Qinghai. According to the latest systems of dating and classification, the Yangshao culture encompassed the whole of

the period from roughly 2500 to 1000 BC, that is from the late Neolithic until the historical Bronze Age, following the valley of the River Wei, in Henan and Shânxi provinces, after which it gave way to a new type of civilisation, the Zhou.

The ware of Yangshao village is a red clay ware, generally consisting of low flared bowls with dark red decorations of vertical or slanting lines. Banpo in Shânxi is a village not far from Xian which was discovered in 1954. The ware here was decorated with geometric motifs such as circles, triangles, spirals, and cross-hatching, the interior being sometimes decorated with stylised fish and men. Banshan in Gansu was discovered in 1923, and is another famous Neolithic village, where solidly made funerary urns with a polished finish were discovered, evidence of the use of the potter's wheel and of the existence of a well-defined taste and sure technique. The clay is very fine in grain and light grey or dull red in colour, the bottom being elegantly decorated in black or reddish-brown, with vertical and horizontal lines in both colours, as well as spirals, zig-zags, symmetrically arranged circles and rhombi painted in circular or square fields, in a truly explosive phase of creative imagination.

The ware of Machang in Qinghai province is light grey, with a coarse grain clay, less elegant and less surely and imaginatively conceived than the preceding type. In spite of this, it is generally held to be later in date, since the two provinces of Gansu and Qinghai lie outside the proto-Chinese area and are not necessarily connected to the same cultural developments.

Even later than Machang is the clay ware of Xin dian in Gansu, which is first found shortly after the middle of the second millennium BC. It lasted until about 1000 BC, and formed in its few brief centuries of existence an interesting variant to the repertory of painted ware from Gansu province.

From Qijaping in the Tao valley in the same province comes a large-scale grey ware with combed geometrical decoration of an inferior quality, suggesting the intrusion of a doubtless semi-nomadic culture which only developed into a settled farming population at a later period. This evidence comes from the highest stratum of Hougang, and is chronologically the latest product of the Neolithic period, dating from the transition towards the Bronze Age.

The Lungshan culture is named after a village in Shandong discovered by Wu Gin Ting in 1928. This was a plains culture, post-dating the Yangshao plateau culture, although both coexisted until the end of the Neolithic, preserving their characteristic distinctions, the red ware of Yangshao and the black ware of Lungshan. This last is a delicate and refined ware, thrown on a wheel and fired in a special way. Lungshan ware was fired in a closed kiln like bucchero, to prevent the carbon dioxide gases escaping and oxygen entering, so that the ware was practically fired in smoke.

When Shang bronze ware appeared around the middle of the second millenium BC, the shapes of the pots, food containers, and bowls were borrowed from the Lungshan culture.

The Shang

TOWARDS THE middle of the second millennium BC – a widely accepted date is 1523 BC – a people known as the Shang appeared in the basin of the Huang river. Many of their artefacts and other traces of their presence have been found at the sites of two cities, each of which was for a time the capital of the empire. These were Anyang and Zhengzhou, in the province of Henan. Their society was monarchical, with a Shang king living in his capital city, where artisans skilled in the working of bronze and jade plied their crafts. Other artisans produced pottery, and horses and carts were used by the merchants to transport their goods. In the countryside, the peasants continued to use Neolithic equipment. Archaeological discoveries have proved the coexistence during the Shang period of bronzes, Lungshan pottery, and grey pottery in the late Neolithic style.

The Shâng social system invested the king with various sacred func-

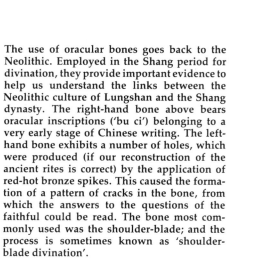

The use of oracular bones goes back to the Neolithic. Employed in the Shang period for divination, they provide important evidence to help us understand the links between the Neolithic culture of Lungshan and the Shang dynasty. The right-hand bone above bears oracular inscriptions ('bu ci') belonging to a very early stage of Chinese writing. The left-hand bone exhibits a number of holes, which were produced (if our reconstruction of the ancient rites is correct) by the application of red-hot bronze spikes. This caused the formation of a pattern of cracks in the bone, from which the answers to the questions of the faithful could be read. The bone most commonly used was the shoulder-blade; and the process is sometimes known as 'shoulder-blade divination'.

tions, giving him the role of an intermediary between man and heaven. Their primitive religion was conceived in terms of the necessity of ensuring a proper correspondence between the cosmic cycle of the seasons and the agricultural cycle of humanity. It was therefore the king's duty to fix the timetable for the farmers' annual tasks. He also had to celebrate the cult of his ancestors' spirits; and the nobles, too, had to worship the spirits of their ancestors in their own homes. Faith in the existence of the spirits of the dead seems to have been limited to those belonging to the nobility. Shang society was formed on the basis of clear distinction between the various classes – the nobles, the artisans, the merchants, the peasants and the slaves.

The spirit of the king's ancestors was called *ti*. It represented the whole community. For every member of Shang society, to render homage to that spirit meant to honour his own past, his own tradition, his own history.

The Shang gradually extended the boundaries of their state westwards as far as the valley of the Wei. They moved up on to the loess plateau. Towards the east, they made their way down into the Great Plain towards the Shandong. The Shang state came to include the whole area of northern China that is included in the basin of the Huang he. The Shang won their victories and subdued the rural tribesmen, because they had weapons of bronze, with which they could easily overcome the resistance of the primitively armed Neolithic peasants.

Bronze

The origin of the Bronze Age civilisation in China still presents some problems. Excavation at Anyang (the later of the two Shang capitals) led to the discovery of bronzes of such refined design and technical perfection that they gave rise to confused speculation about a possible earlier culture which had vanished without trace. Subsequent excavation at Zhengzhou (the first of the Shang capitals) provided an explanation, showing us the technique of working in bronze at an earlier and less perfect stage. But was the technique of casting in bronze invented by the Shang artisans, or was it imported from the West? In the light of the excavations at Zhengzhou, we can be fairly sure that it was invented by the Chinese. This is a reasonable hypothesis, even if it has not yet been finally confirmed. Right from those very early times, the style of Chinese bronze-workers has displayed one special characteristic – an accuracy of detail which borders on perfectionism.

The bronze artefacts of the Shang culture, like those of most early cultures, belong mainly to two categories – weapons and ritual vessels. Bronze axles for chariots, and various bronze fittings designed to strengthen or protect them, belong to a later stage. Ritual vessels were not intended solely for religious services and court ceremonies, but might also be used for domestic purposes by the nobles, who perhaps regarded bronze objects of this kind as status symbols.

The variety of forms used is extraordinary. Most of them are original, though a few repeat the shapes first created by the potters of the Neolithic period. Beauty of form, structural harmony and colour, sureness of line and subtle volumetric balance, combined to make Shang bronzes an admirable artistic achievement. Nor must we forget the decorations and pictographic inscriptions which often are added to indicate the ritual and symbolic significance of the vessel. An impressive example is the *tao tie* mask, which represents the hideous, mouthless face of a terrifying monster, and is intended to frighten away evil spirits. (Some bronzes, probably intended for rural ceremonies, are engraved with the heads of animals such as cats or oxen, normally equipped with mouths.)

Pictographic and ideographic writing

The most interesting phenomenon of ancient Chinese culture is the development of the pictographic script – a form of writing which is derived from representational art. The Chinese legends maintain that it is the product of no mortal intelligence; and it is in fact such an extraordinary phenomenon, so far beyond what any individual could imagine, that we can easily understand why it was formerly believed that magical or divine intervention must have been involved in such a wonderful development.

It was, in reality, a long, slow process. It began with the simplest possible form of communication, namely a rough sketch of a hunted animal – which is, in fact, itself a pictogram. It developed into a highly schematic form of representation, simpler in structure and more stable in shape, which was soon adopted widely enough to form a basis for the communication of concrete facts. It gradually also became capable of conveying abstract conceptions.

This led to the development of the ideographic script, which does not indicate the sounds of speech, but is composed of symbols each of which signifies an idea. If we want a comparison from things within our own experience, we may consider the symbols from 1 to 9 which we use to indicate numbers. When we learn to read, the meaning of each of these numerical symbols has to be learned separately, because the symbol itself provides no clue to the sound of the corresponding spoken word – which varies according to the mother tongue of the reader. The ideographic script has been adopted throughout the vast territory of China; the pronunciation of the characters differs radically from one province to another, according to local linguistic traditions, but the conceptual values are identical everywhere. This has created a formidable degree of cultural unity in every kind of situation and at all periods of history. The ideographic characters themselves have been much modified with the passage of time, and are at present being subjected to a process of simplification. The oldest examples of archaic Chinese writing appear in the late Shang period, in the form of inscriptions, some of which are incised on bronze vessels and are known in Chinese as *jin wen* or inscriptions on metal, while others are found on the bones of animals, tortoise shells, and jade seals. The first inscriptions of the kind known in Chinese as *bu ci* or oracular writings were discovered in the course of excavations carried out in 1899 in the neighbourhood of Anyang, the last capital of the Shang yin. These excavations led to the recovery of materials of the kinds mentioned above bearing inscriptions incorporating a total of about two thousand characters, not all of which have yet been identified.

Jade

Jade artefacts appear in China before the end of the Neolithic period, and from that time on they remain an essential part of Chinese artistic taste and cultural development. It is astonishing that so hard a material should have been worked at all in the Neolithic period, even for the production of simple, undecorated artefacts such as knife-blades, awls, components for weapons, and (most commonly of all) funeral vestments. Magical virtues were attributed to this material in every period. Jade has a hardness index of 6.5 on the Mohs scale. The abrasives used to work it were quartz sand (hardness factor 7), garnet powder (hardness factor 7.5) or corundum powder (hardness factor 9). Today an artificial product is generally used – carborundum sand, which is a mixture of carbon and quartz sand, with very high abrasive properties. Pure jade is white, but the presence of other elements, such as chrome and manganese, imparts various delicate shades of colour to the material, ranging from light green to emerald green and olive green. It is generally translucent, and gives an impression of almost waxy softness to the touch. It occurs naturally in two forms: nefrite and jadeite. Nefrite, which is rich in iron, is the more highly esteemed of the two.

To think of jade is to think of China, but it must be said that jade does not occur naturally in that country at all. Jade was imported from central Asia. Samarkand was one source; others, such as the Khotan region at the foot of the Gunlun mountains, and the southern slope of the Tianshan range, now form part of the Autonomous Uighur Region of Xinjiang and thus fall within the boundaries of the modern Chinese state.

Jade artefacts have been found at the Neolithic site of Banshan in Gansu Province. This shows that nomadic and semi-nomadic peoples from central Asia were on the march towards the regions of the East, including the basin of the Huang he, about the middle of the third millennium BC, bringing with them a culture quite different from that which was taking shape in China itself.

Rather more than a thousand years later a second emigration must have

Ceremonial daggers of the late Shang dynasty (twelfth century BC). Slightly more than 20 centimetres (8 inches) in length, they have blades of white jade and bronze handles encrusted with turquoise mosaic. For the ancient Chinese, jade was the most precious of all stones. Magical properties were attributed to it, and its use in propitiatory rites and in religious ceremonies had a symbolical importance. These daggers, in common with all weapons made of jade, are not to be regarded as offensive weapons, but as ritual objects.

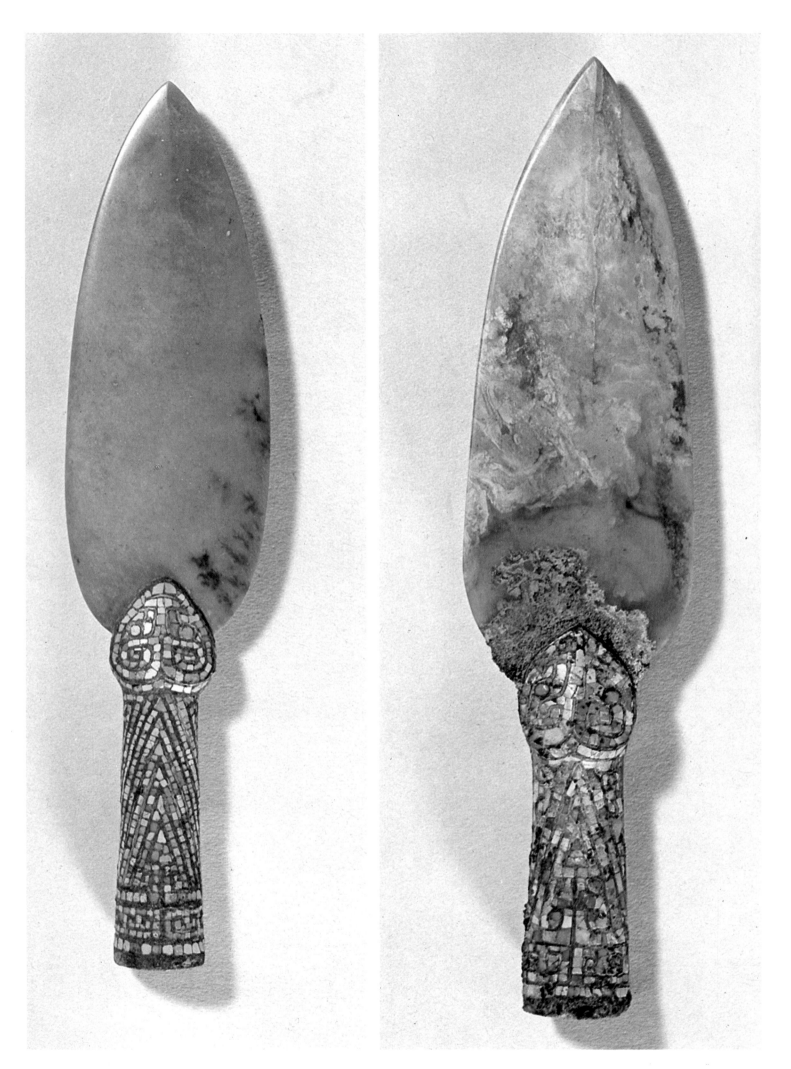

followed the same route, which has left traces of itself in the grey pottery which has been found in the uppermost stratum at Anyang, together with recent discoveries of most sophisticated jade artefacts. There is clearly a gap of many centuries between the artefacts of Banshan and those of Anyang; as is also confirmed by the observations already made in relation to bronzes.

Among the objects found in the Shang yin tombs at Anyang are ritual and ceremonial weapons such as axes, daggers, and knives; rectangular tablets pierced by three holes and designed to be attached to a belt (known to the Chinese as *dagui*); and many kinds of ritual object, such as the pierced disc or the great ring with a flat circular surround (known in Chinese as *bi*), which are symbols of heaven and intended for the use of the king, who is the son of heaven. They are richly decorated with circles and other harmonious geometrical ornamentation; or sometimes with lively little figures of crouching tigers, birds, and fish, together with dragons and other mythological creatures. Most of these objects are made from fairly thin flakes of jade; the exact thickness varies according to the end use.

The Birth of the Middle Kingdom

The Zhou dynasty

The end of the Shang yin dynasty and the coming to power of the Zhou dynasty took place in 1028 BC, as all historians now agree. This meant the end of the refined civilisation of the plains, since the coming of the Zhou, who had grown up in a boundary region on the western plateau, gave a predominant position to the peasant peoples of the uplands, who were much less advanced.

For some centuries the culture inherited from the Shang dynasty continued to develop, though often at a lower level than before. The bronzes of this period, for example, retain the former beauty of line and shape, but have lost the charming imaginative inventiveness that characterised Shang art. The age of the Zhou lasted eight centuries, and falls into many different sections; but the principal division is that between the period of the Western Zhou (1028–771 BC) and the period of the Eastern Zhou (771–221 BC). In spite of what has been said above, the age of the Zhou includes in itself all the elements of the new civilisation of China, which was developing and delineating its philosophical, literary, artistic and social physiognomy at that very time. Four social classes were developed – scholars (*shih*), peasants (*nung*), artisans (*gong*) and merchants (*shang*). These classes remained in existence without any change right down to the present century. We must underline the importance of this subdivision into classes for three reasons. In the first place it is most unusual for the structure of a society to remain unchanged for such a long time; in the second place, the absence of a military caste from the earliest days shows the pacific nature of Chinese society; and in the third place there is no priestly caste armed with magic powers.

These were the conditions which made possible the crystallisation of the society of ancient China. Slavery had existed under the Shang yin dynasty, but now it disappeared. There is progress in the domain of religious thought. The ancient beliefs had been celebrated with ritual objects such as the *tao tie* mask, which were incised with symbols loaded with religious significance; but now they were replaced by a ritual whose symbols inspired nothing but pure veneration. The paint-brush was invented, and replaced the reed pen as a writing instrument; it was also used for pictorial work. No complete paintings of that period have been preserved, although the archaeological excavations at Changsha and Chenjia dashan between 1941 and 1949 have led to the discovery of a lac jewel box and a piece of coarse cloth, both of which bear traces of pictorial work apparently belonging to the final stage of the Zhou period, which is known as the Time of the Warring States. It can safely be said that Chinese painting showed right from the beginning various characteristics which remained typical of its later traditions, such as vigour of line, coherence of structure, skilful brushwork and delicate colours.

Detail of a seventeenth-century silk scroll, depicting two philosophers intently contemplating the symbol of yin and yang, the two elements which express and summarise the bipolarity of Chinese thought. Each of them contains the embryo of its opposite, so that there is a constant possibility of interchange. Yin and yang are often represented in works of art by a visual symbol which expresses their inner meaning. This is a circle divided into two parts: a light-coloured section representing yin, which contains a dark-coloured spot representing the embryo of yang; and a dark-coloured section representing yang, which contains a light-coloured spot representing the embryo of yin. The two sections are spirally intertwined to form the circle.

The Time of the Warring States was a period of very important development in the civil life of the country. Feudalism triumphed and the country split up into numerous small states at war with each other; and yet, at the same time, by a strange paradox, a consciousness of national unity began to establish itself, with the concept of China as the centre of the universe – as *Zhong guo* or the Middle Kingdom, with the twin duties of defending itself from invasion by northern barbarians and of extending its boundaries to the south beyond the basin of the Yangzi.

Chinese thought

Thanks to Confucius, Chinese thought was clearly defined in the sixth century BC, in a form which represented the codification of a tradition and also provided the basis for subsequent development and elaboration.

Two fundamental principles had already been established and absorbed by Chinese culture, and it was with their help that Confucius was able to construct his own logical system. The first principle is based on the idea of celestial harmony. The heavens bear witness to a cosmic order, for which there is ample evidence, from the point of view of an agricultural society, in the recurrence of the seasons and of other natural phenomena, following a pattern which many centuries of observation have established and which may reasonably be expected to continue into the future. Both the ethical laws governing individual behaviour and the official laws of the state must be based on respect for natural order. They must therefore be an interpretation of the divine pattern we read in the sky, which *is* the natural order. From this conception are derived the responsibility and the primary function of man, whether considered as an individual or as the organiser of a community. This aspect of Confucianism ultimately had its influence in the world of art. It left its mark especially on the structure of the Confucian temple, as a place designed for the performance of rituals which celebrated the link between the heavens and mankind 'under the heavens', and also found expression in the exaltation of the human figure, which is given great prominence not only in portraits but also in scenes of individual prowess. The second of the two fundamental principles mentioned above is the dialectic conception of existence. Two cosmic energies cause birth, growth and death in this world. These two energies alternate in the production of union and disunion. They take it in turns to prevail over one another, and their alternation is responsible for all the vicissitudes of existence. Their names are 'yin' and 'yang'. Yin is associated with the female element, with the moon and with shadow; yang is associated with the male element, with the sun and with light. This dialectic conception, which interprets existence as a scientific phenomenon, was of tremendous importance in the development of Chinese thought. It did not encourage metaphysics or belief in God; nor did it favour the attribution of hierarchical values to the beings which exist in the cosmic environment. It did not encourage metaphysics, because there is no 'before' or 'after' in the action of yin and yang, but only an 'always'. There is no conception of life as existence and death as the end of existence, and all the problems which that conception brings with it therefore do not arise. The only reality is that of *becoming* – a process which continually bears all things and all men away with it, regulated by a superior harmony known as the Dao. It is not a God but a Law that controls the universe. Within the framework of the existential equilibrium, the forces of nature are driven by yin and yang, and create flowers, men, trees, water, worms, rocks. . . . There is no hierarchy inherent in nature; for Confucius, hierarchy exists, but it is an artificial product of society, a social convenience.

As we have seen, yin and yang had entered deeply into Chinese thought even before the time of Confucius. On to these fundamental principles were grafted two important schools of philosophy. Confucianism and Taoism. The Taoist school derives from a text, the *Dao de jing*, attributed to an author, Lao zi, whose existence is still a matter of debate. The historical figure of Lao zi is wrapped in an almost impenetrable cloud of legend. The *Dao de jing*, or *Classic Relating to the Virtue of the Dao*, enunciates the principle of the 'void', which is closely connected with the creative and activatory functions of yin and yang, since these are forces operating in the void and producing a reality which can take shape only through the void.

TEACHINGS OF CONFUCIUS

The Master said: 'To study and from time to time to repeat what one has learned – is it not a pleasure? A friend comes from far away – is it not a joy? To be unknown and not to be angry about it – is it not the conduct of a wise man?'

The Master said: 'I am not sad because men do not know me. I am sad because I do not know them.'

The Master said: 'The man who learns the truth in the morning can die happy in the evening.'

The Master said: 'To learn without meditating is useless. To meditate without learning is dangerous.'

The Master said: 'The superior man wishes to be slow in speech, but quick in action.'

Duke Ching of Ch'i questioned Confucius about good government. Confucius replied: 'Let the prince be a prince and the subject be a subject! Let the father be a father and the son be a son!'

When the Master went to the country of Wei, Jan Yü was his coachman. Confucius remarked: 'What a numerous population!' and Jan Yü enquired: 'Since they are already numerous, what more can be done for them?' 'They can be enriched!' was the reply of the Master. 'And when they have been made rich, what else can be done for them?' The Master replied: 'They can be educated!'

Tzu-kung enquired about good government. The Master said: 'Enough food, enough soldiers, and the trust of the people are what is required.' Tsu-kung asked again: 'If you had to renounce one of these three things, which would it be?' Confucius replied: 'I would renounce the soldiers.' Tzu-kung continued: 'And if you also had to renounce one of the other two things . . . ?' Confucius replied: 'I would renounce the food. From the earliest times death has been the common lot of all men; but a people that has no faith in its governors cannot survive.'

From the *Lun-yü* or *Dialogues*, one of the *Thirteen Classics*.

The outlines of things can be realised in the void, and these outlines, or profiles, characterise the things themselves. And things (such as a vase or a house) can only be used through the void. The void is thus the source of reality. The void is Dao. But the process of passing, in conditions of balanced harmony, from the void to the world of concrete reality and of the constant transformations to which that reality is subject, involves a contradiction which could never be resolved but for the existence within the Dao of a particular (otherwise inexplicable) quality. This is the Virtue (*de*) of the Dao.

What did all this mean in the social field? It meant that the individual was separated from the political and moral problems of society. It encouraged man to make himself part of the great harmony of nature, and to take no steps that might disturb it. It encouraged him to adopt the motto '*wu wei*', which means 'Abstain from Action'. The ideal condition of Taoism is consequently asceticism. And what influence does this attitude have on art? For a long time, pure Taoism remained a doctrine of the élite, while an inferior version became widespread among the masses, debasing its ideals into operations of black magic and witchcraft. It was only with the spread of Chan Buddhism, after the sixth century, that a more civilised form of Taoism, closer to the origins, was re-established. Chinese art, and especially Chinese painting, then began to give visual form to the profound depths of the philosophy. From the tenth century on, those depths found expression in the famous series of landscapes (*shan shui*) in which hills and waters play the part of yang and yin, and the mystery of nature, into which man dissolves and loses himself, are represented by the mists and vapours which obscure the more distant figures. Aerial perspective is inherent in the art of the Taoist painter.

The Great Wall

DURING THE prolonged strife of the Time of Warring States (453–221 BC) all the small states of northern China had tried to protect themselves from invasion by the nomadic Turkish and Mongol tribes, and especially from the Xiong nu Huns, by building walls along their northern boundaries. From east to west, along the basin of the Yellow River, the states of Yan, Wei, Chao and Qin were all fortified in this way. The Duke of Qin finally won the long war and unified China, proclaiming himself Emperor with the title of Qin shi Huang di in 221 BC. He then gave orders that the various stretches of wall should be joined up together to form a continuous barrier along the northern boundaries of the new state. He also ordered the destruction of certain stretches of wall which had been built between one small Chinese state and another, since these were no longer necessary. The project employed 300,000 men for ten years, under the direction of the general Meng Qian. The gigantic structure which resulted from their efforts had wooden observation towers at varying intervals, while at certain points there were connecting walls of rammed earth. Some of the succeeding dynasties which ruled over China enlarged the Great Wall or improved its structure; others did not. For example, the Han dynasty, in its earlier years, preferred to make a peaceful settlement with the warlike Huns.

By paying the Huns tribute in bales of silk and granting them other privileges, the Han managed to convert them into peaceful 'allies'. The Tang dynasty, on the other hand, had conquered the Turks of Mongolia and had pushed the boundaries of the Chinese state far to the north of the Great Wall. The Northern Song were persuaded to pay tributes of various kinds to the Tartar tribes along their northern frontiers, to keep them in check and arrive at a condition of relatively peaceful coexistence. For the Southern Song the problem never arose, since the Tartars had occupied northern China and the northern boundary of the Chinese state now ran along the line of the Yangzi jiang, in the heart of southern China. The Great Wall was of little interest to the following dynasty of the Yuan, who were of Mongolian origin and came from north of the Wall. After the expulsion of the Mongols, the Emperors of the Ming dynasty had to guard

Container of the 'fang ting' type from the beginning of the Western Zhou period. (This period lasted from 1028–771 BC.) Containers like this were used for cooking sacrificial foods, and are considered to be a four-legged variation of the ting tripods of the preceding period. The main decorative motifs are horned animal heads, often highly stylised; examples can be seen on the handles and the legs of the container shown here. The side facing the camera is decorated with bosses and geometrical motifs, and its upper panel shows two birds facing each other.

Pages 26–27:
The Great Wall near Badaling, on the boundary to the north of Peking. The Wall begins in the east at the pass of Shanhaiguan, on the frontier between the provinces of Liaoning and Hebei. Snaking its way along mountain ridges and across valleys, deserts and plains, adapting itself to the lie of the land, the Wall extends for 4,000 kilometres (2,500 miles) to the pass of Jiayuguan, in the province of Gansu, at the edge of the Gobi Desert. The average height is 7–8 metres (23–26 feet). Built of large blocks of stone, generally quarried locally, the Wall has a carriageway between 4 and 6 metres (13 and 20 feet) in width, paved with large tiles. Protected by side-walls, this road made it possible for foot or horse patrols to keep a vast expanse of territory under observation. At intervals along the road are towers, several storeys high, to serve as guard-posts and as accommodation for troops.

against the possibility of their return; and they were therefore keenly interested in restoring the Wall, in replacing the rammed-earthed sections with stonework, and generally strengthening its entire structure. The emperor Tai zu gave orders for this work to begin in AD 1368, under the direction of the general Xu Da. The work of extension and reinforcement continued for over a hundred years, almost to the end of the fifteenth century. The defensive system then reached its state of greatest development, and the Great Wall assumed the configuration that it shows today. From that time on, the Chinese called it *Wan li chang cheng*, or the Ten Thousand *Li* Wall. It is a structure built of stone, the rammed-earth sections having finally crumbled away. The pavement is reinforced by the use of large tiles, designed to protect the underlying material from infiltration and erosion by rain-water. All the wooden structures have been replaced with masonry.

At its eastern end, the Great Wall starts from the pass of Shanhaiguan in the province of Liaoning, at its point of junction with the Hebei, near the defile that leads to Manchuria. It snakes its way along mountain ridges, descends into valleys, and climbs back on to the ridges again, following the natural lines of the mountains and valleys, until it reaches the pass of Jiəyuguan in the province of Gansu, on the boundary of the Gobi Desert, in the far west. In the course of its western journey, the Wall divides into two branches at Nankou. One of these is called *bian cheng* or 'Frontier Wall', while the other is known as *chang cheng* or 'Long Wall'. Of the two, the *bian cheng* runs further to the north and takes in more territory. The two branch walls join up again in Shânxi. This is why we find varying accounts of the length of the Great Wall, which vary from 4,000 kilometres (2,500 miles) to 6,000 kilometres (3,750 miles). The Chinese name *wan li*, meaning '10,000 *li*' indicates a length of 6,000 kilometres (3,750 miles), since one *li* is just over 600 metres (650 yards). The Chinese have added in the length of both of the two branch walls mentioned above.

The large blocks of stone used in building the Wall were often obtained locally, but sometimes brought in from distant quarries along the highway provided by the completed portion of the Wall itself. For a road runs along the top of the wall, at an average height of 7.5 metres (25 feet) above the ground. This is the surface which the Ming protected with tiles, as we have already seen. Its width varied from 4 to 6 metres (13–20 feet) – wide enough to allow the passage of three horses side by side or of the heavy carts which were used to carry building stone during the construction of the wall, and to bring in provisions to the garrison at a later stage. The rough mountain terrain provided no other means of communication. The base of the Wall was always about 1 metre (39 inches) wider than the roadway. The road was protected on both sides by thick, battlemented walls, as high as a man on horseback, with observation slits through which the surrounding country could be studied. At irregular intervals, as the terrain permitted, ramps were constructed to provide access to the interior for men, horses and carts. In the provinces through which the Wall passed, special military colonies were set up to cultivate the soil and provide a certain level of local self-sufficiency, and so make it possible for the Wall to resist attack in all circumstances. From these colonies were recruited the troops to man the guard-posts distributed along the Wall, which sent out patrols to cover their respective beats and provide a service of continuous vigilance along the whole northern frontier.

How real a barrier did the Great Wall oppose to invasion or infiltration of China by the peoples of the north?

It is difficult to provide a definite answer. The history of China is punctuated by numerous violations of the northern frontier. Many peoples of proto-Turkish origin carved out kingdoms for themselves from the territory of China, such as the Toba, the Tartars, the Tangutans, the Mongols and the Manchus. This was possible because the Great Wall, despite its solid construction and enormous size, was not always defended by sufficient guard-posts and adequate human resources. Circumstances arose in which it would be easy for the peoples of the steppes to penetrate into Chinese territory, because of the political weakness or indifference of Chinese governments – or because of treachery.

THE FIRST EMPEROR

Then followed kings Hsiao-wen and Chuang-hsiang whose reigns were short and uneventful. After this the First Emperor arose to carry on the glorious achievements of six generations. Cracking his long whip, he drove the universe before him, swallowing up the eastern and western Chou and overthrowing the feudal lords. He ascended to the highest position and ruled the six directions, scourging the world with his rod, and his might shook the four seas. In the south he seized the land of Yüeh and made of it the Cassia Forest and Elephant commanderies, and the hundred lords of Yüeh bowed their heads, hung halters from their necks and pleaded for their lives with the lowest officials of Ch'in. Then he caused Meng T'ien to build the Great Wall and defend the borders, driving back the Hsiung-nu over seven hundred li so that the barbarians no longer dared to come south to pasture their horses and their men dared not take up their bows to avenge their hatred.

Thereupon he discarded the ways of the former kings and burned the writings of the hundred schools in order to make the people ignorant. He destroyed the major fortifications of the states, assassinated their powerful leaders, collected all the arms of the empire and had them brought to his capital at Hsien-yang where the spears and arrowheads were melted down to make twelve human statues, all in order to weaken the people of the empire. After this he ascended and fortified Mount Hua and set up fords along the Yellow River, strengthening the heights and precipices overlooking the deep valleys. He garrisoned the strategic points with skilled generals and expert bowmen and stationed trusted ministers and well-trained soldiers to guard the land with arms and question all who passed back and forth. When he had thus pacified the empire, the First Emperor believed in his heart that with the strength of his capital within the Pass and his walls of metal extending a thousand miles, he had established a rule that would be enjoyed by his descendants for ten thousand generations.

Jia Yi, poet and statesman of the Han period, 201–169 BC.

•••••• 359–352 BC |||||||||||| 215–209 BC

▬■▬■▬■▬ 324–300 BC

▲▲▲▲▲▲▲ about 300 BC   ⌐┐⌐┐ The 'new' Great Wall, 14th to 16th centuries AD

▬ ▬ ▬ ▬ 300–284 BC

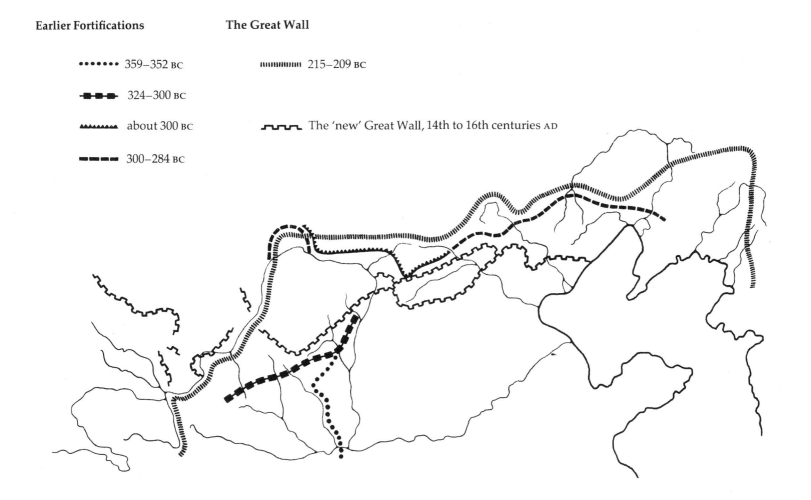

Sketch map of the Great Wall. The left-hand column of the table above provides a key to the fortifications erected against the barbarian tribes between 359 and 284 BC. The right-hand column shows the signs used to indicate the Wall built during the reign of Qin shi Huang di and the 'new' Great Wall built under the Ming dynasty.

The Tombs of Emperors and Nobles

QIN SHI HUANG DI came to the imperial throne in 221 BC, and almost immediately issued orders for the construction of his mausoleum. A work-force of 700,000 men was assigned to the task, all of whom had been castrated as punishment for various crimes. A new city was to be built around the mausoleum, with 300 major buildings within the circuit of its walls and another 400 in the surrounding area. The imperial order was that 30,000 families should be moved into the new city, all of whom would be given ten years exemption from forced labour on public works. The Emperor thought it desirable that life should flourish briskly and happily around his tomb, for he rejected the idea of death as a state of isolation from the world of the living. In the heart of the city, astride an axis running from north to south through the great tomb itself, he ordered the construction of the so-called 'Palace of Sleep', where changes of clothing and various other objects were stored. His stone coffin came from the mountains of the north, and was floated down-river to its destination along the same route as building timber from the regions of Shu and Jing (in other words, from Sichuan and Hukuang). Mount Li was chosen as the site for the mausoleum, because it was near the temple which the emperor had caused to be built to the memory of his ancestors on the southern bank of the River Wei. He had given this temple the name of Ji, which was meant as a reference to the stars of *Tian ji* (the celestial poles). This was intended to be a clear reminder that one of the functions of an Emperor is to provide orientation for his realm, just as the celestial poles provide orientation to the heavens. A connecting road was built between the ancestral temple of Ji and Mount Li. All comparable temples of earlier date were destroyed, so that the temple of Ji might become the only temple dedicated to imperial ancestors. This led logically to the idea of connecting the mausoleum with the temple. Work on the mausoleum went on for ten years: at the foot of Mount Li, two rows of rammed-earth walls were erected, covering an area measuring 2,173 metres (2,370 yards) from north to south, and 974 metres (1,060 yards) from east to west. The tomb itself was situated slightly to the

Lintong, Shânxi. Clay statue of a warrior from the mausoleum of the Emperor Qin shi Huang. This Emperor came to the throne after the conquest of the last six Warring States, which was achieved by the general Zhang Han in 221 BC. The new Emperor immediately gave orders for the construction of his own mausoleum. It took ten years to complete, involving great expenditure and highly skilled labour. In his *Shi Ji* or *Historical Memoirs*, the historian Sima Qian describes the tomb in detail, dwelling on its marvellous appearance and remarkable size. Recent excavations have recovered a large number of wonderful terracotta statues of warriors, horses and chariots – a whole army placed at the service of the defunct Emperor. The sculptures are fully lifesize. The height of the warriors varies between 1.75 and 1.80 metres (5 feet 9 inches and 5 feet 11 inches).

south of the centre point of this rectangle, and the Palace of Sleep was built slightly to the north of it, astride the central axis.

The tomb is a complex structure, built in many sections, and measuring altogether 485 by 515 metres (528 by 561 yards). Above it rises a mound, shaped like a square, truncated pyramid, which is 76 metres (250 feet) in height. The entrance to the tomb is on the east side, along an east–west axis. This is unusual, since imperial tombs normally have the entrance on the south side, along the north–south axis. It seems unlikely that there was an entrance or exit of any kind on the western side of the tomb, because Chinese archaeologists have found definite traces of an ancient factory producing bricks and stonework in that area.

Early historical documents, and especially the writings of the Chinese historian Sima Qian, who died in the first century BC, tell us that the foundations of the tomb were dug out right down to the water-table. To exclude all possibility of rising damp, molten bronze was then poured into the bottom of the excavation to form a sort of gigantic metal bowl. Finally the sarcophagus itself was lowered into the vault. Around the sarcophagus were placed household furniture of exquisite design, jewels, and rare works of art. To discourage thieves, certain artisans were given the secret task of installing special crossbows, designed to function automatically and transfix any intruder who ventured into the immense sepulchre. On the floor of the great bronze basin was a system of channels, filled not with water but with quicksilver, which represented rivers, lakes and the sea itself. A special series of interconnected machines was designed to keep the waters, or rather the quicksilver, in motion, flowing from one channel into another, so as to provide a constantly working model of the hydrographic structure of the Empire. The ceiling of the vault was fitted with long-burning torches. Such is the account given by the historian, who goes on to tell us that, of the Emperor's numerous concubines, all those who had not given birth to sons were put to death in this sepulchre. After the death of Qin shi Huang in 209 BC, when the funeral procession entered the tomb, someone gave the heir to the throne a piece of whispered advice, observing that it would be dangerous to allow the artisans and labourers who had worked in the tomb and knew all its secrets to leave the vault alive. They knew about the treasures buried there, they knew about the wonderful machines that had been installed and understood how they worked. If this information became public property, anyone might be tempted to profane the imperial tomb, with dire consequences for the life of the Empire. This suggestion was taken to heart by the heir to the throne.

When the funeral was over and no one remained in the tomb except the artisans and labourers in charge of the functioning and control of the special equipment, the massive stone door was lowered into position, blocking the entrance to the sepulchre, so that none of those left inside ever saw the light of day again.

The city of Li, which had sprung up partly inside and partly outside the walls of the great mausoleum, was burnt to the ground by Chu Bao Wang (232–202 BC) during his struggle with Liu Bang for the succession to the empire. (Chu Bao Wang is perhaps better known by the name of Xiang Yu.) The city, which consisted largely of houses made of mud and wood, was completely destroyed by the flames and everything was obliterated by its collapse. A layer of earth and detritus spread over the whole of the mausoleum. It was only in 1962 that Chinese archaeologists made the first trial excavations of this vast site, following up the clues given in the historical texts. In the northern part of the mausoleum some flagstones were found, which proved the presence of roads. Stone pillars were discovered which must have supported houses. Stone stairs were unearthed, which had formed part of external staircases. Major excavations began in 1974, starting from the eastern side, and penetrating the double row of rammed-earth walls, which had largely collapsed. These excavations brought to light the now famous army of terracotta statues, with thousands of soldiers, horses and war-chariots, all reproduced in their natural sizes. There was no mention of this in the texts. Excavation is continuing in the general area of the mausoleum, but the tomb itself has not yet been reached. There is consequently as yet no archaeological evidence about the structure of the tomb itself, its special equipment and

Lintong, Shânxi. A haunting glimpse of the army of statues found in the mausoleum of the Qin Emperor shi Huang di, who was buried in 209 BC. The mausoleum is 50 kilometres (30 miles) to the east of Xinjiang, which was the capital of the Qin. The mound containing the mausoleum is 46 metres (150 feet) in height. Excavation of the site began in 1974, and is still in progress, covering an area of 25 hectares (62 acres). There are many underground galleries, about 5 metres (16 feet) in height. These have not yet been fully explored, but it is thought that they contain about 6,000 statues, all standing in orderly ranks. A huge metal roof covers the area of excavation, converting it into a museum, which has been open to the public since 1979.

THE TOMB OF THE FIRST EMPEROR

In the 9th moon the First Emperor was buried in Mount Li, which in the early days of his reign he had caused to be tunnelled and prepared with that view. Then, when he had consolidated the empire, he employed his soldiery, to the number of 700,000, to bore down to the Three Springs (that is, until water was reached), and there a foundation of bronze was laid and the sarcophagus placed thereon. Rare objects and costly jewels were collected from the palaces and from the various officials, and were carried thither and stored in vast quantities. Artificers were ordered to construct mechanical crossbows, which, if any one were to enter, would immediately discharge their arrows. With the aid of quicksilver, rivers were made, the Yang-tsze, the Hoang-ho, and the great ocean, the metal being poured from one into the other by machinery. On the roof were delineated the constellations of the sky, on the floor the geographical divisions of the earth. Candles were made from the fat of the man-fish [walrus], calculated to last for a very long time.

The Second Emperor said, 'It is not fitting that the concubines of my late father who are without children should leave him now;' and accordingly he ordered them to accompany the dead monarch to the next world, those who thus perished being many in number.

When the interment was completed, some one suggested that the workmen who had made the machinery and concealed the treasure knew the great value of the latter, and that the secret would leak out. Therefore, so soon as the ceremony was over, and the path giving access to the sarcophagus had been blocked up at its innermost end, the outside gate at the entrance to this path was let fall, and the mausoleum was effectually closed, so that not one of the workmen escaped. Trees and grass were then planted around, that the spot might look like the rest of the mountain.

Sima Qian, historian of the
Early Han period, second century BC.

its system of quicksilver channels – nor about the mass killing of concubines, labourers and artisans which is said to have taken place in the Emperor's tomb at the time of the funeral. The work of excavation, which requires infinite attention and patience, has not yet been finished; at present only a part of the immense mausoleum has been uncovered. We can look forward to the unveiling of the mystery of the first emperor's tomb in the not too distant future. A wealth of interesting objects will undoubtedly be discovered. The ancient practice of burying useful articles and precious objects with the dead is intimately linked with the belief in the possibility of a future life, in an ill-determined kingdom of the dead, where the individual continued to exist on an indefinite basis, immaterial as a spirit and yet having some of the physical needs of a body. This conception of the other world invested it with feelings of religious mystery and expectation which led to a cult of the dead. This cult took the form of a careful provision for any needs which the dead might have after leaving this world for another. Ancestor-worship was closely linked with this cult of the dead, but broadened its meaning; it threw a bridge between the present era and the past, by underlining the continuity of family, culture, society and nation. The cult of the dead found expression in the placing of objects of personal use in the tomb of the departed, and in ensuring that the spirit continued to receive the attentions to which it was accustomed in life from the spirits of his servants. Ancestor-worship, on the other hand, found expression in the performance of appropriate rites in the ancestral temple or in a private shrine in the family home.

From the Han period onward, a new development appears in the tombs of the emperors and nobility, which is not unconnected with the great terracotta statues in the mausoleum of Qin shi Huang di, those statues being the first example of an inanimate substitute for human victims. In the time of the Shang dynasty, it had been a widespread custom to kill the slaves, concubines and animals of a lord when he died and bury them all with him. The custom was however applied with less rigour during the Zou period which followed, and especially during its final phase, which was the Time of the Warring Kingdoms; but it evidently had not vanished altogether, in view of the information which the historian Sima Qian provides on the subject of the burial of the Emperor Qin shi Huang. But the presence in his tomb of life-sized terracotta statues is the sign of a change of heart, which equates a statue with a human victim. The services of a retainer can be continued into the kingdom of the dead by the sacrifice of a statue instead of the more dramatic method of killing the servant himself. During the Han dynasty, a further step was taken in the direction of symbolism: the size of the images was greatly reduced. This made it possible to represent not only men and animals, but houses and fortified towers, in the form of quite small models. These terracotta images occur in the tombs in great numbers, providing valuable evidence of the dress, customs and stylistic preferences of their period, besides proving the technical ability and the artistry of their makers. They are known as *ming qi* or 'luminous objects', luminosity being conceived as a valuable property in the dark and shadowy kingdom of the dead. These innovations had an influence on funeral rites and the relevant ceremonial. The Emperor Wu (181–47 BC) issued an edict designed to control the materials used for tombs and to establish standards for their construction. Two main types of tomb were specified. First came the type which is hollowed out of a steep mountainside (one of these has in fact been discovered in Shandong). Then came the type of tomb which was dug in a normal piece of flat ground and marked by a mound shaped like a reversed *dou*, or truncated, four-sided pyramid. The side of the square base should measure 240 metres (790 feet) and the height should be 46.50 metres (152 feet). The mound was made of rammed earth, in accordance with contemporary practice. The tomb under the mound consisted of an antechamber leading into the central chamber where the body lay, with a network of corridors and passages around those two rooms, and an approach avenue running along the north–south axis. In conformity with a custom which had grown up during the Time of the Warring States, the deceased, if he belonged to the imperial family, had to be dressed in a jade suit, made up of small tablets of jade held together by gold thread, which was passed through

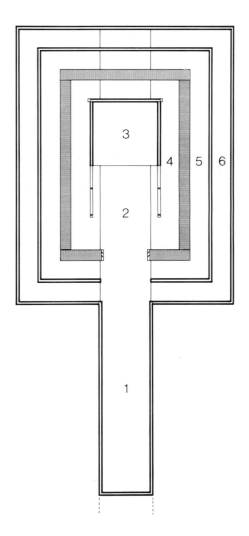

Plan of a wooden tomb of the Han period. 1 Entrance avenue. 2 Antechamber. 3 Mortuary hall. 4 Internal corridor. 5 External corridor. 6 External gallery. The wall between the internal and external corridors was made of square bars of cypress wood, stacked up as shown in the drawing below. Each bar was 90 centimetres (3 feet) in length and 10 centimetres (4 inches) square.

Changsha, Hunan. Wine jar of the 'zhong' type, decorated with lac. This comes from the tomb found at Mawangtui, a village on the eastern side of Changsha; it belongs to the second century BC. Excavation of the tomb began in 1972. Access is by a stairway, which leads to the gallery where the coffin was found. This was a mortised wooden sarcophagus, which contained the mummified body of a woman. With the sarcophagus were various objects decorated in lac, and also clothes, hangings, paintings on silk, and the remains of food. No fewer than 184 lac items were found, all in an excellent state of preservation. The jar illustrated here is decorated with red and black lac, to a design depicting clouds and birds; there are also panels with a zig-zag pattern. The lid has three S-shaped handles.

Changsha, Hunan. A box for cosmetics, decorated with lac. This is another example of the funerary goods found in the tomb at Mawangtui. The outer box is of two-tier construction, and inside it are smaller boxes for rouge, unguents and combs for dressing the hair.

Dahuting, Henan. 'The Hundred Dances of Joy' – a wall-painting in the second tomb, which dates from the end of the second century. The tombs at Dahuting, which is not far from Mixian, were discovered in 1959, and are among the few surviving examples of painted tombs belonging to the Han period. The detail reproduced above represents a banquet at which the Emperor is present.

Dahuting, Henan. The interior of the second tomb, which dates from the end of the second century. This is a large mausoleum, of stone faced with ceramics. A stately entrance leads into a series of magnificent halls. The decoration is largely abstract, but carved human figures appear along the walls of the mortuary chamber; and a tiger's head appears at the centre of each of the pair of great doors which give access to that chamber. Human figures are painted on the walls of some of the other rooms.

four holes at the corners of each tablet. The garment covered not only the body and the limbs but also the head. Clothed in this manner, the body was placed in a coffin of Chinese catalpa wood. This was placed inside another coffin of the same material, and another, and another, until five layers of wood surrounded the body and isolated it from its surroundings. The central chamber had to have double walls and a ceiling of wood, with a thick outer wall made up of 15,000 cypress-wood bars measuring $10 \times 10 \times 90$ centimetres ($4 \times 4 \times 35$ inches). These wooden bars were stacked up to make a wall 90 centimetres (35 inches) in thickness. Along the northern side of the chamber, the wall was to be built up out of thirty layers, each containing 160 wooden bars. On the southern side of the chamber, which contained the doorway, the wall was less extensive. It was still thirty bars high, but each layer comprised only thirty-four wooden bars. In front of the central chamber was an antechamber supported by four columns (two on each side), which carried three long beams per side. Inside this antechamber would be placed two beds and a table with an ivory chessboard. From the chronicles of the time contained in the *Han shu* (Books of the Han) of Ban gu (AD 32–92) we know that, of the eleven tombs of the Western Han emperors, nine are situated to the north of the city of Xian, along the northern banks of the River Wei, in their native Chengyang. The trouble is that over 500 funeral mounds are now to be seen in that area, and there are no outward signs to identify the nine imperial tombs. Archaeological excavations began in 1962, and have led to the discovery of several important tombs of that period. Of the remaining two Han emperors, the tomb of Wen di (180–157 BC) is situated to the east of Xian, and the tomb of Xuan di (74–48 BC) lies to the south-east of the city.

Turning now to the Eastern Han emperors, we find that the tomb of Xian

di (AD 189–220) is on the outskirts of the ancient city of Shanyang (now Jiaozuo, in Henan), but those of the other eleven emperors are in the immediate neighbourhood of Luoyang. It is to be hoped that the tomb of the first of the Eastern Han, Guang Wu di (AD 25–57) will one day be identified from among them. While the tombs of the Han emperors have not yet seen the light of day, various other tombs of the same period (second century BC to third century AD) have been discovered in various provinces, from Henan to Gansu and Hunan. These tombs are not mere wooden structures; they are built of stone or bricks, with frescoes on the inner walls, painted terracotta tiles and stone panels carved in bas-relief. Evidently the development of the arts of moulding in clay and carving in stone had reached a point where imperial restrictions could no longer be applied. Tombs belonging to noble families have yielded up finely worked objects of everyday use, including textiles, brocades, ivories and lac ornaments. Lac objects have not only great intrinsic beauty, but a most remarkable resistance to humidity. Chinese production of lac ornaments goes back to the earliest days of the country's history. The production technique is quite simple, although it demands unlimited patience and gives scope for great artistic sensibility. Lac is a resinous substance formed on the twigs of a certain tree (*Rhus vernicifera*, known to the Chinese as *qi shu*) through the action of an insect. A lightweight wooden skeleton or armature is prepared, and a thin film of lac is spread over it. This first film is allowed to dry, and then the operation is repeated twenty or thirty times. The object is then lightly incised or more deeply carved in accordance with a previously prepared decorative design, and the grooves left by this operation are filled up with a different kind of lac, which has been mixed with pigments or with gold or silver powder. The object is then carefully polished, and one or more final coatings of lac are applied over its entire surface. Generally speaking, the various operations, such as the preparation of the overall decorative design, the application of the main layers of lac, the carving, the application of coloured material, and the final cleaning and polishing are all carried out by different specialists. Many kinds of article can be made from lac, including furniture, highly sophisticated decorative screens, boxes and caskets, cups, ladles, cosmetic boxes, and containers for liquids or for the storage of food.

The natural colour of the resin is generally black, but sometimes red. A wide variety of different pigments was used for decoration. Lac articles of tomb furniture have often survived to the present day in a state of astonishing freshness, partly because of the wonderful intrinsic quality of the material and partly because of the special efforts made by the builders to protect the tombs from damp with thick wooden walls and solid slabs of stone.

Of the twenty-one emperors of the Tang dynasty (AD 618–907), eighteen were buried in tombs situated in the region of Xian, to the north of the River Wei, in Shânxi province. Of the other three Tang emperors, Zhaozong (AD 888–904), who was one of the last of the dynasty, was buried in Henan. The two remaining Tang tombs are situated in the district of Qian, in Shânxi province. These are the tombs of the third Tang emperor, Gaozong (AD 649–683) and of his consort, Wu Zetian (AD 690–705) – one of the very few women in the long history of China who ever took on the burden of imperial rule. A great mausoleum was built for this imperial pair, comprising a square burial mound and a square enclosure measuring 40 kilometres (25 miles) each way. This was protected by a great wall of rammed earth, which delimited an area containing not only the tombs, but also 378 buildings for habitation by the living, the object being to surround the imperial dead with the noisy bustle of life. Few traces of those buildings remain today.

Apart from its magnificent size, the mausoleum adds a new element to the glorification of the deceased, a new conception of the homage due to the dead. The plans of earlier tombs had always included an access road to serve the main entrance on the south side; but this now became the Avenue of the Spirits, or *Shen dao*. On either side of the avenue rose gigantic stone statues, representing high dignitaries of state, horses, and fabulous monsters, together with huge stone stelae. There were over a hundred of these great figures, reverently lining the road as the imperial

'Flying Horse', of the later part of the Han period (second century AD; found at Wuwei, Gansu). This remarkable bronze is 35 centimetres (14 inches) in height. It is an example of the extraordinary skill shown by Han sculptors in the representation of the horse. 'Fei ma' (flying horses) and 'tian ma' (heavenly horses) were names given by the Chinese to the splendid chargers they imported from central Asia. The strength and speed of these magnificent animals was highly appreciated by the Chinese, who found them essential to success in their frequent wars against barbarian tribes, in a period of vigorous expansion towards the west.

Jiayuguan, Gansu. Paintings on tiles from the fifth tomb, end of the third century. One of a group of six discovered 20 kilometres (12 miles) to the east of the town of Jiayu, this tomb has now been reconstructed in the provincial museum of Lanzhou, the administrative centre of Gansu. It consists of two chambers, roughly square in shape. The inner chamber, which contains the body of the deceased person, has a domed roof and walls covered with earthenware tiles; the floor is of ceramic tiles with abstract decoration. On the walls of the outer chamber are ceramic tiles painted with scenes of country life; feasts, ceremonies, dances and the tasks of the farmer. This group of paintings provides a valuable record of the dress and customs of the period.

Jade burial suit found in the tomb of Prince Liu Sheng and his wife Tou Wan (second century BC). Made up of more than two thousand small plates of jade held together with gold wire, it contained the body of Princess Tou Wan. A similar suit covered the body of the prince himself. He was the brother of the Emperor Wu, who reigned from 141–87 BC. Prince Liu Sheng's tomb is situated at Man Cheng (Hebei), and was excavated in 1968. It contained a rich collection of household and other goods, including many works of art from the palace of Chungshan, which had been the residence of the princely couple.

Qianxian, Shânxi. Mausoleum of Gaozong (AD 649–683), the third Emperor of the Tang dynasty, and of his wife the Empress Wu Zetian (AD 690–705). The mausoleum is at Qianling, on Mount Liang; it takes up a huge area, with a perimeter of about 40 kilometres (25 miles). The photograph shows the 'Avenue of the Spirits' or Shen dao. This is the access road leading to the tomb, and is lined by more than a hundred stone statues of dignitaries, horses and mythical animals. The area of the mausoleum was originally surrounded by walls, within which about 400 buildings were constructed as habitations for the living, so that the dead emperor could be surrounded by the bustle of life, in keeping with Chinese tradition. The whole astonishing complex was built between AD 684 and AD 705.

AN ANIMAL FABLE OF THE TANG PERIOD

There were no donkeys in the province of Kweichow until the day when a zealot brought one in by boat. Finding no profit in the animal, however, he turned him loose at the foot of a mountain.

A tigress, seeing how tall and stout-looking the donkey was, took him for a divine being. Hidden in the jungle, she watched him carefully for a while, and then came out for a closer look, though still at a respectful distance. One day the donkey brayed and terrified the tigress, who ran away for fear of being devoured. Frightened as she was, she came back later for another look at him. She became aware in the end that he was not, after all, such an extraordinary creature; she became accustomed to the sound of his braying, and began to approach him more closely, though without daring to attack him. And the closer she came the more confident she felt; she prowled boldly round the donkey until he lost control of himself and kicked out at her.

'So *that*'s all you can do!' cried the tigress happily. She leaped at the donkey with a roar and sank her teeth into his throat. Then she ate him up and went away.

From the *Qian zhi lu*, by Liu Zungyuan, AD 773–819.

 40   CHINA

funeral procession passed by, and symbolising the homage of the State, of the natural world and of the mysterious forces represented by the monsters. The great statues, in their silent, respectful rows, were also intended to guard the entrance to the tomb; in case of need, they could offer their services to the spirit of the Emperor, like the *ming qi*. While on the subject of the *ming qi*, we must mention the glazed terracotta ware which is one of the most important products of Tang art. The tombs of the period have yielded up many examples of this ware, remarkable both for their beauty and for the information they provide about contemporary dress. They represent civil and military dignitaries, foreign merchants, ambassadors, the ladies of the court, horses, mounted horsemen, camels and legendary animals and monsters. They are distinguished not only by harmony of form, effective depiction of movement, and artistic balance and precision, but also by the nature of the coloured glazes. These were generally applied in three layers (*san cai*), but sometimes in five layers (*wu cai*). The glazes were allowed to flow freely towards the base of each piece, allowing an extraordinary liberty of invention. Sometimes glazes of different colours were mixed to give the famous 'egg and spinach' effect.

The magnificence of the Tang mausoleum reflects the political and military power of Tang China. That magnificence survives to a certain extent, although on a smaller scale, in the splendid imperial tombs of the Five Dynasties (AD 907–960). Here the exuberant use of terracotta mouldings and of large slabs of building stone carved with bas-reliefs made it possible to create truly majestic sepulchres, of clear-cut, monumental design. The Five Dynasties (a period also sometimes known as the Ten Kingdoms) was an exceptionally confused chapter of Chinese political history. It includes the reign of the Emperor Li Jing of the Southern Tang

Qianxian, Shânxi. This wall-painting, showing a procession of court ladies, is in the tomb of the Yongtai princess Li Xianhui, a young daughter of the Emperor Zhong Zong; she was killed at the age of seventeen on the instructions of the Empress Wu Zetian. The tomb dates from about the year AD 707. The painting shown here appears on the wall of the long corridor which leads to the mortuary chamber. It is an example of the elegance and essential simplicity of the work of Tang artists. The subject was a common one at the time; but the painter of this group of court ladies shows a remarkable sureness in the handling of space, and provides an interesting record of some of the details of the architecture of wooden buildings in the Tang period.

42   CHINA

A glazed terracotta statuette of the Tang period. The traditional funerary figures in terracotta reached an extraordinary level of refinement at this time, as regards both elegance of form and skilful use of colour. The commonest subjects are dignitaries, court ladies, members of the army and various kinds of animal, such as horses, camels and mythological beasts. The enamel is allowed to flow freely towards the base of the statuette. It is generally of three colours, obtained by adding the oxides of the metals copper, iron and cobalt.

dynasty (AD 938–961). His capital city was Nanking in the province of Jiangsu, where his tomb has been discovered. Similar tombs, belonging to the same historical period, have been found at Chengdu in Sichuan, such as the tomb of Wang Jian of the Early Shu dynasty (AD 907–925).

The emperors of the Song dynasty (AD 960–1127) had their capital at Kaifeng in Henan; and it is extremely fortunate that they did not build their tombs in the neighbourhood of that city. If they had done so, it is unlikely that any trace of the tombs would have survived. For Kaifeng was completely destroyed by a terrible flood in AD 1642, and was not rebuilt until over a century later. The tombs of eight of the nine emperors of the Northern Song dynasty have in fact survived. They lie to the south of the confluence of the River Luo with the Huang he, not far from Luoyang, in the plain of Gongxian, in western Henan. They follow the splendid model provided by the great Tang tombs, with a mound in the form of a truncated square pyramid, surrounded by a boundary wall which included a vast area for the accommodation of ordinary citizens, who would surround the sepulchre with the bustle of life. There were four gates in the boundary wall, and there was a great avenue in the southern part of the complex which was lined with stone statues of civil and military functionaries, foreign envoys, horses, elephants, sheep, lions and tigers. The tomb of a Song emperor was, however, always built after his death, and had to be completed within the next seven months, to conform with the requirements of religion. This time-limit made it difficult to achieve a degree of magnificence fully comparable with that of the Tang tombs which were their model. As mentioned above, there were only eight of these tombs; the ninth and last of the Song emperors, Qinzong (AD 1100–1161) was not buried in China, having been taken prisoner by the Jürchen (known as 'Ruzhen' to the Chinese) and carried away to Manchuria.

The most celebrated and carefully planned tombs of all are those of the Ming emperors (AD 1368–1644). The Emperor Zhu Yuanzhang was the founder of the Ming dynasty. (*Ming* means 'luminous'.) His tomb is situated on the outskirts of his capital city, Nanking, on the eastern side. It is approached by the Avenue of the Spirits, or Sacred Way, as it is often called by Westerners, passing through the Great Red Gate or *Da hong men*, near which is a stele mounted on the back of a tortoise (a symbol of eternity). The statues which flank the avenue begin a little further on, and their effect on the visitor is somewhat oppressive, because the avenue is only about three metres (ten feet) in width. The statues represent camels, lions, horses and chimeras, shown alternately in a standing and a squatting position, followed by civil and military functionaries. At the end of the avenue is a gate leading through a perimeter wall into a courtyard. After passing through three such walls and courtyards, the third of which is over 500 metres (550 yards) in length, the visitor sees the great mound which marks the tomb of the Emperor and Empress rising before his eyes to the north. The tombs of two important counsellors of the Emperor, Xu Da and Li Wenzhong have also been discovered and excavated. These two tombs were situated not far from each other, and contain stone statues of horses accompanied by their grooms, and stelae mounted on the backs of tortoises. Unlike the imperial sepulchres, these tombs are arranged about an axis running from east to west. The dynastic name of Zhu Yuanzhang, the first Ming Emperor, was Hong Wu, and he reigned from AD 1368–1398. He died at Nanking; and so did Jien Wen (AD 1398–1402), the second Ming emperor, who died tragically and very young in a palace fire. His successor, Emperor Yong Le (AD 1402–1424) transferred the capital from Nanking (Nanjing, or Southern Capital) to Yanjing in northern China, which was renamed Peking (Beijing, or Northern Capital). And it is from Peking that the modern traveller sets out to visit the Ming tombs, which are situated in a large valley, called the Valley of the Thirteen Imperial Tombs, or *Shisan ling*. It will be noted that the number of tombs is thirteen, while the total number of Ming emperors was sixteen. The first two emperors, as we have already seen, died at Nanking. The other missing emperor is Taizong, who replaced his brother Yingzong on the throne when the latter was taken prisoner by the Mongols, and reigned under the dynastic name of Jingtai from AD 1449–1457. In 1457, Yingzong returned from imprisonment and regained the throne. He had previously reigned under the name of Zhengtong, but now changed his name again to Tianshun, and gave orders that the throne should be recorded as having been vacant during the years of his absence. The records thus showed a Zhengtong era (AD 1436–1449) and a Tianshun era (AD 1457–1464), both of which in fact refer to the same person, while the Jingtai era is completely suppressed. The effect of this decision was that Taizong lost all right to imperial honours, and was buried like a common mortal. The most important of the thirteen tombs from every point of view – architectural merit, sheer size and state of conservation – are the one known as *Chang ling* (which contains the body of Yong Le, the first of the Ming emperors to die at Peking) and the one known as *Ding ling* (which contains the bodies of the Emperor Wan Li [AD 1572–1620] and his two wives). The visitor approaches this huge group of tombs through a monumental white marble gateway or *shi paifang*, built in AD 1540. It is supported by six square columns, resting on bases decorated with bas-relief carvings of lions, dragons and lotus flowers. Between the columns are five separate entrances. Above, the columns are linked by double architraves, over which rises a series of small, separate roofs, covered with rounded, blue-enamel tiles, in a style which neatly combines the graceful and the monumental, and which, from its association with this particular original building, is now generally known as the *paifang* or *pailou* style – words which indicate a gateway comprising several separate entrances, in isolation from other buildings.

About one kilometre (1,100 yards) beyond the *paifang* gateway, the visitor comes to the Great Red Gate or *Da hong men*. This consists of three archways in the perimeter wall which runs right round the Valley of the Tombs. This vast and magnificent sepulchral complex is characterised by a profound originality of design, which finds expression not so much in the architecture of the individual tombs as in the general concept which combines them into a universal shrine, an independent world of its own within which a worthy place can be found over the centuries for every member of the imperial line. That new concept is undoubtedly based on a well-developed dynastic pride.

About 700 metres (800 yards) beyond the entrance to the vast sepulchral enclosure is the beginning of the Avenue of the Spirits, a road flanked by great stone statues which leads to the tombs themselves. The statues represent traditional subjects such as civil and military dignitaries, horses and camels, elephants and lions, and mythical monsters such as the *qi lin* and the *xie chi* (which are great cats with horns and manes). The avenue is ten metres (eleven yards) in width, flanked by a double row of statues and trees, beyond which expanses of bare plain can be seen. Silence reigns supreme, and all human activities are prohibited.

The tombs are built to various different models. The sepulchre of Yong Le, which is known by the name of *Chang ling*, recalls the structure of the Han tombs, with a corridor leading to an antechamber known as the Hall of Eminent Favours or *Ling en dian*, from which we go on through a small portico, past an altar and the tower of the stele, to the mortuary chamber itself. The mound which marks the position of the tomb dominates the entire complex.

The tomb of Wan Li, which is known as *Ding ling*, has a most unusual star-shaped ground-plan. The visitor passes through the corridor to a small antechamber, and then passes on through a completely empty hall to a central room of rectangular shape. From the central room, he passes into the mortuary chamber itself, which is situated at right angles to it and contains the coffin of the Emperor, flanked by those of his two wives. Two further corridors take off from the sides of the central room, one to the left and the other to the right; they lead to two chambers, lying parallel with the central room, which may have originally been intended to house the coffins of the two Empresses who now lie on either side of their husband. (The Emperor was the last of the three to die.) The two side-chambers are empty, and appear never to have been used. In the central room are a row of three marble thrones and some splendid blue-and-white vases – a type of porcelain which is among the main artistic achievements of the Ming period. Porcelain itself had been invented much earlier, and so had the application of blue pigments under glaze. The delicate modelling of Song

Nanking, Jiangsu. At the foot of Mount Zu Dang, to the south of Nanking, are two imperial tombs of similar size and construction. The first is that of the Emperor Li Bien; the second is that of the Emperor Li Jing, of the Southern Tang dynasty. Both these emperors ruled in the time of the Five Dynasties (AD 907–960). The illustration shows the interior of the mausoleum of Li Jing. This consists of a row of three chambers, with a width of about 10 metres (33 feet) and a total length of about 22 metres (72 feet). The chambers are square in plan, and have domed roofs covered with rectangular or trapezoidal ceramic tiles. The sarcophagus was placed in the third chamber, which was larger than the others. The walls of this chamber are covered with coloured plaster and decorated with pilasters crowned with a motif resembling a trident. The bas-relief image of a soldier can be seen on the far wall of the second chamber; this is probably a compliment to the warlike virtues of Li Jing.

porcelain is unrivalled, and the potters of the Mongol period (Yuan dynasty) had discovered the use of cobalt pigments under glaze. In the Ming period, however, China had very good trade relations with Iran, and began to import large quantities of highly refined Iranian cobalt; and this gave the Ming potters the opportunity to attain perfection in the art of firing cobalt pigments under glaze and to create blue-and-white porcelain of such magnificence that it enchanted Chinese and foreigners, contemporaries and posterity alike, by virtue of the extraordinary elegance of the decoration and the magical beauty of the fusion of white porcelain and blue pigments, which gave the impression of a mysterious natural bloom on the surface of the material.

The three marble thrones may remind us of the beds placed in the antechamber of the Han tombs; but what point could there be in having the thrones there, unless it was believed that the dead emperor and his wives would sometimes come and sit on them? Perhaps the spirits of the deceased would wander about their tombs, wrapped in the intimate comfort of well-guarded peace and security; perhaps they would find pleasure in the linear purity of the cold marble and its expressive, symbolical carvings. . . . Now that the tombs have been opened up, the introduction of artificial illumination and, worst of all, the admission of living visitors has shattered that ancient peace and frightened the spirits away for ever.

The tombs of the Qing dynasty (AD 1644–1911) are at Zun hua (Hebei), at a distance of about thirteen kilometres (eight miles) from Peking. After prolonged study by the archaeologists, they were opened to the public in 1978. The interiors of these sepulchres are very simple and severe, solemn and unadorned in style. The exterior effect is very different; the buildings stand out among the trees with a happy grace like that of an elegant holiday villa. Western cemeteries are full of reminders of mortality, such as crosses, angels, and chilly white marble statues; but the Chinese are tireless in their efforts to project earthly life into the future, and beyond the future.

Chinese tombs of our own century are characterised by a flatteringly monumental quality, an architectural apotheosis of marble statues and structural features climbing up into the sunlight. One example is the mausoleum of Dr Sun Yatsen, which stands on a hill, the sides of which are carved into great steps, just outside Nanking; but the mausoleum of Chairman Mao Zedong, which rises in the heart of Peking, on one side of Tian an men Square (where the imperial palaces also stand), takes us back to a very ancient tradition – that of the tomb situated in the lively, bustling heart of the city. It is as if the city itself had made the choice, welcoming this tomb into its midst in grateful memory of the man who directed the victorious revolution and laid the foundation of the new Chinese state.

Birth and Death of a Famous Capital City

CHANGAN ('LASTING PEACE') was undoubtedly the most famous capital city in the whole history of China. It was situated in Shânxi province to the south of the River Wei and between two of its tributaries, the Feng shui to the west and the Ba shui to the east. It was the first large Chinese city that a wanderer from central Asia would see on his southward journey, and was the eastern terminus of the Silk Road. In the time of the Han, and also during the later period of the Tang, it was a fortified city at the western tip of the territory of the Chinese empire. It was at once the gateway to the world of central Asia and the city most exposed to external attack; and it is probably this dual character that led to its glorification as a capital city. The Changan of the Han dynasty was widely celebrated; and so was the Changan of the Tang. Although the name remained the same, the two cities were not in fact identical. The Han capital, which was founded in 200 BC, was completely destroyed before the Tang capital was built, on a site adjacent to its ruins, in the sixth century AD.

There had been various different capital cities before the Han dynasty.

Peking. This white marble statue of a mythical beast stands by the 'Avenue of the Spirits' – the access road that runs through the valley of the Ming Emperors' tombs, about 50 kilometres (30 miles) from Peking. The avenue is 7 kilometres (4½ miles) in length, and provides access to all the tombs in the valley. These are thirteen in number, and were built in the fifteenth, sixteenth and seventeenth centuries. Along the sides of the avenue are numerous gigantic white marble statues, arranged symmetrically. These statues represent important members of the imperial court, dignitaries and generals; animals such as lions, camels, elephants and horses; and mythical beasts such as the one shown here. The function of these statues was probably that of protecting the deceased from evil spirits.

When the Emperor Qin shi Huang di unified all the Chinese kingdoms under his rule, he had transferred his capital from Luoyang in Henan to Xianyang in Shânxi, to the north of the Wei. He died in 209 BC, and a few years later the weakness and inefficiency of his heirs led to a furious struggle for the succession. In the year 206 BC, the troops of Liu Bang destroyed Xianyang. Liu Bang became emperor under the name of Gao Zu and was the founder of the Han dynasty. He ordered the construction of a new capital. In 200 BC, the new city was ready to welcome its emperor, who gave it the name of Changan. At that time the city contained just the public buildings necessary for the carrying on of government – the Chang lo, where the Emperor himself had taken up residence, the Wei yang, which was occupied by the Grand Counsellor Xiao He, and the Bei gong or Palace of the North; there were also nine ministries, three temples and nine markets. The city was situated on a plain sloping gently towards the north. The royal palaces were built on the high ground towards the south, around the Chang lo – a complex of five buildings, the most northerly of which faced on to the main thoroughfare of the artisans' and merchants' quarters. The merchants' offices and the artisans' shops ran along the line parallel with the north-western side of the city. The north-eastern quarter was reserved for the housing of the common people. The city was traversed by nine great parallel streets, which were intersected at right angles by eight great avenues. This system, based on a network of straight lines running north and south or east and west, is common to virtually all those cities that have been built in accordance with a plan, and corresponds to a heavenly geometrical order. (The ancient cities of Italy, even before the Roman period, were laid out to a similar pattern.) Between the main streets lay a tangled labyrinth of smaller streets and alleys, running in every possible direction and creating a rather chaotic impression. The city was divided into nine wards or *shi*, separated from each other by gates which were always kept shut at night. They could also be closed in the

Peking. The *Shi paifang*, a monumental gateway of white marble which was built in AD 1540 to serve as an entrance to the valley of the Ming tombs. The six columns are connected with each other by double architraves, and rest on pedestals decorated with reliefs representing lions, dragons and lotus flowers. The Chinese word 'paifang' is used generally to denote this type of isolated gateway, designed to offer access through several different openings. With the exception of the Emperor Taizong and the two Emperors who died at Nanking, all the Ming Emperors, with their wives and concubines, are buried in this valley, which was selected for the purpose by the Emperor Yong Le, the founder of Peking, after consultation with his court magicians.

daytime in case of emergency, completely isolating each ward from its neighbours.

Apart from the geometrical rigour of its street-plan, the city does not seem to have had any other special characteristics at that time to mark it out as an imperial capital. Gao Zu died in 195 BC, and was succeeded by his young son Hui di (195–188 BC) whose mother, the widowed Empress Lu, acted as regent during his reign. Astrological factors were taken fully into account in the planning of the city's fortifications, which took place at this time.

Astrological beliefs were (and perhaps still are) closely based on certain astronomical facts. It is therefore relevant to consider the state of astronomical knowledge in China during the second century BC. Ancient Chinese astronomy has been studied by Maspero, Franke, De Saussure and Chatley; but the most important recent work has been done by Joseph Needham and his collaborators at Cambridge. For the Chinese, the science of astronomy was an essential component in their unitary view of the universe. It also provided the essential basis for the calculation of the official calendar for farming operations. The successive stages of the annual agricultural cycle were formally initiated and blessed by the emperor in a series of special ceremonies, which gave a regular rhythm to the life of the empire. Calendar-making and astronomy were orthodox (and consequently Confucian) sciences. They had every right to play an important role in the life of the nation. In the second century BC there were two schools of astronomy in China.

The older of the two was known as *gai tian* ('umbrella sky'), or *Zhou bi* ('Zhou vertex'). According to this theory, the earth is in the form of an inverted, square-sided platter, placed in the face-down position, and the sky is a hemispherical cover fitted over it. The Pole Star is in the middle of the sky, and the habitation of mankind is in the middle of the terrestrial platter. Unlike the Babylonians, Greeks, and Egyptians, the early Chinese astronomers did not devote much study to the rising and setting of the stars, but concentrated their attention more on the circumpolar constellations, which do not rise or set below the horizon. The Great Bear and the Little Bear (which contains the Pole Star) are always to be seen high above our heads in the northern sky. Such was the basis for the development of the Chinese schools of astronomy. When the rain falls on the convex surface of the inverted terrestrial platter, it runs off outwards towards the four oceans which form its boundaries. The four borders of the sky touch the surface of the four oceans; and the heavenly bodies, which appear to rise and set, never in fact pass below the surface of the earth. As we have seen, this theory was given the name of *Zhou bi*, *Zhou* indicating the dynasty during which it was formulated, and *bi* meaning the vertical gnomon which was used to measure the length of the solar shadow; while an alternative name for the same system was *gai tian*, which expresses the idea of the sky as an umbrella open over the earth. The centre of the sky and the centre of the earth were the highest points of their respective cosmic planes; each was the apex of a curved surface which tended to end in a conical peak. The centre point of the sky was marked by the Pole Star, which stood exactly above the highest point of the earth's surface – the point from which the earth sloped away downwards in all four directions. The succession of day and night was the effect of three sources of light, the sun, the moon and the stars, which were sometimes hidden and sometimes visible. The mechanism was as follows: the sky rotates obliquely towards the left; the sun and the moon are attached to the sky and turn with it, but each of them also has a motion of its own in the opposite direction, towards the right. The result is that, although the real movement of sun and moon is towards the east, they are carried along by the rotation of the sky in the opposite direction, so that they seem to move towards the west. For this reason the movements of the sun and the moon are slow, and the motion of the sky is more rapid.

Among the inconsistencies and naïvetés of this theory, two points should be noted. The first is the importance attached throughout to the north pole. The second is the precise statement regarding the inclination of the polar axis, which is supported by a legend according to which the

AN EIGHTEENTH-CENTURY POET

'What, seventy years old,
and still planting trees?'
Dear friend, do not laugh
at my folly.
From the beginning of time
we are fated to die.
By our good fortune
we do not know when!
     Yuan Mei (1716–1797), *Zaishu zichao*
     (Planting a tree).

When I was twelve or thirteen years old
I loved books more than I loved myself,
and if I passed in front of a bookshop
I would stand stock still and gaze at the books.
I had, alas, no money to buy them,
and could possess them only in my dreams!
Yet the notes that I still consult today
were nearly all written by me in those very
    years.
When I was fairly launched in my career, I
    followed my tastes;
I bought books until my house was full of
    them,
and now that I am an old man I still read them,
    even at night,
holding a piece of candle in my hand.
My two sons, who are about the age I was
    then,
are not stirred by the sight of a book.
This is not something that can be taught:
it depends on the *karma* of one's previous life.
You never see two successive generations of
    famous warriors
or of famous men of letters; we found no
    dynasties!
Yet it grieves me when one of my sons
looks at a book and . . . yawns!
    Yuan Mei, *Duishu tan*
    (Sighing at the sight of a book).

Peking. Interior of the central hall of the tomb of the Ming Emperor Wan Li and his two wives (early seventeenth century). This is one of the most imposing Ming tombs, and has an unusual, star-shaped plan. A corridor leads to an outer hall, from which the visitor passes into the central hall; from the central hall two other corridors lead to two smaller chambers. The central hall contains a row of three marble thrones and a number of porcelain vases. The vases are magnificent examples of the technical perfection achieved by Ming artists in the firing of cobalt blue undervarnish.

Pages 52–53:
Peking. A view of the east cemetery at Zun Hua, a few kilometres from Peking, where the emperors and empresses of the Qing dynasty are buried. After restoration, the tombs were opened to the public in 1978. These tombs typically consist of a fair-sized upper section, and a spacious underground section with large chambers decorated with marble carvings and reliefs.

mythical Gong Gung shattered the pillars of the sky and made it tilt towards the north-west.

The other school of astronomy in ancient China was known as *hun tian* ('celestial sphere'). According to this the heavens are spherical, or rather egg-shaped. The earth is like the yolk of the egg, and is entirely surrounded by the sky. The sky is supported by vapours, and the earth is floating on water. The heavenly bodies can all be observed and measured; beyond the heavenly bodies lies the cosmos, of which we can have no knowledge. The cosmos has no limits or boundaries. The sun and the moon move through the sky along an ecliptic path around the North Star. The entire cosmos rotates about the celestial axis. These theories imply an intuitive understanding of some very important concepts, such as the roundness of the earth and the infinite nature of space; and the *hun tian* system also incorporated principles which demonstrate continuity with the philosophical tradition of yin and yang and with the most ancient conception of the universe. The sky had nine possible positions, and the earth had nine continents. Three luminous systems or *chen* (the sun, the moon and the stars) existed in the sky; on earth existed three forms or *xing* (earth, water and air). Phenomena were adumbrated in the sky, while forms (which were nothing but materialisations of the phenomena) came into being on earth.

This system develops a contrast between the two worlds of sky and earth which appears to be a matter of mechanics, but is profoundly dialectic in its deeper nature. It emphasises the close affinity and mutual interdependence of sky and earth, and strengthens the case for a philosophy that has always tried to furnish an explanation of cosmic phenomena and an answer to the problems of human life. The vision of heaven and earth as forming an indivisible harmonic unity, based on the dialectic interplay of substantially interdependent factors, is restated as a scientific fact rather than a philosophical belief. It follows that, since the laws of nature produce harmony and balance on the celestial scale, they must also be respected on earth in the interests of earthly harmony and balance. We find a similar parallel between heaven and earth as far back as the sixth century BC, in the works of Confucius. 'He who governs the people with the strength of his own virtues,' he says, 'is like the Pole Star, which holds its place while all the other stars circle around it.'

In the time of Confucius, the Pole Star was already a useful point of reference; in the second century BC, scientific advance brought confirmation that the Pole Star was the very foundation of Chinese astronomy.

We must now consider the question of determining the position of the stars in relation to the sun. The Egyptians and the Greeks adopted what is known as the 'contiguity system', which is based on observing the position of the stars the moment before sunrise, or the moment after sunset; but the Chinese concentrated their attention not on the rising or setting of the heavenly bodies, but on the North Star and the circumpolar constellations. And just as Chinese science and philosophy pivoted about the concept of the North Star as an essential point of reference, the same was true of the mythology of Taoism. The Taoists, in fact, believed in a 'Lord of the Sublime' – a sort of celestial demiurge, whom they addressed with the title of *Tai Ye* or Supreme Ultimate. 'In the Central Palace of the Heavens,' they said, 'the Pole Star is the brightest of all; and the Pole Star is the dwelling-place of the Supreme Ultimate.' The cultural scene of China in the second century BC may be summed up as a confused mixture of science and myths, of pragmatism and fantasy; but it contains some useful guiding ideas, which were of essential value to an agricultural community. Above all, the universe (composed of heaven and earth) was conceived as a unity; the heavens were regulated by a harmonious divine order centred on the Pole Star and the circumpolar stars, which were also the dwelling place of the Supreme Ultimate.

It follows from this that the capital of an earthly government must also be situated towards the north. For the government has a duty to reproduce on earth the harmony that rules the sky; only thus can the universal order be maintained.

The Chinese historian Sima Qian, who has already been quoted, has something to say on this subject. He tells us that when the master of a

house received a guest, he took up a position with his back towards the east and his face towards the west. The east–west axis indicated a state of equality. When the Han Emperor Wen di (180–157 BC) was originally offered the throne by all the highest dignitaries of the state, he refused it three times, turning his face towards the east each time as he expressed his thanks and declined to accept the nomination. When he finally accepted, he turned his face towards the south. This gesture symbolised the restoration of the cosmic model, the north–south axis, in which he was assuming the role of the Supreme One.

It was against this well-established cultural background that the town planners received instructions to devise a system of fortifications for the capital city of Changan. Their answer to the problem was to build a wall of rammed earth round the northern side of the city which followed a line derived from the movement across the sky of the stars of the Great Bear. Changan became the first Chinese capital to incorporate tangible signs of a deliberate parallelism with the celestial order, so that there should be no doubt about the function that the city was to perform 'under the heavens' (*tian xia*). (This is an expression used by the Chinese down to the present day to indicate the world in general and China in particular.) Thus Changan became the celebrated capital of the Western Han. It also became the eastern terminus of the Silk Road. It was the worthy centre of a vast and powerful empire. It was partially destroyed in AD 25 by the 'Red Eyebrows', and during the following period it ceased to be the capital, except for a few short interludes. Luoyang, a city of Henan, which had long been the capital before the Han dynasty, now assumed that role again.

After the fall of the Han in AD 220, Changan underwent a period of decline and neglect; and in AD 589, when the Sui dynasty wanted to move the capital back into the same district, the ancient and celebrated city of the Han seems to have been in such a lamentable condition as to be past restoration. The Sui accordingly laid out their new capital on a fresh site to the south-east of the old city, but retained the old name of 'Changan'. The city still exists today, as an important centre of activity in the province of Shânxi; its name has been changed to Xian, which means 'Western Peace'.

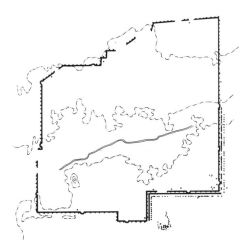

Plan of the ancient city of Changan in the Han period. It was founded about 200 BC by the Emperor Gao Zu, the first of the Han dynasty. As can be seen from the contours, the city was situated on a plain sloping slightly from the south towards the north. The imperial palaces were in the higher part of the city; the north-east sector was reserved for the residence of the common people; and the north-western zone was reserved for artisans' workshops and centres of commercial activity.

The Silk Road

The Silk Road

IN THE second century BC various restless nomadic tribes were on the move to the north of China, beyond the Great Wall, the Xiong nu being the most aggressive. At various times they raided into Chinese territory, in the far north-west. The Han dynasty preferred to come to terms with these uncomfortable neighbours, and agree a sort of truce with them, paying them off with consignments of food and silk. This was the first time that silk had ever left Chinese territory, where it had been produced for about a thousand years. The Xiong nu sold it in central Asia, to the inhabitants of the prosperous oases scattered along the valleys of the Ili and the Tarim, who were, however, not rich enough to make use of such refined and costly goods themselves, but resold the silk to Iranian merchants. Silk had previously been unknown in the western world, but now it made its way across to the markets of the eastern Mediterranean, after passing through innumerable hands and often taking years to complete the journey. The Chinese originally knew nothing about the commercial potential of central Asia, and would probably have continued to ignore it indefinitely, if the Emperor Wu (140–87 BC) had not sent an ambassador, Zhang Qian, to Ferghana (Dayuan), with the task of getting into contact with the Yue ji to discuss the purchase of some of their famous horses. For the Emperor was planning to set up a cavalry corps capable of defeating the Xiong nu.

Zhang Qian set out in 139 BC. He reached the oasis of Qarashahr (Yanqi), made his way up the Ili and was taken prisoner by the Xiong nu, who were grazing their flocks around Lake Issyk-Kul. He was set free ten years later, completed his mission and returned home in 126 BC, bringing with him ample and valuable information about the regions of the west, from the Tarim valley to Sogdiana and from Ferghana to Bachia and the lands of the Pamir. It was not long after his death in 114 BC that the first caravan of Chinese merchants set out into central Asia.

From then on, an average of a dozen caravans per year set out from China, each of which comprised about a hundred men and numerous draught animals, carrying goods of various kinds, including a few bales of silk, for which there was still little demand because few buyers had heard of it. Merchants interested in the great adventure of a journey which, allowing for the return trip, would last several months, and which presented many unknown factors, gathered in the capital city of Changan with their goods, and the noisy, bustling company set out for central Asia on the agreed day. From Changan to Lanzhou, the road ran through Chinese territory and was protected on the northern side by the Great Wall, so that this part of the journey was very safe. After Lanzhou, the road continued to run through Chinese territory up to Yunen and Anxi; but the caravans were now exposed to possible raids by the Xiong nu. The province of Gansu, where the places just mentioned were (and still are) situated, had always been exposed to raids by the nomads and barbarous horsemen of the north. From Anxi they went on towards the west, until they came to Dunhuang, almost on the frontier of the province of Gansu; and then they entered the basin of the Tarim, turning slightly to the north-west towards the oasis states of Iwu (Hami) and Shan Shan (Piqan) and then crossing the great plain of Dulupan or Turfan, the capital of the state of the same name, which also contained the important town of Bezeklik.

Dunhuang, Gansu. A painting in cave no. 45, dating from the mature Tang period (AD 820–907). It shows a group of merchants being attacked by robbers on the Silk Road. All the paintings in this cave are concerned with devotion to Guanyin. The scene shown above is derived from the 'Sutra of the Lotus'; the merchants are dressed in the clothes worn by the people of the north, while the thieves wear Han clothing. When the merchants pronounce the name of Guanyin, they are immediately released.

Pages 58–59:
Turfan, Xinjiang. Ruins of the ancient city of Gaozhang. They lie at the foot of Mount Huoyan, about 45 kilometres (30 miles) to the east of Turfan. The royal city of Turfan was founded towards the end of the fifth century AD by the tribe of the Renqujia. It became an important Chinese military colony for the protection of the Silk Road, and its population increased to over 30,000. It continued to prosper until AD 640, when it was destroyed by the Tang dynasty.

It should be noted that all the oases and other centres of population in the basin were organised as autonomous and independent states, with established, resident populations devoted to agriculture, stock-raising or trade. They were, however, affected by the pressure of the nomads who lived to the north of them, and raided them from time to time. This stretch of the journey along the northern side of the Tarim valley turned out to be very dangerous during the early times; but it was the only route where the provisions necessary for the continuation of the journey could be obtained.

From Dulupan, the caravans went on towards the oasis of Yanqi (Qarashahr), then to Lun tai (Bugur) and finally to Kuqa (Kucha), a large and important oasis state of the Tarim basin, comprising places such as Kezier, Gaha and Qumtura. From Kuqa they went on to Wen Su (Aksu), and then to Wu Shi (Uch Turfan) and Shu le. Finally they arrived at Kashi (Kashgar) which was the most important caravan trading station, where merchants of the east and of the west exchanged their goods.

The first part of the route, which wound its way through the provinces of Shânxi and Gansu between Changan and Dunhuang, had been regarded as safely under the protection of Chinese troops right from the time

of the first Chinese caravan. (As early as 121 BC, the Chinese troops had won control from the Xiong nu of the territory lying between Lanzou in the valley of the Huang he and the salt lake of Lobnor.)

The Xiong nu were not very pleased with the change of policy introduced by the Emperor Wu, who had cut off the tribute of food and silks and established military control of the borderland; and they tried to recover their ancient dominion over those regions. It was then (in 110 BC, to be precise) that Wu decided to protect the land in question with strong boundary walls. The Great Wall had been built up by Qin shi Huang as far as Tao he (the River Tao); and now Wu extended it from Tao he to Yumen guan far beyond Lanzhou, where he built the Huang guan, which is the most westerly of the gates in the Great Wall. The main structure was completed in five years (110–105 BC). Fortifications were then built at regular intervals, with provision for garrisons, along the line from Dunhuang to Lobnor, so that by about 95 BC the whole western Chinese region was protected; this region was known as *He xi*, which means 'to the west of the river'. The trouble was that from that point onwards the difficulties and dangers to be overcome remained quite formidable, for two reasons: the road along the northern side of the Tarim basin was still exposed to attacks from the Xiong nu, while the southern route ran through a waterless and largely uninhabited waste, where there was sometimes a journey of ten days between human habitations, and there was a risk of being refused help even in the utmost emergency. The task that faced the Chinese was the creation of reasonable conditions for transit both to the north and to the south of the basin. Around Lake Lobnor was a terrible salt desert, described by the Chinese as the Dragon Dune Wilderness. The state of Lon lan, which had been set up in this area, was compelled to supply guides who could find food and water for Chinese ambassadors on the way through the desert. In 103 BC a military expedition led by the general Li Guangli took the southern route on its way to conquer the King of Dayuan (Ferghana); a large number of soldiers died, exhausted by the fatigues of the journey and by hunger. In 101 BC another expedition was sent out, but this time the army was divided into two parts, one of which was to take the southern route, and the other the northern. Each was to establish exact points of reference along the route that it took. We know the result of this last part of the expedition's activities. All the states lying along the northern route complied wholeheartedly with every kind of request for help, except for the city-state of Lun Tai (Bugur), not far from Kuqa (Kucha). This city was punished for its hostile attitude by being surrounded, sacked, and permanently subjugated. The Chinese stationed a detachment at this point and founded the first military-agricultural colony to be set up anywhere along the route, in 95 BC. This colony was subject to an imperial commissioner, with the task of supervising the cultivation of the soil, gathering in the grain harvest, and providing for the needs of Chinese ambassadors on their way to central Asia. Later on other states were subjugated, and other military-agricultural colonies were set up. Turfan was occupied in 62 BC; the state of Lon lan no longer existed after 77 BC; and another Chinese colony was founded in one of the oases of Shan Shan. In this way full control was achieved of the whole of the northern route, and the problems of provisions for the journey and security from attack were solved, to the point where some tribes of the Xiong nu themselves began to offer submission. The imperial commissioner now wanted to offer similar services to travellers bound for Pi shan (Guma) or for So che (Yarkand) and to travellers coming from those places to China.

These operations effectively opened two commercial routes through the Tarim valley, one running to the north and the other to the south. The southern route was followed by merchants bound for oases such as Hotian (Khotan) or So che (Yarkand), to buy nephrite or jadeite, which the local people found in the Khohan-darja and Yarkand-darja rivers.

In the year 60 BC, the Emperor Xuan (74–48 BC), nominated the imperial commissioner Zheng Ji to the post of *Du hu* or Protector-General of the two roads, with jurisdiction over the commissioners in charge of the individual military colonies which had now been founded at almost every possible point along both the north and the south sides of the valley, to guarantee

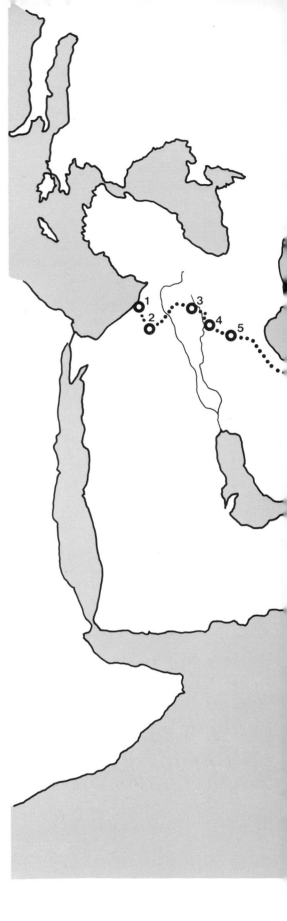

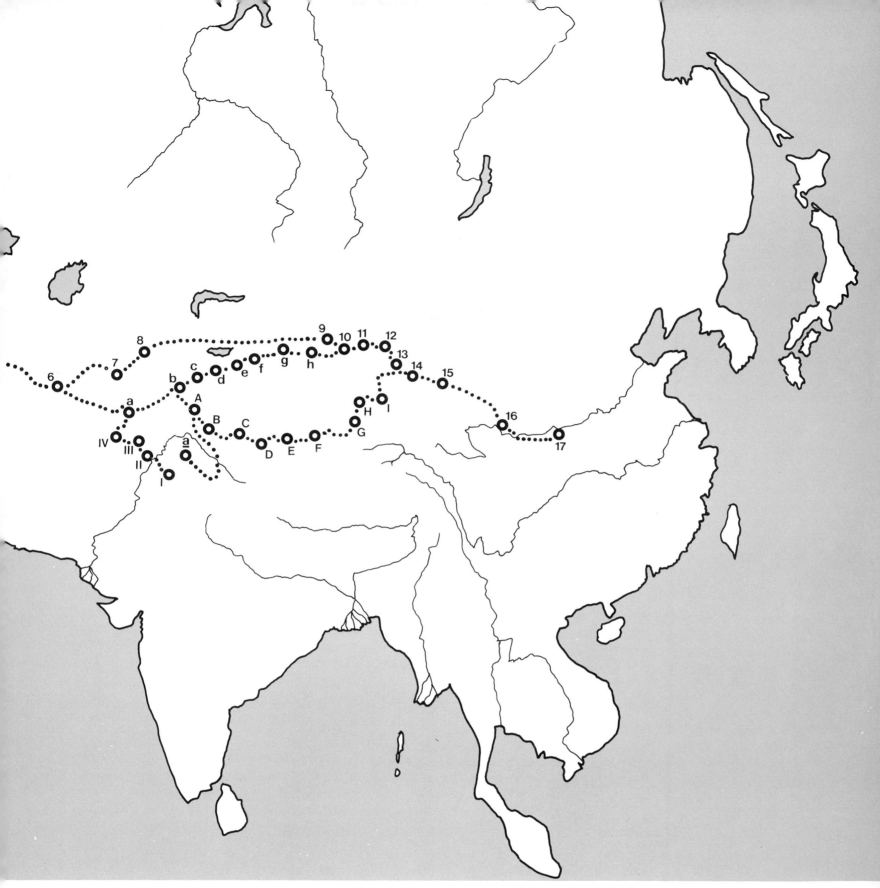

The principal routes of the Silk Road

1) Antioch
2) Palmyra
3) Dura Europos
4) Ecbatana
5) Hekatompylos
6) Merv (Mary)
7) Samarkand
8) Tashkent
9) Urumqi
10) Dulupan (Turfan)
11) Shan Shan (Piqan)
12) Iwu (Hami)
13) Dunhuang
14) Anxi
15) Yumen
16) Lanzhou
17) Xian (Changan)

6) Merv (Mary)
a) Balkh
b) Kashi (Kashgar)
c) Shu le
d) Wu shi (Uch Turfan)
e) Wen su (Aksu)
f) Kuqa (Kucha)
g) Lun tai (Bugur)
h) Yanqi (Karashahr)
10) Dulupan (Turfan)

I) Taxila
II) Peshawar
III) Khyber Pass
IV) Bamiyan
a) Balkh

a) Shrinagar (in Kashmir)
A) So che (Yarkand)

b) Kashi (Kashgar)
A) So che (Yarkand)
B) Pi shan (Guma)
C) Hotian (Khotan)
D) Yutian (Keriya)
E) Minfeng (Niya)
F) Tuholo (Endere)
G) Qiemo (Qargan)
H) Ruoqiang (Qarkilik)
I) Milan (Miran)
13) Dunhuang

the safety of a caravan traffic which had grown with extraordinary rapidity since its beginnings half a century earlier.

In the reign of the Emperor Yuan (48–33 BC), two important military officials were appointed, with the titles of *Wu xiao wei* and *Ji xiao wei*, to administer the most important military colony, which was that of Gaozhang, situated about twenty-four kilometres (fifteen miles) to the east of Turfan. The ruins of Gaozhang (now known as Idikuchari) were discovered by the archaeologist Grünwedel in 1902.

Between the years AD 1 and AD 6, it proved possible to create a direct connection between Turfan and the Yumen Gate, which by-passed the salt desert of Lobnor.

During the crisis of the Han dynasty, the Chinese held out along the northern roads for a long time, maintaining their military colonies at Turfan and Kucha until AD 23. In that year it became impossible to withstand the pressure of the Xiong nu, and the whole valley had to be abandoned to the invaders. Trade relations between China and the Western world were interrupted. In AD 73 the Chinese were on the march to reconquer the lost territory, thanks to the initiative of the general Ban Chao. By this time the Xiong nu had repeatedly invaded the Tarim valley, and had even penetrated into the Chinese district of He xi in the north-west of Gansu province. They had completely destroyed everything that had been achieved by the generals of Wu di. The formerly independent states of the Tarim valley had regained their freedom, and lost it again to the Xiong nu. This was a state of affairs in which there could be no thought of reopening commercial relations between China and the western countries.

The Emperor Zhang (AD 76–88) granted Ban Chao a commission to pacify the area, and in a few years the general had restored the conditions of a century earlier. The military-agricultural colonies again appeared in the valley to guarantee safe travelling conditions for the caravans, which immediately began to ply again. Posting-houses were also set up, with relays of horses for the convenience of travellers. There was also a postal service for correspondents, and even a corps of interpreters, who had to be ready to travel in any direction at any time.

Caravans now began to leave China with large loads of silk, because there was heavy demand from a big buyer in the Western world – namely, the Roman Empire.

Towards the end of the first century AD, the roads of Asia were full of caravans converging upon Kashgar from the east with loads of silk for sale, and of other caravans converging on Kashgar from the west, to purchase the precious material. It was not only merchants and merchandise that were carried by the caravans. Buddhist monks on pilgrimage travelled with them; and so did the ideas, cultures, traditions, languages, costumes and philosophies of many different peoples. An extraordinarily confused mingling of ideas took place in the great caravanserais; and the master idea which emerged from that confusion was the idea of Buddhism. Of Indian origin, and coloured to some extent by the artistic interpretations of the school of Gandhara, Buddhism was now beginning its long march into central Asia and into China. Buddhism travelled on eastwards from Kashgar with the Chinese caravans that were returning home after selling their silk; and at the same time the silk travelled on to an eastern Mediterranean port, where it took ship for Rome.

If we are to understand the nature of the various influences that rolled in long waves over the centres of the caravan trade in central Asia, it is important to consider the staging-points through which the caravans passed on their way to China from the Mediterranean or from India. The routes from the Mediterranean passed through the ancient cities of Antioch, Palmyra, Dura Europos, Ecbatana, and Hekatompylos (which is in Parthia); here they turned towards the north and proceeded to Merv (known today as Mary).

Merv was an important centre of the caravan trade. It offered two alternative routes to China. The first went through Samarkand (in Sogdiana), Tashkent (in Fergana), Urumqi (in Dsungaria), Dulupan (Turfan), Shan Shan (Piqan), Iwu (Hami), Dunhuang, and Anxi. The other route set out for Kashgar, passing through Balkh (in Bactriana). Caravans from

Turfan, Xinjiang. Picture of a standing Buddha, in a wall-painting of cave no. 9 at Bezezlik. It dates from the mature Tang period (ninth to tenth centuries AD). The Buddha is shown in the attitude of debate, turning to the right; he has two attendants on each side and is further surrounded by people offering gifts. The headgear of some of the latter indicates Western origin. In the bottom right-hand corner are a camel and a donkey. The rectangular structure of the scene, the shading of the garments and the precision of the drawing may remind us of the best Buddhist paintings of the late Tang period, but there is little warmth in the line, little expression in the faces, and the shading is no more than a decorative device. This picture is in fact the work of Uighur artists of the ninth or tenth centuries; and, as such, it is an interesting peripheral example of the art of the Tang period.

ON THE SILK ROAD

Leave this province, and let us go to another called Kashgar, that in old time was a kingdom, although now it be subject to the Great Cane. In this province are many fair cities and towns, the best is Kashgar: they be all Mahomets. This province is between the Northeast and the East. In it be many great merchants, fair possessions and wines, they have much cotton-wool there, and very good. The merchants of that country be near, and covetous. In this province, which endureth five days journey, be Christians called Nestorians, and have churches, and speak a language of their own. . . .

Departing from Charchan, you shall travel five days journey in sand, and in the way, fresh and sweet waters, and some saltish. Being passed these five days journey, you shall find a great desert, and at the beginning of it a great city called Charklik, between the Northeast and the East. They be under the obedience of the Great Cane, and be Mahomets. And they that will pass this desert, had need to be in this city a week, for to provide them victuals and other necessaries for them and their horses for a month, for in this desert, you shall find nothing to eat or drink: and there be many sandy hills, and great. After you be entered into it one day's journey, you shall find good water, but after that neither good nor bad, nor beasts, nor fowls, nor anything to eat: and travelling that way by night, you shall hear in the air, the sound of Tabors and other instruments, to put the travellers in fear, and to make them lose their way, and to depart from their company, and lose themselves: and by that means many do die, being deceived so, by evil spirits, that make these sounds, and also do call divers of the travellers by their names, and make them to leave their company, so that you shall pass this desert with great danger.

Marco Polo, *Travels*, Chapters 40 and 36.

India also came to Balkh, following the only available route through the mountain passes. The assembly point was at Taxila in the Punjab, and the caravans set out for Peshawar in Gandhara; from here they went on through the Khyber Pass and across Afghanistan along the Kabul valley before reaching the famous centre of Bamiyan, in whose mountain rocks the first gigantic statues of the Buddha were carved by devoted monks. From Bamiyan the traveller went on to Balkh and then to Kashgar. Kashgar was thus the terminus or final destination of caravans from both India and the Mediterranean. Yet another route led to Kashgar from the north of Kashmir, crossing the Pamir by the passes of Mintaka or Kilik; but it was also possible to go on beyond Kashgar to Yarkand. From Kashgar onwards, the merchants were travelling through Chinese territory, where public safety and public services were guaranteed by the Chinese garrisons that had been planted all along the route. To the east of Kashgar, the road split in two, one branch going to the north and the other to the south, to avoid the desert of Taklamakan. The northern branch was the one that went to Changan, passing through Kuqa (Kucha), Lun tai (Bugur), Dulupan (Turfan), Dunhuang, Anxi and Lanzhou.

The southern route ran along the northern slopes of the mountain chain of Altin Tagh, squeezed between the mountains and the desert of Taklamakan. After leaving Kashi (Kashgar), the main halting-places were So Che (Yarkand) which also had a direct link with Kashmir, and then Hotian (Khotan), Yutian (Keriya), Minfeng (Niya), Tuholo (Endere), Qiemo (Qarqan), Milan, Dunhuang and Anxi.

At Dunhuang, the two roads met again; although sometimes travellers on the northern road by-passed Dunhuang and went straight on to Anxi, where the two routes were finally reunited. The Silk Road, or rather Roads, remained open to traffic between China and the Western world until the tenth century AD, apart from some fairly long periods of interruption, at times when political conditions in China were such that security of transit could not be guaranteed. The whole area comprising the Tarim river basin, from Kashgar to the western boundary of Dunhuang, was known by the name of Serindia. After the fall of the Han dynasty in AD 220, Serindia fell under the influence of the Juan-juan (Avari), until the victory of the Toba in the third century AD. The Toba, having set up the Wei dynasty in China, were in a position to ensure the security of the commercial routes of central Asia. In AD 552, the Tu jue, who had conquered the Avari, set up a great empire in central Asia. But they were defeated and driven back by soldiers of the Tang, who reopened the caravan routes through Serindia. In the middle of the eighth century, the Uighur Turks appear on the scene, replacing and absorbing the Tu jue; and from that time onwards until the tenth century, when the process of Islamisation began, the situation in Serindia changed very little. In the meantime, however, many of the settlements in Serindia were completely abandoned, after a process of decline which in some cases had begun at the end of the third century AD, in others during the eighth century AD, and in others again at a later period. Many of the oases had formerly known wealth and prosperity, and had developed into centres of culture and of original artistic production; but they have become mere archaeological sites, half-buried by the sand which (unchecked by human activities) is so swift to re-establish its dominion over everything in those regions. The buried city of Khotan (Hotian), which was discovered by M. A. Stein in his first journey to Serindia in 1900–1901, is typical of all of them.

Silence reigns supreme today over the sparse ruins of Tuholo (Endere) of Qiemo (Qarqan), of Gaozhang, and of Shicheng (the City of Stone), which the Chinese built near Ruoqiang (Qarkilik). . . . In that silence, in the solitude of bleak, unfriendly places, the stone statues of Buddha and the paintings of Buddha on the walls of the caves seem to contemplate with remote attention the mysterious flow of life and death.

The Signs of the Buddha

Buddhism in China

ACCORDING TO Chinese Buddhist traditions, the first group of Buddhist monks to enter China were Shi Lifang and his seventeen companions, during the reign of Qin shi Huang di, in the third century BC. This, however, was an isolated episode, without permanent consequences. Several more centuries passed before a Chinese embassy to the Iuezhi or Indo-Scythians met the famous Indian missionaries Kasyapa, Matanga and Dharmaratna. Wang Zun and Cai Yin are said to have taken this opportunity to copy the *Sutra of Forty-Two Chapters*, which they then introduced into China in the year AD 68. According to a tradition still alive today, they used a white horse to carry the manuscripts into the city of Luoyang. The event was celebrated by the erection of a Buddhist monastery – the first to be built in China – with the name of *Bai ma si*, or Monastery of the White Horse. Several decades later, an event took place which revived interest in Buddhism on the theoretical and doctrinal plane. This was the arrival at Luoyang of the famous Arsacid prince, An Shigao. (The name 'An' indicates Parthian origin.) According to some sources, he arrived in China in AD 144, according to others in AD 148; he is believed to have remained there about twenty years. He spent that long period in the Monastery of the White Horse at Luoyang, which was at that time the capital city of the Han empire, translating several dozen Buddhist texts, with the indispensable help of his compatriot An Xuan and of a Chinese monk named Yan Fotiao. In order to ensure that the translation was carried out in a co-ordinated manner and with adequate doctrinal control, An Xuan and Yan Fotiao organised their helpers into working groups. Those helpers were an Indo-Scythian called Lokaksema, two Sogdians called Kan Ju and Kang Mengsiang, and three Indians whose names are given as Dharmasatya, Zhu Fosho and Zhu Dali. (The last two have an un-Indian sound and are probably Chinese pen-names.) The translated texts were then made the basis of a synthesis, in which the most essential passages were summarised to improve comprehension and help in the spread of the doctrine.

The impact of this first penetration of Buddhism into China, being based on the compilation of Chinese versions of Indian exegetic texts, was limited to court circles and to intellectuals, who were animated by curiosity about the various aspects of Indian thought, which had already aroused so much interest outside China – in all the towns lying along the Silk Road, where Buddhist monks from India, Kashmir or Persia had settled from time to time. In their miserable baggage would be a *sutra* or holy book; and they were always ready to teach its doctrine and, if necessary, to translate its text into the local language. By virtue of their ability to read and write, the monks became cultural ambassadors, and aroused the interest of the intellectual governing classes. Such was the first impact of Buddhism,

Yongjing, Gansu. The Bingling caves. Discovered in 1951, the 183 caves at Bingling were originally dug out of the vertical rocky side of a narrow valley surrounded by the peaks of Mount Xianji-shi, 20 kilometres (12 miles) to the north of the city of Yongjing, along the Huang he. Not far away are the twelve caves of the Upper Temple. The place is sometimes known by the name of 'Holy Mountain'. It is on the Silk Road and was consequently much visited as a place of pilgrimage by the Buddhists. Near the caves was a suspension bridge across the river, as we learn from a text written between AD 405 and 418 by Qi Fu of the Western Jin period.

which preceded the general evangelisation of the masses; this followed at a later stage, in response to especially favourable historical conditions.

Luoyang, which had been the first Chinese city to welcome Buddhist monks, remained the principal centre of Buddhist studies for several centuries; and it was from Luoyang that more monks set out to spread the doctrine into new territory. One of the products of the school of Luoyang was Zhe Qien, a monk of Scythian origin, who had studied and translated the holy texts with Zhe Liang, a disciple of Lokaksema. After the fall of the Han dynasty in AD 220, Zhe Qien moved from Luoyang to southern China, and settled in Nanking (then known as 'Jien Kan'), the capital of the Wu dynasty (AD 222–280). He continued to work as a translator, and became the head of a school of translation. In AD 241, he was joined by the monk Kang Senghui, who founded the first Buddhist monastery at Nanking – the Monastery of Jien. During the same period of fifty-eight years (which is sometimes known as the Time of the Three Kingdoms), the work of translation at Luoyang continued unabated, with the help of Indian Buddhist monks and of monks coming from Kucha and Parthia. It was during this period that a translation was made of a work that had special importance in China, because it was the fundamental text of the Mahayana, which was the branch of Buddhism that became established in China. This work was the *Sutra of the Lotus*, also known as the *Lotus of the True Law* (*Saddharma Pundarika Sutra*).

An interesting story is told about the introduction of this text into China. It was translated for the first time in the years AD 255–256 by an anonymous monk, but this translation was lost. A second translation was prepared by the famous Dharmaraksha in AD 265, but this was also lost. The third translation, made in AD 286, was the first to survive. It was not, however, the last; many other versions followed. The great interest shown in this text is to be explained by its vital importance to the spread of the doctrine of the Mahayana, and by the authoritative guidance that is offered to the correct presentation and interpretation of events in religious plays, with complete faithfulness to traditional iconography. Among the translators of the *Saddharma Pundarika Sutra* (which in Chinese becomes *Fa Hua Jing* or the *Book of the Flower of the Law*) is the famous Kumarajiva. Born in Kucha, he studied the doctrines of Buddhism in Kashmir, and went on to the Chinese city of Liangzhou. The Chinese monk Daoan later invited him to move on to Changan. The main works of Kumarajiva were written between the date of his arrival at Changan (AD 401) and the date of his death (AD 413 or possibly 417). They made a contribution of fundamental importance to Chinese thought, by providing translations of the text of the major Indian exegetic authorities on Mahayana Buddhism, such as Asvaghosa, Nagarjuna, Vasubandu and Harivarman. Kumarajiva translated a total of ninety-eight works, including one of exceptional importance for China. This was the *Brahmajala Sutra*, a text of the *Mahayana Vinaya*, which lays down the basis of the *vinaya* (discipline) which must be accepted by aspirants to the religious life, such as members of the monastic orders. The work defines not only their religious duties, but also the details of their clothing and the daily routine of their lives.

At the beginning of the fifth century, when Kumarajiva was active, there were already about 17,000 Buddhist temples in China. Most of them were attached to monasteries, inhabited by a religious community which had been set up in response to a popular demand based on historical factors as much as on truly religious considerations.

During the fourth century AD, great changes had taken place in China, which modified the original relationship that had been established between Buddhism and Chinese society. From the year AD 317 onwards, northern China was not governed by a Chinese dynasty. The Jin dynasty (which ruled from AD 317–420) had to move to Nanking, while Luoyang was occupied by the Huns, who founded the Zhao dynasty (AD 318–329), and transferred their capital to Changan, further towards the south-east.

A few years later, power passed into other hands (though they were still the hands of Huns). A new dynasty known as the Later Zhao ruled from AD 329–352.

The Huns were not slow to realise that their power in northern China would soon be undermined if they tried to administer the country through

Buddha said, 'O Subhūti, tell me after thy wit, can a man see the Buddha in the flesh?'

'He cannot, O World-Honoured, and for this reason: The Buddha has declared that flesh has no objective existence.'

Then Buddha told Subhūti, saying, 'All objective existences are unsubstantial and unreal. If a man can see clearly that they are so, then can he see the Buddha.'

Buddha said, 'O Subhūti, if one man were to collect the seven precious things from countless galaxies of worlds, and bestow all these in charity, and another virtuous man, or virtuous woman, were to become filled with the spirit, and held fast by this *sûtra*, preaching it ever so little for the conversion of mankind, I say unto you that the happiness of this last man would far exceed the happiness of that other man.

'Conversion to what? To the disregard of objective existences, and to absolute quiescence of the individual. And why? Because every external phenomenon is like a dream, like a vision, like a bubble, like shadow, like dew, like lightning, and should be regarded as such.'

Kumarajiva (AD 344–413), an Indian Buddhist missionary and scholar from central Asia; he translated Buddhist texts into Chinese at Changan.

the Chinese intelligentsia, for the obvious reason that the Chinese intellectuals knew the traditions of the country, the Confucian rules of conduct, and Chinese society in general better than their barbarian conquerors. In order to govern a people so different from themselves, the barbarians were historically compelled to turn to Buddhism as the source not only of a religious doctrine but also of an alternative culture to replace the culture of Confucianism and the culture of Taoism. The Huns themselves, like many other pastoral peoples of central Asia, had become Buddhists as a result of the missionary eloquence of the Indian monks who arrived with the caravans in the oases along the Silk Road, and stayed there to preach their gospel.

Those monks created centres of culture which often provided the translators of the canonical texts which appeared in China. The Huns were culturally inferior to the Chinese and strangers to their traditions; they adopted Buddhism as a manifestation of a culture of their own. In this way they tried to establish the fact that they had not only conquered China with superior military force, but were also capable of governing the country with the help of the superior culture introduced by the Buddhist monks. The Chinese, on the other hand, were probably amazed and shocked by the thought that a significant doctrine could be of non-Chinese origin, and could in fact have been imported from abroad. Many attempts were made by the Chinese to prove that Buddhism had sprung from a Confucian root or flowered on a Taoist tree.

About the end of the third century AD, the *Mahaparinirvana Sutra* was translated into Chinese (probably from the Pali) by Be Fazi. (A French version of this text has been edited by Carlo Puini under the title *Le livre de l'extinction totale de Buddha*.) The ethics and beliefs of Buddhism are adapted in this work to the rules of Confucianism, in such matters as the importance of filial piety, the respect due to the aged, the worship of Heaven and Earth, respect for the tutelary deities of one's country, and the performance of ritual ceremonies corresponding to the agricultural activities of the four seasons.

The hostility of the Taoists towards Buddhism is well known, and arose from a feeling that they were confronted with a system competitive with their own. There was a real affinity between the two doctrines which made it natural to use Taoist terms to translate Buddhist concepts into Chinese, on both the epistemological and the ethical planes; and both Taoists and Buddhists practised asceticism and monasticism.

In the end, the Taoists came to regard Buddhism as an offshoot of their own system, which was now returning home after a period of wandering in foreign lands; they claimed that the doctrine which they had elaborated had spread out into the various regions of Asia, including the distant land of India, and was now returning to China in the guise of Buddhism.

This aspect is emphasised in *Laozi hua zhu jing* (*The Book of Laozi, the Converter of the Barbarians*), which was written by Wang Fu towards the end of the third century AD, and which claims that Sakyamuni is an immortal spirit who was converted to Taoism by Lao zi when he visited India. Subsequent writers affirm the same ideas. Buddhism is nothing but a reflection of Taoism; and Buddhism is consequently of Chinese origin. It will however be readily understood that these are purely literary affirmations and ideas, supported by the political power attained by the Taoists in Chinese society after a rebellion they had themselves directed. This was the Rebellion of the Yellow Turbans (184 AD), which left the Taoists in a strong position, thanks to their profound links with the peasants and their capacity to give expression to the sufferings and discontent of country people in difficult times.

The Rebellion of the Yellow Turbans inflicted irreparable damage on the Han dynasty, and conferred tremendous prestige on the Taoists. The Taoists were far from ready to give up that prestige – least of all in favour of a foreign religious doctrine. But their efforts to combat it were unavailing.

When northern China fell under foreign domination, her barbarian masters gave their official support to the spread of Buddhism. Shi Le, a king of the Later Zhao dynasty, issued a decree stating that, being bound to follow the customs of his people, it was his duty to pay homage to Buddha, since Buddha was a god of his own barbarian stock. Buddhism was also favoured under the Qin dynasty (AD 352–394), which a general of proto-Tibetan origin had founded on the ruins of the Later Zhao empire. Monasteries were built, and more work was done on the study and translation of Pali and Sanskirt texts under the direction of the monk Fo Tudeng. (Chinese names beginning with 'Fo' are a clear indication of their owner's religion, since 'Fo' means 'Buddha' in Chinese.) These efforts, together with the pacifist ideology of Buddhism, which was expected to discourage hostile sentiments and political demands of every kind, formed the basis of a policy of encouraging the spread of Buddhism. They also helped to convert Buddhism from a doctrine whose main appeal was to the curiosity of intellectual circles into a religion with wide penetration among the masses, embracing ever larger numbers of poor peasants, to whom the new faith might offer a consolation and a refuge from the calamities of the times. After the year AD 385, the Qin dynasty underwent a rapid decline, coinciding with the rise to power of yet another outlandish tribe – that of the proto-Turkish Toba, who had been settled for some decades in one Chinese province, namely Shanxi. In AD 386, they set up a state of their own and founded the Wei dynasty. At this time northern China was divided into many small barbarian states; but the Wei soon embarked on the long and gradual task of bringing the whole area under their control, which they completed in AD 439. The Wei dynasty was a great patron of Buddhism. From its earliest days, it was able to devise a policy well calculated to maintain its own power and at the same time to strengthen the Buddhist church in every way. One by one, and often after a bitter struggle, the states of northern China submitted to the Wei, who followed the subtle policy of allowing the Chinese landed proprietors to remain on their estates, and nominating them *tai shou* or governors of their own property. The landowners, who had expected to suffer confiscation, were thus reassured about the future intentions of the government, now that they had been given this responsibility towards the state. In this way, they became personally involved in government policy and in the future fate of the dynasty. The Chinese landowners, in fact, became members of the Toba hierarchy. Since Buddhism was the religion of the royal court, they had no alternative but to favour the expansion of Buddhism and to support its growth by giving donations to the monasteries and accepting Buddhist monks as advisers. At this point the Taoist monks realised that they were in danger of irretrievable ruin, and succeeded, at least temporarily, in reversing the situation. Perhaps the Taoists softened up the Wei by telling them that they were now fully accepted as a Chinese regime and fully capable of governing in accordance with Chinese tradition; and perhaps the Wei responded with an impulse of honest pride, an urge to prove that they could fulfil this expectation, so deeply flattering for a foreign dynasty. Be that as it may, a series of edicts by King Tai Wu (AD 424–451) unleashed a policy of repression against Buddhism, which was outlawed as being a 'foreign religion'! (This took place in the years AD 444–446.)

This is the first instance in history of a persecution directed against Buddhism. The second such persecution took place exactly four centuries later, in AD 845. By that time, no one could have maintained that Buddhism was still a foreign religion in China; and so there had to be a different reason for the second persecution. Its causes were in fact socio-economic. Out of every five mouths to feed, one belonged to a soldier and one to a monk, which made for an excessively high percentage of 'parasites'. The monasteries had also become centres of power and privilege, being exempted from the duties and obligations to which other landowners were subject.

The second persecution will be discussed more fully in the chapter on architecture.

The first persecution did not cause irreparable damage (unlike the second which saw the destruction of most of the monasteries). It seems, in fact, to have produced something like a feeling of guilt in the royal family. When Tai Wu died, his successor Gaozong (AD 452–465) at once issued a new edict which made Buddhism legal again. In the year AD 460, he also commissioned a series of religious sculptures in the caves of Yungang, in Shanxi province. The idea of digging out caves and decorating them with

Dunhuang, Gansu. Northern wall of cave no. 275 (Northern Liang period, AD 400–420). As the rock out of which they were dug is unsuitable for sculpture, the main artistic wealth of this large group of caves lies in wall-paintings of extraordinary beauty; the few statues found there are modelled in coloured plaster. The various works date from different periods, ranging from the fifth to the first half of the eighth century AD. Cave no. 275 is rectangular in shape, and its ceiling is held up by beams. The niches of the northern wall of this cave have frames like the doors of an imperial palace, and contain statues of the Bodhisattva Maitreya, which combine the strength of the Buddhist cultural tradition with the originality of Chinese art. The paintings show scenes from the lives of various mythical characters. On the southern wall of the cave is a painting of a scene from the life of the Buddha. The style of painting and the appearance of the figures are not typically Chinese; like all the works of art at Dunhuang, they show the influence of central Asiatic tradition.

Pages 72–73:
Baicheng, Xinjiang. The caves of Kezier. The photograph shows a lunette in cave no. 17, with paintings dating from the fourth and fifth centuries AD. The rock is very friable in this cave, but the walls are covered with frescos. The ceiling is divided into three areas. To the left and right are large panels illustrating scenes from the life of the Buddha; the smaller central panel depicts an unaccompanied standing figure of a Buddha, with a full-length, oval aureole behind him. The lunette, lower centre, shows a Bodhisattva sitting with crossed legs; to his left and right are other Bodhisattvas in attitudes of adoration. The style is typical of central Asian art of the late fourth and early fifth centuries; the strong outlines emphasise the anatomical structure of the figures, while their attitudes suggest an inner serenity.

Buddhist religious art had probably been suggested to the Wei dynasty by the caves at Dunhuang, in Liang province, which they had conquered in the years AD 435–440. At Dunhuang, the Buddhist monk Luo Zun had begun work in AD 366, digging out and decorating the caves in accordance with a tradition which had grown up in India and was well suited to Indian climatic conditions and the poverty of Indian monks. The same tradition imposed itself in China as well, in spite of the very different climatic and political conditions. The Wei dynasty (who reigned from AD 439–535 and whose full historical name is the Northern Wei) gave much encouragement to the construction of Buddhist cave-temples and to their decoration with frescoes and sculptures. In AD 494 the Wei transferred their capital from Datong in Shanxi to Luoyang in Henan; and it was only a year later that they commissioned the construction of the cave-temples at Longmen, just a few miles from the new capital.

The wealth of images of the Buddha himself and of the numerous other religious personages associated with him by the Mahayana branch of the faith, together with the many representations of the narrative passages contained in the sacred texts of Buddhism, combined to form a powerful instrument for the conversion of the masses, to whom the images spoke a mysterious language, full of arcane significance and dazzling flashes of illumination. In northern China, as we have already indicated, various historical and political factors favoured the spread of a great wave of literary, philosophical and artistic interest in Buddhism; but the effects were not confined to northern China. The great wave also swept over southern China, to which the Jin dynasty had withdrawn in AD 317. In the south as in the north, centres of study had sprung up for the perusal and the translation of the canonical texts, of works of exegesis and of religious literature in general. Temples and monasteries had also been built in the south, including two very early examples at Nanking. These were the famous monasteries of Wa guan si and Long guan si, with accommodation for one thousand resident monks. Here, too, a centre of religious studies was organised and many translations were produced during the fourth century AD. This fervid intellectual activity found its emotional counterpart in a passionate desire to spread the gospel of Buddhism, by building new monasteries to attract more disciples and scholars, and also by obtaining the co-operation of famous artists, such as Gu Kaizhi (AD 345–405), whose paintings on Buddhist themes have unfortunately been lost – as have the Buddhist paintings of Zao Buxing about one century earlier. The monk Huiyuan, who lived at Nanking in the fourth century AD, exercised an important influence on the intellectual Buddhism of the whole of southern China. Born in Shanxi in AD 334, Huiyuan had studied at Luoyang under the monk Daoan, who had himself been a disciple of the famous Fo Tudeng. Huiyuan thus represents the continuity of a great Buddhist tradition. He founded the monastery of Lu shan at Nanking; but perhaps his greatest merit is that of having stimulated the special interest in a more profound investigation of the Buddhist concept of reality. The intellectual climate of the time was in fact already favourable to such a development; and the extra impetus provided by Huiyuan bore fruit in a very important project, which was welcomed by, and later given the full backing of, the Emperor An di (AD 396–419 of the Jin dynasty). This was the despatch of a monk to India on a special mission. The monk Fa Xian, born in Shanxi but living in Nanking, was appointed to carry out the project. He set out in AD 399 and returned from his journey in AD 414. He brought back with him from India a set of canonical texts, which he subsequently translated. He also wrote a detailed account of his journey under the title *Tian zhu shi*, which was first translated into a European language in 1883 – see *Record of the Journey of Fa-hsien* by Bunyn Nanjo, published at Oxford.

Fa Xian's journey to India, to the fountainhead of Buddhism, may seem to deny, but in fact confirms, the complete doctrinal maturity, the philosophical independence and the spiritual depth of Buddhism in China, as a part of the Chinese cultural heritage at that time, which had outgrown the incomplete and second-hand materials provided by the leading Buddhist teachers of the central Asiatic schools. Though it might still wish to draw additional sap from its Indian roots, Chinese Buddhism was now well

established on Chinese soil, like a great tree branching out in all directions, bearing a rich philosophical and artistic harvest, and drawing its main strength from the essentially Chinese traditions of Confucianism and Taoism. If the introduction of Buddhism into China was the effect of a chain of specific historical events, its success was due to certain particular characteristics of earlier Chinese cultural tradition.

One of the fundamental principles of Buddhism is atheism, for the negation of the Self involves the negation of God.

There is no such thing as *existence*; everything is in a state of continual flux or *becoming*. When we watch a flame burning, it does not remain the same flame from one moment to another, but nor does it become another flame; and the same is true of our life. The Self is similar to the flame that burns and to the candle that feeds that flame. The Self therefore contains nothing which remains the same from one moment to the next, or from one moment to the moment before. And the same is true of the experiences of the Self – and consequently of its cognitions.

Kucha, Xinjiang. The caves of Qumtura. A ceiling painting from cave 46 (3rd or 4th century AD). Diamond-shaped panels are set in a chequer-board design. Each panel is outlined with a pattern of petals, and has as its central figure a seated Buddha complete with halo, in a circular frame. A second figure kneels alongside the Buddha. The background between the panels is decorated with animal figures of remarkable realism.

Tianshui, Gansu. External view of the caves of Maijishan, at the western end of the Qinling mountain range, about 40 kilometres (25 miles) south-east of the city of Tianshan (known as 'Qinzhou' during the Qin dynasty). At the beginning of the fifth century AD, the Buddhist monk Xuan Gao came here from Changan to carry out a vow of ascetism. A large part of the hill has been carried away by landslides; the surviving caves are to be found on its eastern and western faces. The oldest of these caves date from the middle of the fifth century AD.

Datong, Shanxi. The caves of Yungang. The seated Buddha in cave no. 20. Dug out of sandstone cliffs, these caves extend for about one kilometre (1,100 yards) along the northern bank of the River Wuzhou, about 15 kilometres (9 miles) from the city of Datong. There are 42 caves in all, dating from the period between AD 460 and 535. This particular Buddha was carved between AD 460 and 465, as one of a series of five huge statues, commissioned by the Emperor Wen Chang of the Northern Wei dynasty. The statue is given a particularly impressive appearance by the reflective properties of the sandstone from which it is carved. The position depicted is that of 'dhyana' or meditation, the Chinese name for which is 'chan'. By the side of the main figure is a smaller statue of a standing Buddha. The lower part of the main figure has been damaged by a landslip affecting the front part of the cave.

Left: Datong, Shanxi. The caves of Yungang. Buddhist figures on the eastern wall of cave no. 18, dating from the time of the Northern Wei dynasty (AD 439–535). In the middle of the cave is a large statue of a standing Buddha. The eastern and western walls are carved with Buddhas and Bodhisattvas arranged symmetrically in relation to the central statue. The illustration shows a section of the eastern wall; the huge head (1.80 metres or 6 feet in height) in the bottom left-hand corner of the picture belonged to a statue of the Bodhisattva Guanyin, most of which has disintegrated. Around the head of the Bodhisattva are five standing figures representing followers of Buddha; three of them are shown in the photograph. Although the style of these works owes much to the Indian artists of Mathura, the visitor cannot fail to be impressed by the creative imagination and mental independence of the sculptors of the Northern Wei dynasty – qualities which find full expression in the freedom and variety of the attitudes of the figures. These statues date from the years AD 460–465.

Above right: Datong, Shanxi. The caves of Yungang. Seated Buddha in cave no. 19B (period of the Northern Wei dynasty). The cave is made up of two separate chambers – 19A to the east and 19B to the west. The eastern chamber belongs to the period of the great statues (AD 460–465). The western chamber was for some reason left incomplete, but contains the statue shown here, which is the largest at Yungang, being 16.48 metres (54 feet) in height. The Buddha is seated in a normal attitude. Both he and the small figures of the faithful which stand on either side of him are dressed in the Chinese style. His face, however, shows traces of the style of an earlier period, being affected by Indian influences, and in particular by the example of the great statues at Bamiyan in Afghanistan, which have inspired so much monumental sculpture. The western half of this cave has been carried away by landslips, together with the front wall of the adjacent cave no. 20. It is only recently that these figures have recovered their original beauty thanks to a programme of skilful restoration.

The Buddhist disproof of *existence* can be summed up in the following logical terms: *action* and *creation* both imply *becoming*, and *becoming* is, by definition, different from *being*. That which *becomes* cannot be said to *be*.

The process of *becoming* includes birth and death – two ambivalent terms, the meaning of which varies with the point of view of the observer, just as we may call a door an entrance or an exit according to where we stand in relation to it. Ambivalence thus reinforces the concept of relativity.

In this way, the concept of relativity is supported even by pairs of phenomena (such as birth and death) which appear at first sight to be opposites of a most definite character, but are in fact no more than two identical moments forming part of a single, vast process. That process is the cycle of reincarnation: a vital force or *karma* invests us with the will to live and with life itself, and implants the love of life in us, although life is pain, as can be shown by an objective consideration of its four phases – birth, sickness, old age and death. If the *karma* put into a given life-cycle

Datong, Shanxi. The caves of Yungang. The antechamber of cave no. 12 (period of the Northern Wei dynasty). The illustration shows part of the northern wall and part of the ceiling which is decorated with huge lotus flowers and flying angels. The square niche in the middle of the photograph is directly above the doorway. It is flanked by two more niches with flattened arches. In the one on the right, we see the preaching of the first sermon on the Wheel of the Law in the Park of the Wild Deer. In the left-hand niches, we see the Buddha flanked by the four Kings of the Sky bearing offerings. The upper part of the wall has a frieze of angels making music. The decoration of this cave is thought to have been carried out in AD 480.

does not use up all its energy, it regenerates to form another life. The wheel of reincarnation is known as *samsara*. There is no salvation for man as long as he is the victim of the *samsara*. Salvation is a matter of breaking the cycle; and for this it is essential to become aware of the truth of our situation, to see that what appears to us as reality is an illusion, and to unmask it for what it really is – a chance series of false and deceitful moments. The end of the *samsara* is the end of passion and sorrow, the achievement of supreme happiness, and is called 'Nirvana'. This is the one and only unqualified reality, which frees us not only from the pain of believing in illusions, but from every kind of physical and mental condition. The meaning of Nirvana is in fact 'non-existence'.

The idea of God the Creator had never been established in China. (In India, on the other hand, this doctrine was present in the thought of Brahmanism and, later, of Hinduism.) If such a belief had been native to China, Buddhism would never have got beyond the stage of being a minor sect, with little appeal to the masses. In China, however, the hierarchy of God, man and nature had never existed. The Chinese had a profound feeling for nature, which made it easy for them to accept, at least on the mythological plane, the idea that a man could be turned into an animal, an insect, a plant or a stone – or vice versa. To put it another way, nature had always been considered as a homogeneous complex, within which the animal, vegetable and mineral kingdoms differ from each other only incidentally, being moved by mysterious inner energies. These energies create a harmonious state of *becoming* in nature as a whole, within which metamorphosis, or an exchange of roles, is quite possible. That is why the Chinese have always been deeply convinced atheists.

The Buddhism that spread through China is known as the Mahayana or Great Vehicle, in contradistinction to the sect known as the Hinayana or Little Vehicle. For followers of the Hinayana, the message of the Buddha is historical and ethical, since his teachings contain a moral system on which we can base our lives. For followers of the Mahayana, on the other hand, his message is metaphysical and religious. They therefore do not consider Sakyamuni to be the historical Buddha, but rather a hypostasis, an epiphany of the Truth vouchsafed to one particular era, or one particular phase of the cycle of cosmic eras. There must therefore be many other Buddhas, other hypostases of the truth vouchsafed to various cosmic epochs, including a Buddha of the Future. Amid this multitude of Buddhas, the Buddha of history loses the physical solidity of a human life, and fades away into the impalpable mists of legend and myth.

But that is not the whole story. The number of Buddhas is infinite, since every living creature and every inanimate object has in itself the quality of a Buddha, although this is generally hidden by the deceitful veil of ignorance. If we try to tear that veil away, we need not be alone in our efforts; we can count on the merciful assistance of a Bodhisattva – a being peculiar to Mahayana Buddhism, and unknown to the Hinayana.

This belief in the essentially Buddhic nature of everything also has its parallel in the cultural tradition of Taoism, which regards the void as the natural origin of every kind of force. Living creatures and inanimate objects exist in the form in which they appear to us because the void is there to delineate their shapes; and from this it follows that the void is reality. The Buddhic nature of things is therefore closely parallel to the void, because the objective which the Buddhic nature enables us to achieve is Nirvana, or non-existence.

In matters of art, and especially in matters of iconography, the two doctrines of Mahayana and Hinayana take different roads.

According to the Hinayana, it is not possible to depict the Buddha because he does not exist. During his life as recorded in history, he was a mere illusion, subject to constant change, like everything that falls within our experience. The end of this phase was immediately followed by the beginning of Nirvana – and how can we depict non-existence? The flowering of Buddhist art developed with the spread of Mahayana Buddhism. Paradoxically enough, the earliest images of that art represented purely metaphysical subjects, which existed only in the field of religious belief and lay right outside the world of human experience. At the moment when a philosophical theory (the Hinayana) was transformed into a

Datong, Shanxi. The caves of Yungang. Antechamber of cave no. 9 (period of the Northern Wei dynasty). The antechamber is rectangular in plan; the decoration of the eastern and western walls includes an upper row of niches designed to look like buildings, with tiled roofs. Below these are other niches, about halfway down the wall, containing statues of the Buddha in various attitudes. Below these again is a relief frieze, running right round the room, and depicting scenes from the life of Prince Shama, the son of King Dharma. In the centre of the northern wall is the opening of a corridor, decorated with a festooned frieze topped by a representation of a tiled roof. On one side of the corridor, which leads into the next cave, is a carving representing a tutelary deity. It is thought that the decoration of cave no. 9 was completed in AD 475, for the first visit by the Emperor Xiao Wen of the Northern Wei dynasty.

Bas-relief representing a pagoda, from cave no. 2 at Yungang (beginning of the sixth century AD). Among the decorations of the Yungang caves we often find these small pagodas at the sides of the niches. The design is that of a series of pavilions, open on all four sides, piled on top of each other, and is derived directly from the structure of guard-towers of the Han period. (See also the illustrations on page 134.)

Luoyang, Henan. The caves of Longmen. A general view of the 'Cave of the Ancient Dragon' (Laolongdong) and of the many other caves that surround it, in the valley of the River I Shuei to the south of Mount Longmen. The niches contain large statues of the Buddha, carved in the limestone of the cliff-face. The statues and reliefs cover a very long period, starting with AD 495–534, when Luoyang was the capital of the Northern Wei dynasty, and going on to the middle of the eighth century AD. Many statues of the Buddha have been lost.

A CHINESE PILGRIM IN THE LAND OF THE BUDDHA

The pilgrims now arrived at the city of Gaya, also a complete waste within its walls. Journeying about three more miles southwards, they reached the place where the Bôdhisatva formerly passed six years in self-mortification. It is very woody. From this point going west a mile, they arrived at the spot where Buddha entered the water to bathe, and a god pressed down the branch of a tree to pull him out of the pool. Also, by going two-thirds of a mile farther north, they reached the place where the two lay-sisters presented Buddha with congee made with milk. Two-thirds of a mile to the north of this is the place where Buddha, sitting on a stone under a great tree and facing the east, ate it. The tree and the stone are both there still, the latter being about six feet in length and breadth by over two feet in height. In Central India the climate is equable; trees will live several thousand, and even so much as ten thousand years. From this point going north-east half a yojana, the pilgrims arrived at the cave where the Bôdhisatva, having entered, sat down cross-legged with his face to the west, and reflected as follows: 'If I attain perfect wisdom, there should be some miracle in token thereof.' Whereupon the silhouette of Buddha appeared upon the stone, over three feet in length, and is plainly visible to this day. Then heaven and earth quaked mightily, and the gods who were in space cried out, saying, 'This is not the place where past and future Buddhas have attained and should attain perfect wisdom. The proper spot is beneath the Bô tree, less than half a yojana to the south-west of this.' When the gods had uttered these words, they proceeded to lead the way with singing in order to conduct him thither. The Bôdhisatva got up and followed, and when thirty paces from the tree a god gave him the kus'a grass. Having accepted this, he went on fifteen paces farther, when five hundred dark-coloured birds came and flew three times round him, and departed. The Bôdhisatva went on to the Bô tree, and laying down his kus'a grass, sat down with his face to the east. Then Mara, the king of the devils, sent three beautiful women to approach from the north and tempt him; he himself approaching from the south with the same object. The Bôdhisatva pressed the ground with his toes, whereupon the infernal army retreated in confusion, and the three women became old. At the above-mentioned place where Buddha suffered mortification for six years, and on all these other spots, men of after ages have built pagodas and set up images, all of which are still in existence. Where Buddha, having attained perfect wisdom, comtemplated the tree for seven days, experiencing the joys of emancipation; where Buddha walked backwards and forwards, east and west, under the Bô tree for seven days; where the gods produced a jewelled chamber and worshipped Buddha for seven days; where the blind dragon Muchilinda enveloped Buddha for seven days; where Buddha sat facing the east on a square stone beneath the nyagrodha tree, and Brahmâ came to salute him; where the four heavenly kings offered their alms-bowls; where the five hundred traders gave him cooked rice and honey; where he converted the brothers Kasyapa with their disciples to the number of one thousand souls – on all these spots stûpas have been raised.

Fa Xian, a Chinese Buddhist pilgrim who made an adventurous journey to India, lasting from AD 399 to 414.

Luoyang, Henan. The caves of Longmen. The northern wall of the 'Cave of the Ancient Yang' (Guyangdong). Engraved on each niche is its date of construction. These dates range from AD 500 to AD 515 (Northern Wei dynasty). The northern and southern walls are each divided into three horizontal panels, each of which contains four niches. All the niches contain statues of the Buddha of almost equal size. An inscription records the fact that each niche was sculpted by a different artist. The figures in the top rows show the Buddha in the attitude of meditation (chan); in the middle rows we can recognise the Bodhisattva Maitreya; but the figures in the bottom rows cannot be identified. The Buddhas are examples of an elaborate style, and the same is true of the very detailed decorations inside and outside the niches.

Pages 90–91:
Luoyang, Henan. The caves of Longmen. Interior of the central chamber of the 'Cave of the Submission of Yang' or 'Pinyangdong' (period of the Northern Wei dynasty). The central statue is more than 8 metres (26 feet) in height, and depicts Sakyamuni in the seated position. Behind him is a huge, flame-shaped aureole, the pointed tip of which reaches the ceiling. On either side of the Buddha are symmetrical groups of standing figures which include his followers Kasyapa and Ananda and various Bodhisattvas. On the side walls to left and right are two large statues of standing Buddhas, flanked by Bodhisattvas whose faces have been badly damaged. In all these figures, we can see the same monumental qualities that we have already noticed at Yungang; but the completely Chinese artistic presentation of the whole group, and the pyramidal structure and upward thrust of the great central figure serve to date the decoration of this cave to the beginning of the sixth century AD, probably between AD 505 and AD 523. In the following period, the element of upward thrust is used to emphasise the spiritual nature of the images, and becomes a more and more prominent feature of Chinese sculptural style.

religious faith (the Mahayana), the artistic imagination was set free to celebrate, with true religious fervour, the ineffable beatitude in Nirvana of beings unknown to the world of human experience. According to the doctrine of the Hinayana, Nirvana is conceived as the negation of *samsara*: Nirvana begins when *samsara* ends. For the Mahayana, however, Nirvana cannot be opposed to *samsara*, just as the one cannot be opposed to the many, or being to not-being. When we try to oppose one idea to another, all we can achieve is to concentrate attention on the two of them taken together. The same argument is valid for being and non-being: they cancel each other out, and neither of them has any value in isolation from the other, because the conceptual nature of their existence is dialectic (which means that it feeds on its opposite). The Nirvana of the Mahayana is accordingly not conceived as the end of all things, but as the sum of all things, gathered up into a synthesis of opposites, in which Nirvana equals *samsara*. This may be why the Nirvana of the Mahayana lent itself (and still lends itself) to representation in samsaric terms – a garden of delights, with flowers, music and flying dancers, all depicted with a wealth of imaginative colouring. Buddhist iconology could draw on inexhaustible sources of ideas, scenes and episodes from the sacred text of the faith. Deeply religious artists used this material to build up a rich mixture of reality and fantasy, of experience and imagination and of history and metaphysics. With the passage of time, their work became organised into increasingly perfect patterns, and was finally standardised by the introduction of canons, which it was not safe to break. Such was the birth and the growth of an iconography which has no equal in the world for wide and varied choice of subject, expressive power and rich symbolism. The details given enable us to distinguish between Buddha and Bodhisattva, and to go on and identify the individual by name. The hands of the figures are placed in significant positions (*mudra*) which often remind us of the historical experiences of the Buddha Sakyamuni, and the most significant or dramatic moments of his life or his teaching.

In addition to historical references, more or less mingled with mythological elements, we have the endless series of episodes belonging to the Jataka or previous lives of the Buddha. Their main theme is that of love, as manifested by the voluntary sacrifice of an animal, such as a roe-deer or a hare, in which the Buddha had been incarnated before his birth as Sakyamuni. Among the products of the Buddhist imagination were various Paradises, the Lands of the Pure, and many Buddhas not recorded in history, led by Amitabha or Infinite Light, who is in charge of the Western Paradise. All the Buddhas are recognisable by their mysterious, ineffable smile.

Both the doctrine of Buddhism and the art based on it were imported from abroad by the Chinese; but they re-invented both the doctrine and the art in a way which invested them with a completely Chinese physiognomy. They always, however, cultivated feelings of special respect towards the country from which this wonderful philosophy had come. On a number of different occasions, the Chinese Buddhists sent out scholarly missions of investigation. In AD 518, the Buddhist monk Songyun left China for the central Asian regions which had previously sent so many teachers to China. The most famous of all these missions is the one carried out by the Chinese monk Xuan Zang (AD 602–669), from the celebrated monastery of Zu En (Changan). His memorable mission to India in the years AD 629–644 is recorded in numerous documents and literary legends of a later period.

Another example of the Chinese Buddhists' respectful desire to deepen their knowledge of the doctrine of their faith is to be found in the special relationship set up for the purposes of religious collaboration between the monasteries of China and the Indian monastery of Nalanda (known to the Chinese as 'Nalanto'), in the Sui and Tang periods.

Also relevant is a journey in the opposite direction, from India to China, carried out in the year AD 520 by the Indian monk Bodhidharma, who was the twenty-eighth Buddhist patriarch of India and became the first Buddhist patriarch of China. Putidamo (to give the Chinese version of his name) came to Luoyang, which was then the capital of China, bringing with him the original teachings of the Buddha. His message was based on a very

Baicheng, Xinjiang. The Kezier caves. The illustration shows the defeat of the demons by the Buddha; it is taken from a wall painting in the 'Cave of the Peacock'. This cave was discovered at the beginning of the present century by a group of German archaeologists. This painting was subsequently removed from the wall and taken to Berlin, where it was destroyed during the Second World War. The walls of the main chamber of this cave were subdivided into panels on which various scenes from the life of the Buddha were represented. Though subjected to trials that had reduced him almost to a skeleton, the Buddha succeeds in resisting the temptations of the daughters of Mara (the spirit of evil), and converts them into white-haired old women, as we see in the right-hand section of the illustration. The lack of brilliance in the colours and certain other characteristics of this style show the influence of Kushan art. The date of the painting is about AD 500.

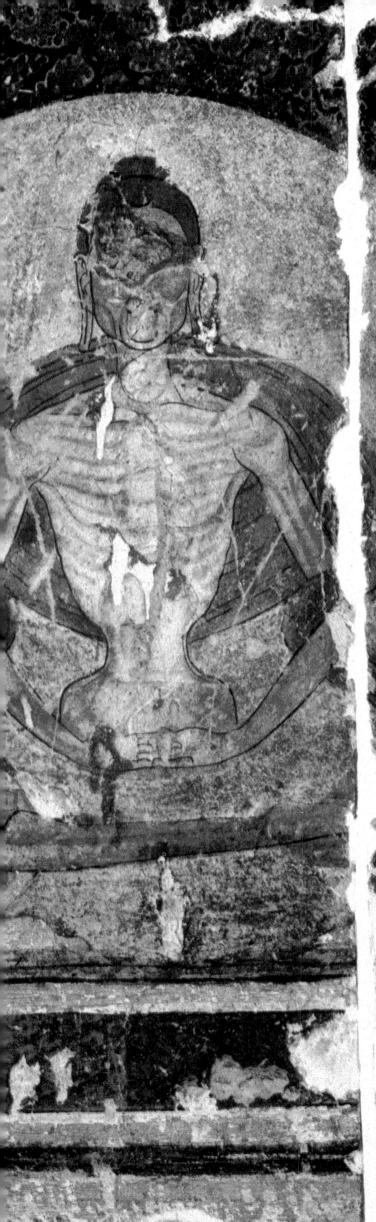

simple and obvious principle: in order to acquire awareness of one's own ignorance, there is no need of study (even of the scriptures) or of any form of external help; all that is needed is meditation. This doctrine was known as *chan*, a Chinese approximation to the sound of the Sanskrit word *dhyana*, which means 'meditation'. By a strange and potent paradox, *chan* became one of the most refined and subtle intellectual movements that the world has ever seen. In the field of art, it had a marked influence on painting with brush and ink, but otherwise had little effect. As a religious doctrine, it became more important at the beginning of the thirteenth century, when it was established in Japan under the name of Zen – a further phonetic approximation.

Cave Temples

BUDDHIST MONKS had reached the valley of the Tarim at a very early stage, travelling with caravans that were making the return trip to China after taking silk to Kashgar. It was at the beginning of the second century AD, when commercial traffic was at its heaviest and the oasis states were at their busiest and most prosperous, that the monks began to settle at various points along the route, founding missionary schools, from which pilgrims later began to set out for China, to tackle the more difficult task of missionary work in a land where culture and social organisation had reached a much higher level. While some of the oases had become centres of Buddhist studies, virtually all the tribes in the valley had yielded to the fascination exercised by this strange new religion, and had been converted to Buddhism. This was true not only of the settled population, but also of the nomads. The Huns who founded the Zhao and Later Zhao dynasties in China in the fourth century AD were Buddhists; and so were the proto-Turkish Toba, who settled in Shanxi, inside Chinese territory, during the same century. Culturally speaking, both the Huns and the Toba were much more closely linked with central Asia than with Confucian and Taoist China. This situation had two important consequences. Buddhism was strengthened both in central Asia and in China itself; and a link sprang up between China and central Asia, or at least between China and Serindia, providing a basis for improvement in the security of the area, which was an indispensable condition for the development of commercial relations.

These conditions were also favourable to the cultural development of Serindia (taking culture as equivalent to Buddhism). Opportunities arose for the beginnings of artistic production among its peoples. By a fortunate chance, several relatively advanced countries, such as Iran, India and Gandhara, were not too far away. Together with the merchants from those countries came the influence of advanced cultures, which easily took root in a region where there was no established culture of a different kind. Another favourable factor was the general prosperity of the peoples of the valley, who were benefiting both from trading activities which had reached a higher level than ever before or after, and from the provision of the services required by the caravans. Artistic activity was also encouraged by the economic and political support afforded to the peoples of the valley by the dynasties reigning in China, especially the Wei and the Tang. But the beginning of this extraordinary chapter in the history of art was quite fortuitous. In the year AD 336, the monk Luo Zun began digging out a rock-face at Dunhuang in order to create caves which could be used as Buddhist temples. The fortuitous element in this event consists in the fact that there was no cave temple tradition either in China or in central Asia. It was in fact a purely Indian tradition. The Buddhist monks of India had originally turned to the construction of cave temples for lack of anything better, because they were too poor to finance the building of temples of brick or stone in the open air themselves, and because they were too isolated, in the midst of a predominantly Hindu population, to raise the necessary large sums locally. In the hot, damp climate of India, cave temples also had the advantage of offering a cool, dry retreat. In China, on the other hand, the traditional practice was to build the temples of

Gongxian, Henan. An external view of caves nos. 1 and 2. These caves are not far from the city of Gonxian. Dug out of the steep southern side of Mount Dafang, they look out over the valley of the river Luo shuei. During the Northern Wei period, this group of five caves was known as the Temple of Xi Xuan. On the outside wall of cave no. 1, on either side of the entrance, are standing statues of *jinganjlishi* – tutelary saints of the Buddhist religion, who are often to be found at the entrance to temples. These statues are about 3 metres (10 feet) in height, and date from some time after AD 520, in the final period of the dynasty of the Northern Wei.

Confucianism out of wood, which was a suitable material in the dry northern climate.

The cave temples of Dunhuang were the first to be constructed in an area under Chinese influence; and a century elapsed before the example was followed elsewhere. It was between AD 435 and 440 that the Wei conquered the province of Liangzhou, which included Dunhuang, and had their first sight of cave temples; and it was in AD 460 that they ordered the construction of similar cave temples at Yungang, near Datong, as an act of reparation for their persecution of the Buddhists fifteen years earlier.

The Yungang cave temples
No fewer than 40,000 Turkish families were moved from Serindia to Yungang to provide the labour necessary for the work of excavation, while a team of monastic artists was given the task of decorating the caves with Buddhist sculptures.

The artistic model for the first sculptures at Yungang was provided by the splendid statues of the Buddha carved in the living rock at Bamiyan, an important caravan station in Afghanistan. The statues are of gigantic size, with precisely stylised features in harmony with the magnificent, static quality of the great figures, which stand out powerfully from the mountain wall and dominate the surrounding world. Their clothing (especially over the upper part of the body), is characterised by a series of deep folds, represented by parallel grooves cut into the rock, which clearly recall the Graeco-Roman style of Gandhara. This stylistic tradition is continued in the earliest statues to be carved in the rock of Yungang.

In the next phase Chinese tradition also makes itself felt. There is a happy meeting of two styles. First there is the style of Gandhara, which is robust and monumental, with some artificial elaboration of decorative motifs such as the folds of clothing. In the second place, we have the Chinese stylistic tradition, developed in the time of the Han dynasty

Gongxian, Henan. A relief on the southern wall of cave no. 1 (period of the Northern Wei dynasty). The subject – a religious procession – is a common one in the Gongxian caves. A priest leads a group of nobles accompanied by their servants, who carry ceremonial fans. Representations of groups of the faithful on their way to render homage to the Buddha are also to be found in the reliefs of Longmen and at Binyang. These reliefs provide most valuable evidence regarding the costume of the period.

Gongxian, Henan. The western wall of cave no. 1 (Northern Wei dynasty). The illustration shows the pointed arch above a niche. A row of statues depicts the Seven Buddhas of the Past; the Buddha himself sits in the centre on a covered throne. Above his head, in a large panel extending to the roof, are rows of smaller niches containing statues of the Thousand Buddhas, all shown in the position of meditation. These sculptures were completed in the period between AD 517 and 523.

Pages 98–99:
Dunhuang, Gansu. Wall-painting in cave no. 249 (dynasty of the Western Wei, AD 535–556). The illustration shows the central part of the arch that frames the most important niche in this cave. The Buddha is shown at the centre of the picture, among decorative motifs based on the lotus and the dwarf palm-tree. Celestial musicians appear on either side. The lively colouring (which has unfortunately been affected by oxidation) and the general elegance of the style are typical of the art of this period.

(202 BC–AD 220) which depends on the realistic, mobile, solid, dynamic representation of the figures. Yungang thus offers the visitor a wonderful spectacle composed of two types of image of the Buddha. One is static, monumental and overpowering, heavily charged with magnetic force and depicted with racial characteristics which are foreign to China. The other expresses the dynamic qualities of Chinese sculpture, shows us Chinese faces and Chinese clothes, and depicts the dignified attitudes and impressive charisma of the typical Chinese magnate. As time goes by, the artists cease to shape their style entirely by the imitation of earlier works, and develop a mature artistic tradition based on its own technique and its own taste – always retaining the superior ability of the Chinese artist to depict the human figure in all its rich expressiveness.

Towards the end of the fifth century AD, the Wei were preparing to transfer their capital from Datong (Shanxi) to Luoyang (Henan) – a better centre from which to adminster the government of northern China. Chinese sculpture had just achieved a dramatic qualitative advance, which was itself a proof of the Chinese artists' extraordinary grasp of the philosophical contents of Buddhism, and also of their extraordinary mastery of the technical methods required to give adequate artistic expression to that philosophy. The dramatic qualitative advance was linked with a rejection of the idea that the images of Buddhism should affect the physical, dynamic reality of a terrestrial world, the solid safety of which was guaranteed by a mighty empire. For Buddhism and the images of Buddhism could not belong to a world of certainty and of solid, dynamic reality. Both the spiritual essence of Buddhism and its intellectual content were bound to focus the attention of mankind on different values, totally alien to human affairs. The artists of the day had to face the problem of using solid images of stone to express the spiritual significance of the

Dunhuang, Gansu. 'The Story of the Five Hundred Thieves', a wall-painting in cave no. 285; painted in AD 538–539, during the Western Wei dynasty. The various scenes of this traditional Buddhist legend are shown against a blank background. To the left we see the capture of the five hundred thieves by soldiers on horseback. To the right, the thieves are punished by having their eyes put out; their cries of pain move the Buddha to pity, and he gives them back their sight. The thieves are converted, and become monks. The staves which they have used as weapons grow up into a wood, which is known as the 'Wood of Eyes'. An inscription dates the picture to the years AD 538–539, at the beginning of the Western Wei dynasty. This dating is also confirmed by the typically Chinese style of the painting, and by its rich, dynamic but never heavy composition.

figures themselves and of a whole world that had to be simultaneously depicted and denied. Among the factors contributing to the achievement of this end were the sensitive imagination of the Chinese artists and the artistic tradition that central Asia had recently inherited from the regions corresponding to present-day Iran, Afghanistan and northern India. (Part of that heritage was the technique of working in polychrome stucco.) The Chinese artists soon understood that a spiritualising doctrine must be represented by figures the very materiality of which displays a tendency towards the immaterial. This understanding found expression in the use of vertically elongated forms, and of triangular figures tapering from a wide base to the apex formed by a long, narrow face and head. This tendency is clearly visible in the sculpture of the Yungang caves, although it was to find better and fuller expression in the following decades in the cave temples of Longmen and Dunhuang, where the artists had scope to achieve a further development of the intuitive understanding they had acquired at Yungang. That intuitive understanding was now associated with a joyousness of composition that bore witness to the prospect of a radiantly happy future opened up by the teachings of the Buddha. As regards subject matter, the elaborate works of art in these caves are packed with flying dancers and other cheerful and decorative motifs, which are well calculated to arouse feelings of happy expectancy in relation to the world of Buddhism. On the technical side, these works are characterised by the use of polychrome stucco. Some of the figures were hewn out of the living rock and then covered with a thick layer of plaster or stucco, to which the sculptor added the final touches. Other figures or decorative motifs were composed entirely of stucco, which could be worked more easily and more rapidly than stone. Pigments of mineral or vegetable origin were then applied to the plaster, creating an effect of

THE SIGNS OF THE BUDDHA   101

Tangshui, Gansu. The Maijishan caves. A triad in cave no. 133 (period of the Western Wei dynasty). The external height of the entrance to this cave is 20 metres (65 feet); the chamber itself is 6 metres (20 feet) in height, and 11.5 metres (38 feet) in depth from front to back. It is the largest cave on the western side of the hill. Eighteen inscriptions are carved vertically into the rock of the cave, all of them illustrated with figures of the Thousand Buddhas. For this reason, the cave was formerly known as the 'Cave of the Ten Thousand Buddhas'. The photograph shows a detail of the decoration. Horizontal panels above and below the triad are carved with figures of the Thousand Buddhas. The triad itself appears in the centre, surrounded by a rectangular frame. It consists of a figure of the Buddha seated in the 'covered throne' position, flanked by two Bodhisattvas standing on lotus flowers. The Buddha's face is relatively long and narrow, in keeping with the style of the artists of the Northern Wei dynasty; but the treatment of the mantle, (shown as falling loosely over part of the throne), suggests a period of transition between the Northern Wei and the Western Wei periods. The soft folds of the Buddha's mantle in fact show the flexibility of line which is characteristic of Western Wei artists; and the same is true of the flying angels shown outside the frame and of the two Bodhisattvas that make up the triad.

vivid luminosity, rich in delightful chromatic contrasts and harmonies.

The cave temples of Yungang were abandoned after the Wei dynasty moved from Datong to Luoyang; but they are still part of the national heritage, bearing invaluable witness to the state of the arts in China during the second half of the fifth century AD.

After moving their capital to Luoyang in AD 494, the Wei quickly decided to create a new series of shrines comparable with those at Yungang. In AD 495 work began on the excavation of cave temples at Mount Longmen, on the bank of the River Yi, not far from the new capital. Work continued at Longmen for the forty years from AD 495 to 535. The Longmen group of cave temples represents the summit of Wei art, and one of the supreme triumphs in the history of Chinese sculpture.

The Longmen cave temples
The stylistic development of Chinese sculpture through the Wei, Sui and Tang periods can be studied in the art of these caves, which also reflect contemporary changes in Buddhist doctrine. First one and then another of the holy books of Buddhism came to be regarded as of supreme religious significance; and this had its effect on literature and art. During the first phase of artistic development, the dominant holy book from which the artists drew their inspiration was the *Sutra of the Lotus* (which is undoubtedly the most famous of all the Buddhist sutras). This book is largely concerned with Sakyamuni, the historical Buddha, and consequently tended to inspire works of art depicting his life, his meditations and his spiritual illumination. One chapter is however devoted to Guanyin, who is also frequently depicted in the art of the cave temples, and becomes an increasingly important figure in Chinese thought. Guanyin represents a spirit of serene and conscious sacrifice inspired by love for humanity; and he is depicted in the guise of a human figure whose beauty expresses the

Dunhuang, Gansu. A figure of the Bodhisattva Manjusri in cave no. 276 (Sui dynasty, AD 581–618). This figure is one of a pair painted on the western wall of the cave, placed symmetrically on either side of the niche. Our illustration shows the Bodhisattva Manjusri in the act of replying to the questions of Vimalakirti, who is the other member of the pair. The harmoniously elegant standing figure is vaguely cylindrical in shape; the face is turned slightly to the left; and the hands are raised in an explanatory attitude. Painted in cinnabar, the picture has kept its red colour well. The treatment of the veils and of the folds of the garments, which often end in an acute angle, remind us of the Wei style; but the classical balance of the forms and the use of trees, flowers, rocks and mountains to frame the central figure look forward to the Tang style, which did in fact begin to take shape during the Sui period.

canons of divine perfection. Guanyin is for Chinese artists what Apollo was for the artists of Greece – making due allowance for different national criteria of beauty, perfection and physical and psychic harmony.

Towards the end of the sixth century AD, another of the sacred books of Buddhism began to take the lead. This was the *Amitayus Dhyana Sutra*. This text introduces a new figure, abstract and metaphysical in character, but full of fascination and mysterious power. This is the Lord of the Western Paradise; his name is Amitabha or Amida, but the Chinese call him Omito. The text contains instructions for sixteen different kinds of meditation that can lead to rebirth in the Land of the Pure. In terms of the visual arts, the rise of Amitabha is accompanied by a decline in the importance of Sakyamuni. The role of Guanyin, however, is undiminished; he becomes one of the two main supporting figures associated with Amitabha, the other being Mahasthamaprapta. As the years go by, other Buddhas acquire increasing importance – the seven Buddhas of the Past, the fifty-three Buddhas, the thousand Buddhas. . . . The Buddha Phabhutaratna and the Bodhisattva Maitreya had played a prominent role during the domination of Sakyamuni, but also shared in his decline, and were ultimately replaced by other figures. In the seventh century AD a new Buddhist sect arose, called *Chen Yen*, or the True Word; and with it came the Buddha Vairocana, who is regarded as the origin of all things. All the other Buddhas, including Sakyamuni, are thought to be emanations of Vairocana. The Buddhist religious system is somewhat complicated; and Buddhist iconography naturally became complicated too. The multiplicity of religious themes gave unprecedented freedom to the imagination of the artists of Buddhism.

The Longmen caves provide a clear-cut and well-articulated conspectus of the development of the changing themes of art and the changing styles used to express them – both of which reflect the changes in the contemporary historical scene. The caves begin with the Wei style, which they develop and bring to maturity. Whether the Buddha is shown standing or sitting, the base of the statue tends to become wider and wider, as the skirt of his robe billows out more and more. The shoulders are narrow and the slightly elongated head forms the apex of a symmetrical triangular composition. Statues of this kind are in themselves full of spiritual dignity; and this is often enhanced by the presence on the wall behind them of a huge halo or aureole, extending around the entire figure and rising to a point above its head, to impart an additional feeling of upward movement and profound spirituality.

The folds of the Buddha's robes form a lively, balanced symmetrical pattern, the effect of which is to lighten the mass at the base of the statue. The sculpture of the Wei period may be regarded as the Chinese equivalent of Gothic art. The Wei style emerged and reached full development in the space of a few decades, during which there was an increasing tendency towards refinement and spiritualisation of the image. The elegance and grace of the figures, and the dynamic rhythm which imparts an upward surge of movement to them, are typical features of Wei sculpture, which is the glory of Chinese art in the sixth century AD.

The same stylistic methods were employed wherever the dynasty decided to use the magic of art to express and propagate its religious beliefs. One example of this is to be found in the caves of Gongxian (Henan), excavated and decorated in the early part of the sixth century, where the images are completely Chinese in facial appearance, clothes and personal ornaments, and the objects that surround them are also Chinese. Another example is provided by the cave temples of Kezier, which were excavated at the beginning of the sixth century near Baicheng (Xinjiang), a staging-post on the Silk Road. In these caves, as at Dunhuang, the walls are still decorated with frescos of the Wei period. The style of these paintings resembles that of Wei sculpture in certain respects, such as the upward movement of the figures; but the treatment of clothing is very different. Belts, scarves, the hems of robes and the borders of upper garments are all arranged so as to form trailing, triangular points. The vigorous handling of line accentuates the angular severity of the figures, and helps them to attain a flat, incorporeal quality – almost as if they had been cut out of coloured paper. In the art of painting, no less than in the

Dunhuang, Gansu. Triad of standing figures in cave no. 427 (period of the Sui dynasty, AD 581–618). Two similar triads stand against the north and south walls of this cave; each consists of a standing Buddha flanked by two attendants. Our illustration shows the triad on the northern wall. The plump faces and bodies may remind us of the art of the Northern Zhou (AD 556–581); but the balance of the composition, the erect position of the Buddha and a certain general rigidity of attitude are typical of Sui sculpture. The red and white paints that we see on the faces are in fact layers of undercoat; and this means that the top layer of colour, expressing the artist's final intentions, is missing. Also typical of the Sui period are the thousand small Buddhas painted in many different colours on the wall behind the triad.

Dunhuang, Gansu. Triad in cave no. 244 (early part of Tang period, AD 618–683). The triad, situated on the western wall of the cave, consists of an enthroned Buddha flanked by disciples and attendants. The florid and imposing appearance of the Buddha and the generous volume of his statue suggests the style of the early Tang period; while the stiffness of the disciples and attendants is typical of Sui art. The Buddha is seated on an octagonal throne. The base of the throne is painted with sacred images, which is a somewhat unusual form of decoration. The circular halo behind the head of the central figure is painted with many small images in different colours, to symbolise the Thousand Buddhas; and the same theme is taken up on a larger scale on the ceiling. The paintings on the wall behind the statues show the preaching of a sermon under the branches of a tree. Typical of both the Sui and the early Tang period is the use of motifs derived from pearls and lotuses to decorate the edges of the wall-paintings.

arts of sculpture in stone and in bronze, the Wei style is the loftiest expression of the Buddhist faith, which denies the corporeal and aspires to a celestial world where there will be no room for sensory reality.

The figures are spiritualised by reduction to little more than flat silhouettes, and the handling of line is of a kind which creates no illusion of solidity. These two factors tend to negate the image in the very moment of its creation. It remains true, however, that the Buddhist faith would never have become established in China, if the story and teachings of the Buddha had not been translated into visual form by the country's artists.

Another typical feature of Wei painting is a certain special attitude of the figures. Though full of movement and impetuous grace, they seem as if frozen by the rigidity of the lines in which they are expressed. When we look at a group of these figures, we see all the vigorous movement of a joyous festival, full of colour and rich in allegory; but when we look at the individual figures, each of them is stationary and motionless, although poised to spring. The Wei style continued to flourish, with its intellectual basis intact, for another twenty years after AD 535, when the empire and the dynasty split into two parts, known as the Eastern Wei and the Western Wei. The figures continue to appear against a colourless back-

Dunhuang, Gansu. 'The Flight of Prince Siddharta' is the subject of a painting on the western wall of cave no. 329; it dates from the early Tang period (AD 618–683). This painting occupies the upper part of the wall, above the niche containing the main figure of the Buddha. (The tip of his pointed auroeole can be seen at the bottom of the illustration.) The figures are placed on a background covered with clouds and flowers. To the right is the Bodhisattva Sakyamuni on an elephant and to the left is Prince Siddharta Gautama on a horse. Between them are two hermits riding dragons and a number of *apsaras* (female spirits of the clouds). Siddharta is fleeing by night from his palace, where he has left his wife and the ladies of the court asleep; angels are muffling the hoofs of his horse to prevent them making any noise. The horse is followed by a figure carrying a ceremonial fan. The fluttering folds and ribbons, and the swirling, brightly coloured clouds and flowers that fill the background, impart a stong sense of movement to this lively, imaginative painting,

which is typical of the art of the early Tang period. The men's faces were originally light-coloured, and the horse and the elephant were white; but the colours have deteriorated as result of oxidation.

ground, in a rarefied atmosphere, surrounded by an airy void containing fluttering symbols and decorative motifs.

A noteworthy feature of early Chinese art is the almost complete absence of landscape. This makes its first timid appearance in the fifth century AD, with the sole object of enhancing the presentation of the human figure. The first real example of Chinese landscape is considered to be *A Walk in the Springtime* by the seventh-century painter Zhang Ziqian.

We have said that the sculpture in the Longmen cave temples illustrates all the artistic styles that have arisen in China in response to the changing intellectual and aesthetic climate of successive historical epochs. After the Wei period, the figures lose their upward thrust, and new ideas and new technical developments begin to appear, especially in the field of sculpture. During the time of the Sui dynasty (AD 581–618) we may become aware of indications that Buddhism is in decline, or at least that the Chinese Sui are not providing it with encouragement or stimulus comparable with that formerly received from the barbarian Wei. In the art of sculpture, religious sentiment begins to be overtaken by a feeling of the respect due to the state. Figures become narrower at the base and slightly wider at bust level, creating a new kind of image, cylindrical rather than

Above: Gongxian, Henan. A niche in the outside wall of cave no. 4 (early Tang period). The carvings depict the nine natures of Amitabha, the Buddha of Unlimited Light. In the space below is a carved inscription containing 190 ideograms, from which the reliefs can be dated to the year AD 662.

Left: Dunhuang, Gansu. Tutelary divinity in cave no. 322 (early Tang period). The features and the clothing of this figure suggest a northern origin; and the armies of the Tang dynasty were in fact recruited in northern Asia.

Pages 112–113:
Luoyang, Henan. The caves of Longmen. The illustration shows Buddhist statues from Fenxian cave (early Tang period). The inscription on the pedestal of the Buddha tells us that these statues were carved in the years from AD 672 to 675, on the orders of the Tang Emperor Gaozong.

triangular in shape, and perfectly symmetrical – an elegant, aristocratic, harmonious figure, radiating confidence and an agreeable, courtly authority.

The Sui style is a transitional one, like the dynasty from which it takes its name. With the advent of the Tang dynasty (AD 618–907), the system of ideas that had produced the Sui style developed deeper roots, and drew its sustenance from the solid strength of the new state. China was now fully conscious of her own might, her safety from enemy attacks, the prestige and power that she enjoyed in central Asia, and her position as undoubtedly the greatest power in the whole continent. All this finds expression in the art of sculpture. The human figure loses its cylindrical quality, and becomes slightly wider again at the base – a change which is not intended to give an impression of movement, but to emphasise that the statue is firmly based on a solid foundation. At the same time, the suggestion of movement conveyed by the figure as a whole is astonishingly free and varied, and this effect is emphasised by the handling of the

folds in the robes. Horses and other animals also exhibit solidity of structure combined with freedom of movement. The statues of the Buddha are again on a gigantic scale, like the Buddhas of Yungang, but without their rigidity of attitude; they express a concept of divine grace and power which may owe something to the spectacle of the earthly majesty of the Emperor.

The Longmen cave temples are not the only ones to present a variety of styles extending over a long period of time. The same is true of the caves at Dunhuang in Gansu. Being situated in the most westerly region of China, on the boundaries of Serindia, the Dunhuang cave temples were subject to central Asiatic influences as well as Chinese. Discovered in 1906 by Paul Pelliot, the Dunhuang caves count among the great artistic treasures of the world, with their magnificent wall-paintings and their wealth of sculpture (much of which has, alas, been stolen).

The Dunhuang cave temples

The frescos on the walls of these caves cover a period of nearly one thousand years, from the fifth to the fourteenth century AD. Over the years there has been considerable damage, from the oxidation of certain pigments, from damp, and from the smoke of camp fires lit by passing soldiers; but a large proportion of the pictures are still in a more or less tolerable state of preservation. The whole vast range of Chinese imagination and invention, enriched by the influences that came in through Serindia along the Silk Road, finds expression in the two hundred caves of Dunhuang. From the festive, mystical, intensely decorative art of the Wei we pass on to the measured, classical, realistic style of the Tang. The figures acquire a priestly dignity, the folds of the robes fall with ample, solemn grace, and liveliness of imagination is combined with balance of composition. Tang painting reaches new heights in the depiction of the human form. Its realism is such that each figure appears to be a portrait; its sureness of touch is such that each figure is filled with vitality and grace of movement. At the same time, the balance of the composition is maintained with absolute mastery. The figures are sometimes depicted against an empty background, in accordance with an ancient and powerful tradition; but more often the background is a natural one, a landscape appropriate to the episode which is the subject of the painting. During the fifth and sixth centuries AD, landscape is still conceived in terms of theatrical scenery, decorated with plants arranged in a formal pattern, to provide a background for the action of human figures or animals, the latter being often used as symbols of the process of reincarnation. In the seventh century, landscape acquires independence, dignity and a special artistic function of its own. The Chinese for 'landscape' is *shan shui*, or 'mountains and waters'; which is a clear reminder of the Tao doctrine of earth and water as elements. The new status of landscape painting consequently marks a resurgence of Taoist influence in the cultural sphere. In the tenth century, the element of water came to be represented in various guises, such as mist, rain, snow, clouds, and so on.

The concept of landscape and the methods of representing it were clearly of great importance to Chinese thought. As Buddhism spread across China, it blended with the Taoist conception of the universe and enriched the ideology of Confucianism with a wider panorama of values; all of which tended to transfer the focus of artistic attention from man to nature.

As time went by and the new values were fully absorbed by neo-Confucianism, Chinese artists began to study and interpret nature and the meaning of nature more and more deeply. During the Five Dynasties (AD 907–960) and the Song period (AD 960–1279), they raised the art of landscape to the highest level it ever reached.

In the caves of Dunhuang, as at Longmen, there is a succession of sculptural styles corresponding to the changing ideologies of the various historical periods. But Dunhuang, being situated at the point where China and central Asia meet, also exhibits developments which are foreign to Chinese tradition, such as the use of coloured stucco. When this technique is applied to the representation of the Buddhas and the world of Buddhism, it creates an effect of festive worship, which is reinforced by the

AGAINST THE BUDDHISTS

Your servant has now heard that instructions have been issued to the priestly community to proceed to Fêng-hsiang and receive a bone of Buddha, and that from a high tower your Majesty will view its introduction into the Imperial Palace; also that orders have been sent to the various temples, commanding that the relic be received with the proper ceremonies. Now, foolish though your servant may be, he is well aware that your Majesty does not do this in the vain hope of deriving advantages therefrom; but that in the fulness of our present plenty, and in the joy which reigns in the heart of all, there is a desire to fall in with the wishes of the people in the celebration at the capital of this delusive mummery. For how could the wisdom of your Majesty stoop to participate in such ridiculous beliefs? Still the people are slow of perception and easily beguiled; and should they behold your Majesty thus earnestly worshipping at the feet of Buddha, they would cry out, 'See! the Son of Heaven, the All-Wise, is a fervent believer; who are we, his people, that we should spare our bodies?' Then would ensue a scorching of heads and burning of fingers; crowds would collect together, and, tearing off their clothes and scattering their money, would spend their time from morn to eve in imitation of your Majesty's example. The result would be that by and by young and old, seized with the same enthusiasm, would totally neglect the business of their lives; and should your Majesty not prohibit it, they would be found flocking to the temples, ready to cut off an arm or slice their bodies as an offering to the god. Thus would our traditions and customs be seriously injured, and ourselves become a laughing-stock on the face of the earth – truly, no small matter!

For Buddha was a barbarian. His language was not the language of China. His clothes were of an alien cut. He did not utter the maxims of our ancient rulers, nor conform to the customs which they have handed down. He did not appreciate the bond between prince and minister, the tie between father and son. Supposing, indeed, this Buddha had come to our capital in the flesh, under an appointment from his own State, then your Majesty might have received him with a few words of admonition, bestowing on him a banquet and a suit of clothes, previous to sending him out of the country with an escort of soldiers, and thereby have avoided any dangerous influence on the minds of the people. But what are the facts? The bone of a man long since dead and decomposed is to be admitted, forsooth, within the precincts of the Imperial Palace!

Han Yu (AD 768–824), *Lun Fugu Biao*
(Memorial on the Bone of the Buddha).

Luoyang, Henan. Fenxian cave (AD 675, during the early Tang period). The two statues shown here are on the southern wall of the cave, and are about 10 metres (33 feet) in height. The smaller statue on the left, which is shown more fully in the illustration on page 113, is the royal and heavenly spirit Lokapala, who is holding the 'Precious Pagoda' in his right hand, and is trampling an evil spirit under his feet. The larger statue is Dvarapala, a tutelary divinity who can be recognised by the angry expression and muscular body which are his distinguishing characteristics. The long necklace which hangs down over his chest indicates that the temple of which he is guardian was built at the express wish and initiative of the Emperor Gaozong himself.

Pages 116–117:
'The Paradise of Amitabha', at Dunhuang, Gansu. This is a wall-painting in cave no. 217 (middle Tang period, AD 756–820). From the middle of the seventh century onwards, the caves at Dunhuang contain many paintings of the Land of the Pure, which is the paradise of Amitabha, the Buddha of Unlimited Light. An especially important source is the *Amitayurdhyana Sutra*, which has been used for the picture shown here. It is painted on the northern wall of the cave. In the middle is the figure of Amitabha, surrounded by attendants standing on lotus flowers. The throne of the Buddha emerges from a lake, beyond which rise splendid palaces, the dwellings of celestial spirits. In front of the central group of figures we can see concerts and dances in progress, and meetings between fathers and sons. The whole composition is majestic, solemn and deeply moving. In the left side-panel we can see, above, the Buddha on Mount Qidu and, below, King Ajase shutting his father up in a fortress. In the right side-panel, thirteen figures in the attitude of prayer appear in a fantastic landscape.

THE SIGNS OF THE BUDDHA 115

colourful and fantastic composition of the frescos on the walls of the caves. The statues, each on its own pedestal, are in perfect complementary harmony with the paintings that accompany them. This is a special characteristic of the cave temples at Dunhuang.

The cave temples of Maijishan, Turfan and Bezeklik

The Maijishan caves are in Gansu province, south-east of Thianshui. The name 'Maijishan' means 'Wheat-Sheaf-Mountain', and describes the shape of the hill into which more than 180 Buddhist cave-temples have been dug. This is another example of the religious enthusiasm of the Wei, who constructed many cave temples in the northern provinces of China, from Shanxi to Henan and Gansu. The Maijishan caves are less famous than those at Longmen, because of their remote geographical situation; but they too contain a series of works of art in various styles, from the idealism and mysticism of the Wei (AD 386–556) to the classical realism of the Tang (AD 618–907) and the Song (AD 960–1279), and must be regarded as one of the most impressive historical monuments of Chinese art. Great statues of the Buddha carved in the living rock of the heights of Maijishan dominated the surrounding plain with their solid, physical presence. In past centuries, these statues imposed themselves on the consciousness of peasants and herdsmen, who revered the majestic dignity of the Buddha and his superhuman, eternal stillness, seeing these things as the outward signs of One who had known the humiliation of penitence and undergone the annihilation of death, to become a mysterious force of goodness and love.

We have deliberately grouped the Maijishan caves with those of Turfan and Bezeklik, although Maijishan is inside the territory of China, while the other two lie beyond its frontiers. Turfan and Bezeklik were situated in Serindia, along the Silk Road, and were originally subjected to non-Chinese cultural influences. The conquest of the Tarim valley by the Han, and its successive reconquest by the Chinese under the Wei and, later, the Tang dynasties had helped to promote a mixture of cultural influences and artistic styles in the whole area, with elements of the Graeco-Buddhist art of Gandhara, the art of India (especially that of the Gupta period), and the art of Iran. There was also, of course, a Chinese contribution, the importance of which varied from place to place and from time to time, being especially strong during the Tang period.

Turfan and the surrounding region, including Bezeklik, was subject to almost continuous Chinese influence, so that the style of the works of art found in those oases can hardly be distinguished from contemporary works found in China. During the ninth century, however, there was an exceptional period, during which the Mohammedan Uighurs were the dominant power in those parts, and Buddhist art suffered a setback.

At the end of the ninth century, the Tang regained control, and Buddhism and Chinese art returned to the region.

Foreign influences frequently had a marked effect on Chinese art. The sculptural style of the Gupta, for example, spread out from India across Asia and into China during the Wei and the early Tang periods. It underwent some modifications at the hands of Chinese artists, and then spread to all the regions of China, including those on the frontiers. This is what is sometimes known as the 'wet Buddha' style. The Buddha is depicted in monastic robes which cling so tightly to his body that the anatomical details can be seen through the tight folds of the garment, which gives the impression of being soaked in water.

The same type of imagery makes its appearance in painting as well as in sculpture, for stylistic developments in these two arts always go hand in hand. In the same way, there is always a close relationship between the ideology of a given period and the arts which give it visual expression within the framework of contemporary and historical conditions. And that close relationship gives rise to the formal concepts which constitute what we call the 'style' of the period in question.

One example of this interdependence of art and ideology is the fact that the Chinese artists refused to follow those of India and Gandhara in their use of the nude. Even semi-nude figures were unacceptable to the Chinese, and the 'wet Buddha' was the greatest compromise they were

Dunhuang, Gansu. 'The Conversion of Vimalakirti' is a wall-painting in cave no. 159 (middle Tang period). This detail shows a Tibetan king with his suite. The picture is on a wall near the entrance to the cave, and illustrates a common theme of Buddhist art. The figure of Vimalakirti appears in the upper part of the painting, which is not shown in this illustration. The Tibetan king, wearing a white robe, is standing on a platform and listening to an argument between Vimalakirti and Manjusri, who can just be seen in the top right-hand corner of the photograph. After An Lushan's rebellion against the Tang dynasty, the Tibetan king shown here had conquered the western region of Huang he, and had gone on in AD 781 to occupy part of Yunnan. A servant stands behind him holding a ceremonial fan, with a long handle ending in a dragon's head; this was a popular motif both in China and in Japan at that time. The stylistic maturity of the painters of this period is shown by the free handling of the figures, the vivid expressiveness of the faces, and the subtlety of the colours. This painting also provides valuable information regarding the costume worn by nobles during the Tibetan occupation of Chinese territory.

Dunhuang, Gansu. Statues of a seated Buddha and his attendants in cave no. 328 (late Tang period, AD 820–907). A large niche has been cut into the northern wall of the cave to accommodate this group of statues. In the middle is the seated Buddha, in the attitude of debate; on either side of him stand two symmetrical pairs of figures, each made up of one Bodhisattva and one *lohan*. Further to the right is another Bodhisattva, bearing an offering of food. The Buddha has a serene, abstracted expression and a dignified torso; the skirt of his robe falls over the lotus-shaped throne in a complex traditional pattern of folds, typical of the period. The two figures standing next to the Buddha with their memorably expressive faces are his two favourite disciples, Kasyapa to the right and Ananda to the left. Other *lohans* are depicted on the wall behind the statues. The Bodhisattva with the offering of food to the right of the picture was originally balanced by a similar figure on the opposite side of the group; but this is now in the Fogg Art Museum at Harvard.

THE SIGNS OF THE BUDDHA   121

Above: Turfan, Xinjiang. The caves of Bezeklik (middle of the ninth century AD). The illustration shows the ceiling of cave no. 19. The ceiling was first primed with ochre paint and then a series of large circles were drawn on this surface. In the middle of each circle are the petals of a huge lotus flower, around which is a complex pattern of linked hearts alternating with leaves. This type of decoration was very popular in China in the eighth century AD. It seems probable, however, that this picture is somewhat later in date, perhaps about the middle of the ninth century AD, during the first period of Uighur rule over Turfan. The same decorative motif appears again on the ceiling of the adjoining cave no. 2.

Left: Turfan, Xinjiang. A general view of the Bezeklik caves, about 50 kilometres (30 miles) to the north-east of the fortified city of Turfan. This group of caves was dug out of the rockface of Mount Huoyan, overlooking the valley of the River Murtuk. Chinese archaeologists have opened up fifty-seven of them. According to the leading expert Yan Wenru, these belong to four separate periods, ranging from the end of the sixth century AD to the beginning of the thirteenth century AD. The period of greatest artistic splendour runs from the ninth to the thirteenth centuries AD, which is the time of Uighur rule.

prepared to make in this respect. In Chinese tradition, the ideas of holiness and imperial majesty are totally incompatible with the idea of nakedness.

Viewed against this background, the cave temples must be regarded as primarily the expression of a system of thought which is specifically Buddhist, although it has been enriched, deepened and made more complex by frequent contributions from Chinese artistic traditions lying outside Buddhism.

The cave-temples have also preserved works of art that would otherwise have been lost, like so many masterpieces placed in more accessible sites. Such losses are very common in the history of Chinese art, down at least to the end of the Song period in the thirteenth century AD.

The cave-temples have survived invasions, revolutions and every kind of destructive disturbance; although in some cases, as at Dunhuang, they have been used as accommodation for soldiers, who have damaged the frescos with smoke from their camp-fires and have sometimes vandalised the statues. Apart from these unfortunate episodes, which are generally confined to the more accessible caves, these temples have long performed – and still continue to perform – the function of museums, preserving works of art to bear witness to the imagination and creative originality of the Chinese people.

Turfan, Xinjiang. The Bezeklik caves. 'The Procession of the Uighurs' is a wall-painting in cave no. 9. The Chinese society of the Tang period was exceptionally open to foreign influence, and had close contacts with the neighbouring peoples. The Uighurs succeeded in establishing themselves in Turfan towards the middle of the ninth century AD, and gradually adopted Chinese dress. In this picture, which dates from the end of the ninth or the beginning of the tenth century AD, three Uighur noblemen are wearing ceremonial clothes which conform with Chinese fashion of the Tang period, except for the head-dress, which is in a different style. This painting measured 62.5 by 55 centimetres (25 by 22 inches), and was reported by Le Coq. It was removed from the wall and taken to Germany by the German archaeologists who discovered the Bezeklik caves, and was destroyed during the Second World War.

Pagodas, Temples, Palaces

Architecture

THERE IS a deep-seated idea that art imitates nature. In fact Aristotle excluded architecture from the class of arts precisely because it is not imitative. By this he meant to express the fact that art does not imitate the appearance of nature but its work. Whereas nature exists for itself alone, in flowers born to die unseen, and shells hidden for ever at the bottom of the sea, human works of art exist for man's eyes and thoughts. So, more or less, wrote Laurence Binyon, some seventy years ago. Should architecture then be considered as an 'art' or not? While accepting as valid Aristotle's opinion that there can be no art without close links with nature, a principle which has nonetheless been abandoned in modern developments in every field of expression, one may still include Chinese architecture among the arts, since the conception on which it was based was that every building should be in harmony with nature. The Chinese builder always took the configuration of the land, the presence of any streams or lakes, and the type and quantity of any vegetation into consideration, laying out his building in harmony with these. There can thus be no doubt that Chinese architecture is art.

Buildings

Chinese houses had three basic parts, the platform, main structure, and roof.

The platform. This is a terrace on which stood the main body of the house, usually only one storey high. More important buildings had higher platforms, with the further distinction that humbler houses had platforms of rammed earth, whilst in larger buildings they were of stone or brick. The latter type was often made even higher by the addition of terraces, balustrades and wide staircases.

The main structure. The main structure of the house consisted of wooden columns and walls which served to divide the rooms rather than support the house; sometimes the internal walls were sliding. The roof was supported by the wooden columns, of pine or cedar, joined at the top by one or more rows of beams fitting into one another and forming a solid structure. This lent strength to the roof and walls, which were usually very thin, and made of woven bamboo covered in mud or parchment, or best of all in wood. This type of dividing wall made the rooms of a house private from the view of others, but did not protect them from smells and noises, as is apparent from Chinese novels.

The rooms were arranged in perfect symmetry, and each one had a specific function in the family rites of Confucianism which punctuated the life of the household. Even the house itself might properly be defined as Confucian, since the rooms into which it was divided were arranged in

Zhaoxian, Hebei. The Anji or Zhaozhou bridge, which was built about the beginning of the seventh century AD. The bridge, which crosses the River Jiao, is of stone construction and is 51 metres (56 yards) in length. It is famous for the technical sophistication of its structure. According to an inscription of the Tang period, bearing the name of Zhang Jiazhen, the bridge was built by Li Chun, who was one of the greatest Chinese architects, in the Sui period. It was repeatedly restored under the Tang, Song, Ming and Qing dynasties, and was completely rebuilt after the proclamation of the People's Republic in 1949. The span of the central arch measures 37.4 metres (123 feet). On either side are two small arches which lighten the structure and provide a passage for flood water. On the inner side of the balustrade are carvings of lions, dragons and mythical beasts.

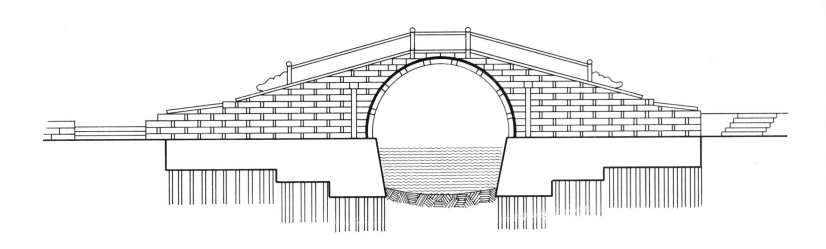

Elevation of a single-arch stone bridge. The 'scissors wall' serves to isolate the arch from the ramps and to reduce the weight borne by the arch. This makes it possible to build very steep-sided bridges, which are often equipped with steps and consequently used only by pedestrians.

size according to a hierarchical arrangement which also governed all the rules which gave the house its appearance. As well as the connecting beams, the upper part of the columns supported the fitted *dou gong*, 'corbel bunches' or superimposed corbels, the upper one projecting slightly beyond the lower on which it rested, and supporting both the roof and the beams which branched out from it on both axes. The column and tie-beam system is extremely ancient, dating back to the Warring States period (453/403–221 BC). The columns were the basis of the whole structure, and so needed protecting from insects and other forms of atmospheric decay. To ensure this they were usually painted with red lac dye, whilst the beams, corbels, sloping roof rafters, ceilings, and all functional parts, far from being concealed, were decorated in other bright colours, creating a pleasingly light ornamental effect.

The façade of the house extended along one of the longer sides, accentuating the rhythmic effect of the horizontal and vertical lines, and creating a rather different impression from that of European houses built on several storeys. The horizontal line was the constant in Chinese architecture, since this blends into the natural line of the surrounding countryside better than the vertical. Even such tall and elegant tapering constructions as towers and pagodas should not be seen as violating the general rule of harmony with the landscape. The towers above city gates and the pagodas of Buddhist monasteries always had secondary roofs, balconies, and mezzanine levels, interrupting the vertical thrust with their emphatic horizontals, and thus producing an impression of the horizontal in the vertical structure, which was always light and flowing, and tapered gently towards the top.

The houses of the common people were traditionally rectangular and opened on to a courtyard, on to which other houses also looked. All the families who shared the court had to pass through it, so that they lived in close contact, not to speak of the snooping and gossiping which provide so many delightful episodes in Chinese novels. Such houses were of course not roofed with glazed tiles, but were built of poorer and less durable materials such as earth (Chinese *tu*) or wood (*mu*). This type of house thus came to be called *tumu*, a word which came to mean 'building' in the wider sense, and finally 'architecture'. A group of such houses and courtyards made up a quarter, which was either rectangular or square in shape, and surrounded by a wall dividing it off from the rest of the city. Each of the four surrounding walls was pierced by a gate which was shut at sunset and opened again at dawn so that the inhabitants' sleep should not be disturbed by robbers or other malefactors.

The houses of the rich and the nobility were distinguished by their greater than usual height, being built on taller platforms. Such buildings were built along a north–south axis, and, if there was more than one such large building, arranged in rows along the same axis. Generally there would also be lesser buildings for housing servants, and these would be situated to the east and west of the main building, and stood lower. Every building had its own court on the south on to which its main entrance opened, and the whole group of buildings belonging to a single owner would be surrounded by a wall within which the private property of buildings, courts, and gardens could be defended and protected.

The roof. The beams and corbels supported horizontal beams with a circular section, on which rested the sloping bamboo roof rafters, also circular in section, and covered with panelling. This enclosed the house space, but needed protection in its turn. First came an insulating layer of clay, and then from the late Han period (202 BC to AD 220) two layers of tiles. In the north these were generally grey, but elsewhere they were glazed in a variety of colours, blue, purple, green, and yellow, all of which were imbued with different symbolisms. The roofs were monochrome, that is to say only one colour was used in a single roof. Before tiles came into general use roofs had been made of thatch. The roof ridge was not necessarily angular, since the post at the centre of the cross-section resembled a king-post and supported the sloping rafters, so that the ridge might be flat, with the angles at each side. If two posts were set at either side of the centre the roof could form a gentle curve without a ridge. To conclude, the posts and beams could be arranged to produce a straight flat roof, a completely curving roof, or one with both techniques combined, the straight type being used for humbler houses, and the curved in larger buildings. The curved roof which has become a symbol of Chinese culture first appeared at the beginning of the Tang period (AD 618–907) in south and south-central China, although some scholars believe that it originated much earlier during the Han period. In the north, the curved style of roof was only adopted under the Song dynasty (AD 960–1279) in Kaifeng in Henan, which was the capital during the first period of the Song dynasty (AD 960–1127). It seems to have been introduced by Yu Hao, an architect from the southern city of Hangzhou, who collaborated with the famous painter Liu Wentong. Curved roofs were built in four basic shapes: with a tympanum; in pavilion-style; mixed, half tympanum and half pavilion; and tent-style. There were two variants on the last type, one pyramidal, the other conical, the latter being found in round buildings. Ceremonial cult, and other public buildings of any size often consisted of a single hall, which might be octagonal, circular, or domed. The roof thus had to follow the ground plan. The ridges, except in the case of conical roofs, were decorated with numerous zoomorphic figures in enamelled pottery, especially on public buildings. These figures were decorated in the same bright colour as the roof, and reached right down to the outer edge of the guttering on the eaves. They fulfilled both a symbolic role, as tutelary figures, and at the same time a decorative function. Since the buildings were usually only a single storey high, the roof was necessarily low, and every part was clearly visible from every side.

Gardens

Chinese gardens are as famous as the curved roofs, and are a characteristic part of Chinese culture. As we have seen, the interior of the house

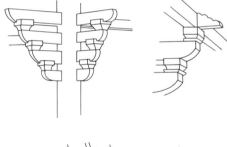

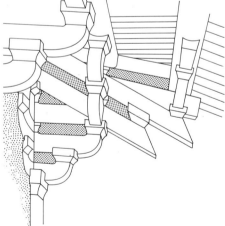

The drawings on this page illustrate some of the types of truss and corbel used in Chinese wooden buildings. The use of overhanging roofs made of heavy materials led to the development over the centuries of a complicated system of wooden supporting structures. Identical designs were later used for similar structures in stone.

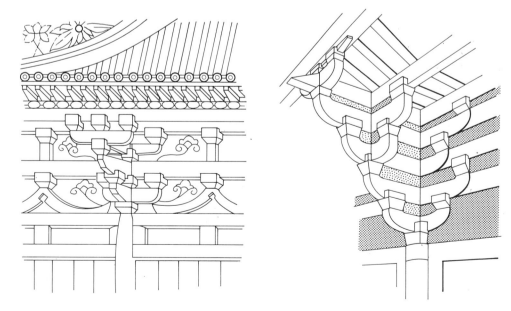

followed precisely defined rules of symmetry and hierarchy, so that we have been able to define the structure of a Chinese house as 'Confucian'. The garden, in contrast, reflected all the mystery, imagination, and unexpectedness of nature, expressing at the same time man's respect for nature and his deep understanding of it. Account had to be taken not only of the appearance of the site, but of how it altered with the different seasons, with the changing shape of the trees and colour of the leaves, and with the appearance of flowers.

This type of relationship with nature is Taoist in inspiration, and the Chinese garden is an organised expression of it. Respect for the landscape created by nature does not, however, prevent man from completing the chosen site with all the elements so necessary to make it a perfect microcosm of nature. If the garden is flat and without natural rises, a few large boulders will be arranged to simulate mountains. If the ground is nowhere high enough to create a waterfall, the stream will wind in graceful curves before debouching and gathering in a small lake. Little bridges in brick or stone will flank the watercourse. If the chosen site lacks water, both watercourse and lake will be dug, beside which little bridges may still be built even if they remain dry. The garden paths are never straight, so that one can never see where they end when setting out along them. By winding round them one gains unexpected glimpses around every corner. Trees, shrubs, and flowers are all chosen to harmonise with the desired landscape, taking into account the changes of the seasons and their effect on the plants. Shrubs are planted to conceal the layout of the garden, and preserve the mystery of its design. There are no lawns, but, if the garden is large enough, there will be small wooden pavilions at appropriate places, their tent-shaped roofs clad in enamelled tiles, where one may rest and enjoy the solitude and sounds of nature. These summer-houses fit perfectly, indeed magically, amongst the plants, shrubs, rocks, earth, sand, water, and flowers which make up the garden. In order to achieve this balance, the pavilions must not be heavy or cumbrous in their structure. Usually they are open, with verandas and roofs supported by four slender wooden columns, surrounded by a low balustrade of sections of wooden trellis work. If they are enclosed, they will have many windows, which like the doors will also be formed of lattice work. The lakes are edged with similar balustrades consisting of wooden trellises in an infinite variety of geometrical patterns, and pierced so as to confer a lightness, delicacy and harmony which make nature itself more beautiful. Sometimes there are covered alleys meandering in twists and curves, never straight, which cross uncultivated tracts of land, lending it an air of joyful contrast with their bright roof-tiles and lacquered columns. The walls surrounding a lord's domains also formed part of both architecture and landscape design. They too were irregular in appearance, wandering freely, altering height, and never appearing grim or monotonous, although they still fulfilled their defensive and protective role. The doors which pierced the walls and led into the gardens were never rectangular; usually they were oval, hexagonal, circular, fan-shaped, or any other strange or curious shape which might lend the spot an air of fable or mystery by concealing any overall view. All these winding ways, fantastic designs, asymmetries, apparent accidents, and air of anarchy represent the projection of the dialectical encounter of the cosmic energies of yin and yang. It is from these that the mysterious creativity of nature is constituted, in all its uniqueness and romance; the air of a Chinese garden is scented with the perfume of the Tao. The origins of gardening in China are lost in time, since we have no paintings to guide us. The only early description to have come down to us is of the huge and magnificent park built at Luoyang in AD 607 by the emperor Sui Yang (AD 604–618), from the *Zhong guo yingzao xue* (*The Teachings of Chinese Architecture*, translated by Alexander Soper and published in 1934). In AD 607 the first Japanese embassy arrived in Luoyang, and four years later a landscaped garden with water of Chinese inspiration was built at Nara, the Japanese capital at that time.

Printing was invented in China in the tenth century AD, and the first architecture book to be published was the famous *Yingzao fa shi* (*The Methods and Forms of Architecture*) printed at Bianliang, Kaifeng, in AD 1103.

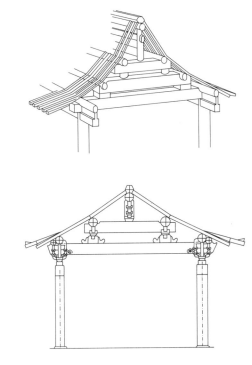

An example of the Chinese method of constructing roofs. The supporting beams are laid horizontally, and the sloping rafters are mounted on top of them. The positioning of the beams determines the profile of the roof, which may be either rectilinear or concave.

Dengfeng, Henan. Brick pagoda at the Songyue temple, built in AD 523, during the Northern Wei dynasty, at the foot of Mount Songyue. It is the oldest brick pagoda in China. It was built during the enlargement of the temple in the fourth year of the reign of Zheng Guang of the Northern Wei dynasty. The exterior is twelve-sided and has fifteen storeys; the interior is octagonal and has ten storeys, with an overall height of about 40 metres (130 feet). The space between the different roof levels is greatly reduced. This pagoda is an example of the style known as 'miyan' or 'hidden eaves': the upper part of the external wall of each storey tapers outwards to meet the edge of the roof above. This style was already somewhat archaic at the time when the pagoda was built. The choice of brick as a building material was very unusual in China at that time, and may have been inspired by an Indian example in the contemporary Gupta style.

The author was Li Mingzhong, an architect, painter, and calligrapher from Zhengzhou in Henan. The book's thirty-four chapters cover stone masonry, wood construction, the buildings of stairs, doors, and windows, the preparation of tiles, how to arrange them on the roof, the techniques of painted decoration, the use of architectural materials such as stone, wood, clay, metal and pottery, the creation of parks and gardens, and finally how to assess the work-force. The methods for constructing ceiling beams are still taken from this amply illustrated text today. It was republished in Suzhou in 1145 after the destruction of the first edition in 1126 when the Song dynasty was forced to abandon Kaifeng because of barbarian invasions. The Suzhou edition was lost in its turn, and the current edition is a photolithographic reproduction made in Shanghai in 1920 of a text which was copied in 1821. This has recently been translated into Japanese, whilst in Europe the essence of the book was culled and edited by the Russian Sinologist F. A. Aschepov in *Arkhitektura Kitaya-Ocherki*.

From the same period comes the *Mu jing* (*The Book of Wood*) which preserves architectural rules, and was written by Yu Hao (twelfth century AD), the architect of the first Song period mentioned above who introduced the curved roof, already widespread in the south, into the north. One other famous work dealing with the problems and techniques of

Above left: Xian, Shânxi. Dayan ta, the Pagoda of the Great Wild Goose, in the Ci en temple (middle of the seventh century AD). The building of the pagoda was begun on the initiative of the Buddhist monk Xuan Zang, during the third year of the reign of the Emperor Gao-zong (AD 649–683). It was extensively rebuilt in AD 704, and the outside wall was refaced with brick during the Ming period.

Above right: Xian, Shânxi. Xiaoyan ta, the Pagoda of the Little Wild Goose, in the Jian fu temple, built in AD 707, under the Tang dynasty. The top two storeys were destroyed by an earthquake in AD 1555. In its truncated form, the pagoda is about 50 metres (160 feet) high. It is square in plan; the high plinth, walls and roof are of brick. The roofs are of the 'miyan' or 'hidden eaves' style and consequently do not overhang very much. They are supported by a system of tapering terracotta trusses.

Right: Xian, Shânxi. Sepulchral pagoda of the monk Xuan Zang in the temple of Xing Jiao ('Flourishing Doctrine'). It was built in AD 669 as a resting place for the mortal remains of Xuan Zang, and was largely rebuilt in AD 828.

Nanking, Jiangsu. The Sheli ta, the Pagoda of the Relics of the Buddha in the temple of Qixia ('Resting Clouds'). The pagoda was built by the Southern Tang (AD 937–975), during the Time of the Five Dynasties, at the foot of Mount Qixia. It is built of limestone to an octagonal plan, with five storeys and a double base. The edges of the roofs are rounded off in the 'miyan' style.

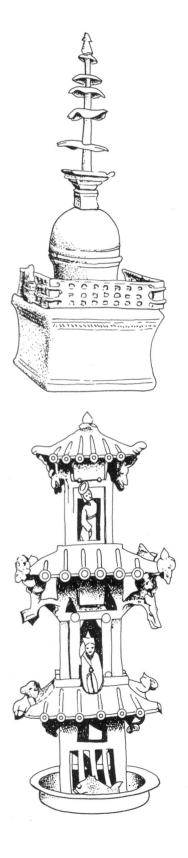

Suzhou, Jiangsu. The pagoda of the temple of Yunyan ('Cave of the Clouds'). The pagoda stands on Mount Huqiu ('Tiger Hill'). Construction began in AD 959, during the Time of the Five Dynasties, and was finished in AD 961, at the beginning of the period of the Song dynasty. Octagonal in plan, it has seven storeys and is built in the 'louge' style. The base and the main structure of the pagoda are in brick. The outer part of the roofs was of wood and ceramics, and was completely destroyed by no less than seven fires during the Song and Qing dynasties. Today only the central structure of the pagoda survives. The interior is of brick, but its structure is closely imitated from that of wooden buildings; the colours used are red, black and white.

The drawings on the left illustrate the prototypes from which the Chinese pagoda is thought to be derived. Above is an Indian stupa from Gandhara (AD 200 approx.). The series of discs of diminishing size that decorates the central post rising above the dome symbolises the Buddhist heavens, and probably inspired the system of tapering roofs which characterises the pagoda. Below is a drawing of a Han tower with superimposed roofs, based on a funerary model in terracotta.

architecture, the *Gong Cheng Zuo fa zi li*, published in 1734, is worthy of mention.

Bridges

The shape of Chinese bridges is as typical as that of the roofs, both in the shape of the span of the arch and in the way in which it was executed. The principle of the arch, with one or more spans, whether pointed or depressed, is an integral part of the nature and function of the bridge itself.

There are two possible architectural methods of creating an arch, one of which is universally known and used, the other being a purely Chinese development. In the first type bricks are laid fanning out from and so creating the curve of the arch; the greater the weight exerted above them, the more they are forced together. There is nothing in this technique which is not known to and applied by every bridge builder. In the second type, the arch is formed of vertically laid slabs shaped so as to form the soffit of the arch, and pressed together by the opposing thrusts of the arch stones, which stick perfectly together, and of the blocks which form the two abutments which thrust down on the road surface. The resulting arch is elegant and refined. The bridge-beams follow the line of the arch to a certain degree, so that the rise of the bridge is hump-backed, like a number of Roman and medieval European bridges. If the rise is particularly steep, the approaches to the bridge may be stepped, a system which restricts the use of the bridge to foot-passengers. This however increases the beauty of the bridge's proportions, making it both a more serene and at the same time more functional part of the landscape. On either side of the rise there was frequently a parapet consisting of little pilasters alternating with stone sculptures of monstrous and mythical beasts. There were also wooden bridges in several spans, resting on great stone piers, which crossed slow-moving rivers, but these do not merit special attention. Turbulent or very wide rivers were generally crossed by ferry, using rafts.

When in AD 589 the Sui dynasty united North and South China, they set about creating links between the two regions to improve trade relations and communications in general. The centrepiece of this enterprise was the Grand Imperial Canal, which crosses central China longitudinally, linking the Huang he, Huai he, and Yangzi jiang. This canal carried a huge volume of trade, and beside it wound a road shaded with trees. Bridges had to be built to cross it, and one of these has won great renown, and still survives in ample testimony of the considerable technical skills which the Chinese had attained by the seventh century AD. This is the Anji, the passage – or crossing – of peace, bridge, which spans the River Jiao near Zhauxian in Hebei, and was built between 605 and 616 by the architect Li Chun, as we read in the Tang period inscription on the bridge sculpted by Zhang Jiazhen. It is more than 50 metres (160 feet) long, with a depressed arch and open spandrel, thus anticipating by seven centuries a technique which was to appear in Europe only in the fourteenth century. The arch is a most daring piece of architecture, with a span of more than 37 metres (120 feet). Two small arches were inserted into each of the two abutments in order to lighten the weight of the bridge and ease the thrust on the road surface. The soffit of the arch, the abutments, and the parapet are all built in stone slabs, those in the abutments being fixed by means of butterfly-shaped iron joints. The parapet consists of alternating small columns and slabs sculpted on the inside with bas relief figures of the heads of mythical and symbolic animals whilst the outer side is sculpted with ornamental festoons.

After the proclamation of the People's Republic in 1949 the bridge was completely restored as a monument of China's past, and today passage is restricted to people only, heavy traffic being diverted to a modern pier bridge close by.

Pagodas

Since the first Song period in the tenth century Europeans have called the towers which dot the Chinese landscape, and are frequently depicted in paintings, pagodas. The word may be derived from a corruption of the Indian word *dagoba*, a kind of hemispherical mound under which the ashes of the Buddha were interred. Pagodas are slender and elegant rather than hemispherical, but they are indeed sacred buildings, dedicated to the use of Buddhist devotees, which follow the canons of Chinese architecture.

Through the medium of Buddhism India had very close links with and considerable and continuous influence upon China, one of the results of which was a change in the use of building materials. Chinese pagodas were built in wood until the sixth century AD, but thereafter they began to be constructed in stone or brick, following the Indian model. After the sixth century AD Buddhist China came of age, developing its own forms and techniques, both in doctrine and in the connected field of art.

The architectural model for the pagoda was developed out of the towers with rising roofs of the Han period. The conception of a series of roofs diminishing in size as they rose constituted one of the elements of harmony for the Chinese, and was probably derived ultimately from the small circular umbrellas of decreasing size which crowned the central summit of the hemispherical Indian domes of stupas like those at Sanchi, which were symbols of the Buddhist heavens. The Chinese inherited not only the architectural form but the whole complex of meaning, symbol, and reference which invests every Indian religious monument. Sacred buildings were capped with a pinnacle, symbolising the axis of the universe, and ending in a cone-shaped lotus bud, symbolising the belief in virtue and in the unity of the many. For this reason the Chinese gave the name of *boa ta*, tower of preciousness, to the pagoda. When this is preceded by a proper name or the name of the temple in which it stands, the pagoda is called not *bao ta*, but simply *ta*. At first the pagoda was part of the monastery, which consisted of a group of wooden buildings separated from the rest of the town by an enclosure. This contained dwellings for the monks, such services as were necessary to ensure that the monastery would be self-sufficient, and the temple where the sacred statues were kept and religious services held. It was only later that free-standing pagodas were built, and even then only rarely. One might compare the relation between temple and pagoda to that between church and spire. The interior of a pagoda is usually plain, with wooden stairs joining the different storeys; and floors, which were also usually of wood, divided the storeys at the level of the roofs. The earliest 'towers of preciousness' were wooden, not only out of respect to tradition, but also because they were conceived as a series of square wooden pavilions built one above the other, each one being slightly smaller than the one below.

No trace remains of any of the wooden pagodas predating the sixth century AD in China. If we wish to form an impression of how they must have appeared we must turn to Japan, to the pagoda of the Horyuri temple in the ancient capital of Nara, which was faithfully rebuilt every time it was destroyed, and has preserved the features of those Chinese pagodas from which the Japanese architects of the beginning of the seventh century AD drew their inspiration. Another, more fertile, source for the appearance of buildings now vanished is illustrations, as is the case with the destroyed stupa of Prabhutaratna; or the Buddhist temple which is carved in the stone architrave on the ground floor of the pagoda of the Great Wild Goose (Dayan ta) at Xian, which provides a precious picture of the type of wooden architecture current in the Tang period. Today there are some 550 stone, brick, and terracotta pagodas scattered more or less evenly across China, and many more would have survived but for the famous anti-Buddhist persecution of AD 845. At that time an imperial edict was issued ordering the demolition of 4,600 monasteries and convents and 40,000 Buddhist buildings. Although the edict was revoked in AD 847, when the work of destruction was still incomplete, the loss was tremendous. Thousands upon thousands of buildings were burnt, and the caves of Dunhuang in Gansu only escaped catastrophe from this iconoclastic frenzy because between AD 757 and 850 they were in the hands of the Tibetans. We know that the Emperor Xuan Zung (AD 712–756) had built a stupa in honour of the Buddha Prabhutaratna, much spoken of in the *Saddharma Pundarika Sutra* (Chinese title *Fa Hua jing*, or *Lotus of the True Law*), and that this great building was completed in AD 745 under the auspices of the Buddhist monk Chu Jin; but not a trace of it now survives. According to the Japanese art-historian Matsumoto, the representation of a nine-storeyed stupa with a hexagonal base painted in a cave at

Kaifeng, Henan. Tie ta ('The Iron Pagoda') in the Youguo temple, built in AD 1049 (Northern Song dynasty). The temple was at the north gate of Kaifeng; it was completely destroyed towards the end of the tenth century AD. Later the Emperor Ren Zong (AD 1022–1063) of the Northern Song dynasty ordered the reconstruction of the pagoda. Being built of red brick and covered externally with bluish enamel tiles, the pagoda gives a colour effect similar to that of rusty iron, which is the reason for the present name of the building. Octagonal in plan, it is about 57 metres (187 feet) in height. It is built in the 'louge' style; each of the thirteen storeys has a small balcony and an overhanging roof supported by a decorative feature resembling those used in wooden buildings. The picture on the right shows a detail of the exterior.

Yingxian, Shânxi. The Sakyamuni Pagoda in the Fogong temple, or 'Palace of Buddha'. The pagoda was built in AD 1056, during the Liao dynasty. It is the oldest surviving wooden pagoda in China. The plan is octagonal, and the general impression is of a building relatively wide in proportion to its height – an impression strengthened by the presence of large columns and pilasters placed internally and externally at every corner of the building. More than sixty different kinds of truss have been used in the construction of the ceiling. Thanks to its unusually robust structure, this pagoda has been able to withstand a number of earthquakes. The height, without the pinnacle, is 67 metres (220 feet). The pagoda stands on a double base of brick, and has five external storeys, each with its own balcony. Internally, most of the storeys are divided into two by a sort of mansard, raising the total number to nine. A statue of the Buddha stands in the middle of each floor.

Dunhuang probably illustrates the stupa of Prabhutaratna which was burnt down in a fire. Space is clearly insufficient to describe all 550 pagodas in China, and we shall restrict ourselves to surveying only the most important of those which illustrate the characteristic features of their respective periods. The earliest brick pagoda in existence in China dates from the beginning of the sixth century AD, and is part of the Songyue temple in Dengfeng, Henan, which was at first built without a pagoda. The latter was erected only in AD 523, in the fourth year of the reign of Emperor Zheng Guang of the Northern Wei dynasty, when the monastery was enlarged at his orders. It has twelve sides, stands some 40 metres (130 feet) high, and has fifteen external storeys. Unlike preceding versions, this pagoda was entirely built in fired brick, and while still preserving the probable outline of its wooden predecessors nevertheless shows many features derived from Indian tradition.

This tendency to imitate wooden construction techniques in other materials is extremely marked in the most famous monument of ancient Changan, the Dayan ta or Pagoda of the Great Wild Goose, which is part of

Songjiang, Shanghai. The pagoda of the Xing sheng jiao temple. The pagoda was built in the years AD 1068–1077, during the Northern Song dynasty, and was restored in the Ming and Qing periods. It is square in plan, and has nine storeys in the 'louge' style. The main structure of the pagoda, including the columns, the massive capitals and the corbels, are of ceramics, while the balconies and other external features were rebuilt in wood in the Qing period. The round capitals of the corner columns, on the other hand, are original features dating back to the Song period.

Left: Peking. Pagoda of the temple of Tianning ('Heavenly Peace'), dating from the beginning of the twelfth century AD (Liao dynasty). The temple is situated on the outskirts of Peking, to the south-west of the centre. The pagoda was built towards the end of the Liao period, and is an elegant example of its architecture, in spite of the restorations to which it was subjected during the Ming and Qing periods. About 58 metres (190 feet) in height, the pagoda is built of brick, and has thirteen storeys with roofs in the 'miyan' style. The building is octagonal in plan, and the space between the storeys is greatly reduced. Only the first storey is comparatively high; it is decorated on all eight sides with niches and reliefs of Buddhist figures.

Above: Luoyang, Henan. The Qi Yun ('Regular Clouds') pagoda in the Baima ('White Horse') temple, built in AD 1175, during the Southern Song dynasty. There is a legend that the temple was built in the first century AD, at the very beginning of the introduction of Buddhism into China. In reality, however, it was not built until the twelfth century AD.

the temple of Ci en, the Great Mercy. This was built around the middle of the seventh century AD on the initiative of the Buddhist monk Xuan Zang, and was subsequently much reworked, so that today it creates an impression rather different from its original appearance. The structural details recall features of wooden buildings, particularly in the way in which the decreasing series of square pavilions are placed regularly one above the other, and in the way the pilasters and beams are placed. During the next fifty years the number and activity of the Buddhist monks was perpetually on the increase, and to meet the problem of housing them the Jian fu (Offering of Fortune Temple), a twin of the Ci en, was built in Xian, containing the Xiaoyan ta, or Pagoda of the Little Wild Goose, which was finished in AD 707, and damaged in the earthquake of 1555 which destroyed its two topmost storeys. Even without its top, the slender pagoda stands out from the countryside on the southern edge of the ancient capital, with its short roofs in the *miyan* or 'hidden eaves' style. Another famous Buddhist temple with attached pagoda was built at Changan in the period between the construction of the Dayan ta and that of the Xiaoyan ta. The occasion was the death of the monk Xuan Zang in AD 664. His remains were buried in a funerary pagoda built in AD 669 as part of the Xing Jiao

Right: Quanzhou, Fujian. Zhenguo ta, the Pagoda of the Stabilisation of the State, in the temple of Kaiyuan, or Beginning of Principle. Built in AD 1238, under the Song dynasty. There are two twin pagodas in this temple; the one illustrated here stands to the east and is 48 metres (157 feet) in height. The other is known as Renshou ta, or Pagoda of Virtue and Longevity; it stands to the west and is 44 metres (144 feet) high. Both these pagodas were built in the years AD 1237–1238 under the Southern Song dynasty. They are constructed of stone, in the 'louge' style; they are octagonal in plan and have five relatively high storeys. Every alternate side of each storey has a doorway, and the sides without doorways have windows. On either side of the doorways are carved tutelary divinities and heavenly kings. The building technique employed is an imitation of that used for wooden structures, as can be seen from the corbels that support the projecting roofs.

Left: Peking. Bai ta, the White Pagoda, in the temple of Miaoying or Sublime Duty (AD 1271–1279). The temple is situated near the Fucheng Gate, and was built in the Liao period on the site of an earlier pagoda built by the Qidan and destroyed by the Mongols. Construction of the pagoda that we see today was begun in AD 1271 on the orders of the Emperor Qubilay. The close links between the Mongol dynasty and Tibet led to the introduction into China of this type of pagoda (designed by the Nepalese architect Anigo). The conical shape is derived from that of the Tibetan 'chorten'. The White Pagoda is 63 metres (206 feet) in height. The colour is also typical of the 'lama style' of Tibet.

(Flourishing Doctrine) temple which dominates the southern plain of the city from a hill. The pagoda was rebuilt at the beginning of the ninth century AD.

In AD 487 a Buddhist monastery was founded in Nanking in Jiangsu at the foot of Mount Qixia (Resting Clouds), after which it was named. Some five centuries later the pagoda of Sheli ta (the Relics of the Buddha) was built next to the monastery at the command of the Southern Tang dynasty (AD 937–975). The present appearance of the temple and monastery derive from the reconstructions carried out in the last century, so that it is difficult now to determine their original form, but the stone pagoda still preserves its original appearance, and is one of the most important and exquisite monuments of ancient Chinese Buddhism.

At Suzhou in the same province of Jiangsu there are still many traces of the intense religious endeavours of the monks, who were particularly fond of octagonal forms. This is the shape of the two 'twin pagodas', Shuang ta, built in brick between AD 984 and 987, as well as of the pagoda of the Yunyan (Cave of the Clouds) temple, which was begun in AD 959 and finished in AD 961 on Tiger Hill, Huqiu. This is a most beautiful construction, with seven tapering storeys still visible today, in spite of the loss of the original wooden roofs which were burnt in various fires. The pagoda leans slightly following an earthquake which occurred in Ming times.

Of particular note and thoroughly characteristic is the pagoda known as the Iron Pagoda, Tie ta, built in Kaifeng in Henan in AD 1049, when the city was the capital of the Song kingdom. The monastery with its temple and pagoda had been destroyed around the end of the tenth century, and the Song emperor, Ren Zong (AD 1022–1063) ordered the pagoda alone to be rebuilt. The building material was red brick, with a covering of blueish enamelled ceramic, so that the pagoda has an iron-colour, explaining its name. The plan is octagonal, following the most widespread pattern, and the ceramic roof-beams recall ancient techniques of construction in wood, but the elevation with thirteen storeys is most unusual, reaching a height which few later pagodas were to emulate. The same Song emperor completed another very tall pagoda some 70 metres (215 feet) high. Although this was connected with the Kaiyuan (Beginning of Principle) temple, it was built on the borderland of Dingxian in Hebei province, its main purpose being to survey from its top the movements of the Qidan, from whom the Liao dynasty was drawn. It was named the Liaodi ta, or Pagoda for Controlling the Enemy (see frontispiece) in token of this. During the same period the barbarians who were thus kept 'under control' built a wooden pagoda at Yingxian in Shânxi, dedicated to Sakyamuni and linked to the temple at Fogong (Palace of the Buddha). This was built on a double octagonal base of brick, and the body alone, excluding the pinnacle, stands a full 67 metres (220 feet) high, in five storeys, with many unique details. First and foremost, it is the oldest wooden pagoda still in existence in China, and second, the internal division into floors does not correspond to the outer divisions, since there are nine internal storeys, which are divided into two by a kind of attic. Another unusual feature is the presence of a statue of the Buddha at the centre of each floor. In addition it was reinforced with internal columns and external buttresses which enabled the pagoda to withstand the earthquakes which occur in the area. One final exceptional feature is that it was never burnt down, either by accident or design.

Another pagoda dating from the period of the Northern Song (AD 960–1126) is that in the city of Songjiang, linked to the temple of Xingshengjiao (Prosperity of the Holy Doctrine), which was built between AD 1068 and AD 1077 in a mixture of wood and ceramic, the latter being used in the balustrades. It was restored during the Qing period.

The pagoda of the Temple of Heavenly Peace (Tianning si) near Peking, was built under the barbarian Liao dynasty at the beginning of the twelfth century, and, like the other pagoda built by the Liao and dedicated to Sakyamuni, was endowed with numerous statues of the Buddha. These were on the outside of the tower, housed in niches designed for the purpose in the ceramic body of the first storey, which was particularly high in comparison to other storeys, and stood on a solid base. The tapering shape, rich decoration, and the series of thirteen close roofs all unite to form a quite unique piece of architecture, and it was this which gave rise to the name 'Tianning style'. The temple to which the pagoda was joined has been destroyed.

The Qi Yun ta or Regular Clouds Pagoda, linked to the Bai ma or White Horse Temple in Luoyang in Henan, is famous not so much for its thirteen ceramic storeys as for the legend which maintains that it was the first pagoda built in China, at the same time as the first Buddhist temple, in the first century, in memory of an occurrence which gave the temple its name. The monks Weng Zun and Cai Yen are said to have entered Luoyang carrying their manuscripts of the sutras on a white horse. There may be an element of truth as well as charm in the account, but there is no doubt that the pagoda as it now stands was built only in the twelfth century AD.

The Zhenguo ta (Stabilisation of the State) pagoda, linked to the Kaiyuan (Beginning of Principle) temple in Quanzhou in Fujian, was built in stone at the same period as its twin, the Renshou (Virtue and Longevity) pagoda, in 1238. Stone lacks the warmth and colour of enamelled and fired ceramic, but the bas reliefs adorning the doors on every floor, the exquisite curve of the roofs, and the mimicking of wooden beam-construction all lend such an impression of movement that this five-storeyed pagoda delights us with its charm and originality.

Another original pagoda which subsequently became the model of its type was the White Pagoda, Bai ta, in the Temple of Miaoying (Sublime Duty) in Peking, erected on the orders of the Mongol Emperor Qubilay during the second half of the thirteenth century on the ruins of an earlier pagoda which had been built by the Qidan and thrown down by the Mongols themselves. This pagoda is of unusual form, imitating that of the conical Tibetan *chorten*, which was equally derived from the Indian stupa. The Liao maintained particularly friendly relations with the Tibetans, even in the religious sphere, where they favoured lamaist Buddhism. Even the white colour of the pagoda is attributable to the so-called 'Lama style'.

Each new stylistic innovation during the succeeding centuries and dynasties was brought to bear on a Chinese model which remained substantially the same through the centuries. The most noticeable features and details of each epoch were the construction material (as when wood

Zhaocheng, Shânxi. Feijiang ta, or the Rainbow Pagoda, in the upper temple of Guangsheng ('Ample Remainder'). The pagoda was built in AD 1515. This temple is on the side of a mountain, at the foot of which is the lower temple. Both temples are constructed of wood, and were built in the Yuan and Ming periods. The Rainbow Pagoda is octagonal in plan, and has thirteen storeys. It owes its name to the richly coloured decoration of enamelled ceramics that covers its entire surface. Some of its tiles carry an inscription recording the fact that it was built in the tenth year of Chengdu, which corresponds to AD 1515. Inside the pagoda is a narrow, tunnel-like set of steps, which can best be climbed on all fours.

Zhaocheng, Shânxi. Detail of the decoration of the Rainbow Pagoda.

was replaced by enamelled ceramic), the emphasis placed on the use of differing colours, and variations in the pedestal.

The Rainbow Pagoda or Feijiang ta, linked to the upper temple of Guangsheng or Ample Remainder (the lower temple stands at the foot of the hill), was built under the Ming dynasty in Zhaocheng in Shanxi. It is obviously named after the fantastically rich colours of the enamelled ceramics which cover the main body and roofs of the building and make up the many sacred sculptures which decorate the eight façades on all thirteen storeys. Another building with dazzling enamelled ceramics is the Duobao ta, or Pagoda of the Many Jewels, on the outskirts of Peking. It has one innovation introduced by the Qing dynasty (1644–1911) architects in that it rests on a base which consists in its turn of a wide pavilion with full projecting wooden roofs, the two structures being set off and at the same time knitted together by the marble balustrade which surrounds the pavilion roof and the base of the pagoda.

PAGODAS, TEMPLES, PALACES   145

Peking. Duobao ta, the Many Jewels Pagoda, was built in the Qing period. It is situated on Mount Xiang, on the outskirts of Peking, to the north-west of the centre, in an area known as the Garden of Tranquillity and Law. The pagoda is faced with ceramics in five different colours, and has seven storeys. Like many pagodas of the Qing period, it has a very wide pavilion at the base, which is connected with the central tower by a white marble balcony. Of similar structure was the Enamelled Pagoda of the Pao en temple in Nanking, which was built in the reign of Yong Le during the Ming period; although it has been destroyed, its appearance is recorded in various paintings.

Innovative as this structure may seem and destined as it was to alter the outline of the pagoda, it was in fact merely the final Chinese variation on the original Indian theme. If one mentally replaces the polygonal Chinese tower with the hemispherical cupola of the Indian stupa, one is left with a building of remarkable similarity. We may therefore take this as an example of innovation by returning to the original conception underlying the ancient prototype. The Indian stupa had itself evolved into slender forms, with brick mouldings where the Chinese pagoda had wooden roofs, in the distant past.

This return to ancient models nevertheless took place within the framework of the religious independence which the Chinese won after the sixth century AD, when the native philosophical and artistic traditions burst into flower. From that time on Chinese sacred architecture, of which the pagoda is the finest expression, developed along lines which were always deeply rooted in Chinese culture, producing creative forms which were consistent with the past yet ever new.

Town-Planning

IN EVERY age and land the most basic indicator of social differentiation among men, the most concrete and obvious symbol of the exercise of power, has been a man's house. In towns and villages, the basic constituents of agrarian life, the headman's house has always occupied the site with the widest prospect, identifiable by the wide surrounding area which separates it and divides it from the rest of the town. These are in fact not merely the outward signs, but the prerogatives of those who have long held power, be they political or religious dignitaries. In larger towns those social groups which manage to achieve individual recognition occupy separate quarters, although the way in which the town is organised to house the various groups which wield power is the more complex since the power structure is itself more complex, and is regulated along well-defined hierarchical lines.

The most interesting and characteristic type of settlement from the point of view of town-planning and from the social and political viewpoint is of course the state capital. Here every element which plays a part in the efficient running of a city appears almost as a prototype or symbol. Furthermore it is possible to see in the capital city the entire state, or rather the entire universe, in microcosm.

At least since Confucius systematised their ancient religious and philosophical beliefs the Chinese have believed that man's life should be regulated by Heaven, and that it should be ordered in imitation of the heavenly order. Confucius defined what he meant by 'order', with a confidence justified by the extreme rigour and wisdom which characterise his system, as being carried out in Heaven, and to be carried out on earth. Thus Heaven has an efficient, well-organised, disciplined, and morally impeccable bureaucracy, which forms a model to be imitated. Other theories adopted by the Taoists also maintained that there was a cosmic bureaucratic and hierarchic order, and that this fact was reflected in the seat chosen by the supreme authority of Heaven and the Universe. The place where the heavenly powers are concentrated is said to be the Great Bear, with the Pole Star where the Supreme Ultimate resides. All this has been amply explained in the chapter on Changan, where the reader's attention was drawn to this topic because the subject under consideration was the foundation of a new Chinese capital. This followed an event of great historical significance, the unification of China after more than three and a half centuries of division, internal warfare, and foreign occupation, with the exception of a brief and tortured period of national unity under the Jin dynasty (AD 285–316). After that date northern China fell under barbarian rule, separated from the territories of the south, the latter meanwhile preserving the ancient traditions and culture. The two branches were united in AD 589 by the Sui dynasty (AD 581–618), which brought the whole territory of the entire Chinese world once more under the sway of a single national government. This was indeed a work of the 'Supreme Ultimate'. To complete the work the Sui emperor ordered the famous architect and town-planner Yu Wen kai (AD 555–612) to draw up plans for a new capital which would make plain the cosmic character of the city. Chinese history had already had one capital of great interest in the Han city of Changan, which had now been long abandoned. Yu the architect drew up plans for a second Changan, not far from the first, with a roughly rectangular plan, the east–west axis being about one kilometre (1,100 yards) longer than the north–south axis, the former measuring in total roughly 9.5 kilometres (6 miles), and the latter 8.5 kilometres (5.3 miles). The whole area was almost twice that of Han Changan. The streets were wide and straight, and ran parallel to one another from north to south, on the by now traditional pattern. To the north, corresponding to the Great Bear, was the site of the public and private buildings where the emperor was to dwell with various of his close advisers, and where public events and government acts took place. This area, more simply the Imperial Palaces, occupied an area of some 3 kilometres (1.9 miles) by 1.5 kilometres (0.9 miles). The Imperial Palace was separated from the rest of the city by a thick and impenetrable wall. The roads running north and

THE CITY OF QUINSAY (i.e. Hangzhou, former capital of the Southern Song)

And I Marco Polo was in this city of Quinsay, and did learn the customs of it, and it was declared unto me, that it was one hundred miles in compass, and had 12,000 bridges of stone with vaults and arches so high, that a great ship might pass under, and the people of this city every one of them must use the science of his fathers and of his predecessors. In this city there standeth a lake which is in compass thirty miles, and in this lake there is built the fairest palaces that ever I saw: and in the midst of this lake standeth two palaces wherein they do celebrate all the weddings of that city, and ever there remaineth within them all the things necessary which belong unto the weddings. Upon every one of the 12,000 bridges of stone, continually there standeth watch and ward, because there shall be no evil done, and that the city do not rebel. In this city there is an high mountain, and upon there standeth a very high tower, and upon it there is a thing to sound upon, and it is sounded when there is any fire or any rumour in the country. There is in this city fourteen baths; and the Great Cane hath great watch and ward in this city. . . .

There is in all the province of Mangi [southern China], 1,202 cities all subject unto the Great Cane, and all those which be born in this province of Mangi, are written by days and hours, that the province may know the number of the people, and that they may not rebel. When they do go on any journey, they consult with the astrologers, and when any dieth, the parents do clothe the dead in canvas, and burn the bodies with papers, whereupon is painted money, horses, slaves, beasts for their houses, apparel, with all other things; for they do say that the dead useth all this in the other world, and that with the smoke of the dead body, and of those papers, whereon there is painted all those things rehearsed, believing that it goeth all with him, into the other world, and when they burn those bodies, they sing and play upon all kinds of instruments and music that they can find, and say, that in that order and pleasure, their gods do receive them in the other world.

Marco Polo, *Travels*, Chapters 97 and 100.

south were crossed by the network of east–west roads forming the various quarters, from that of the artisans to that of the merchants, or that of the lower classes who performed more menial tasks, and so on, all of which were sub-divided by a lattice of streets, alleys, and courtyards. Each quarter was generally enclosed by a wall with four gates, one on each side, although some had only two gates on the east and west walls, which were shut at sunset and reopened at dawn. The whole city was surrounded by a great wall and moat. Under the Tang dynasty (AD 618–907) the city developed into a metropolis seething with trade and organised into its constituent quarters, so that the name of Changan became famous in its day throughout Asia, just as the Han capital of the same name had been in its day. The two cities shared a single strange destiny, as if linked by some mysterious thread of fate. For two centuries the first Changan was the capital of the Western Han empire (202 BC–AD 9), a large and solidly based national empire which succeeded in welding diverse populations into a single nation, and was able to govern competently the unified nation which it had inherited from the preceding dynasty of the Qin (221–206 BC), which had created the union in battle but survived too short a time to enjoy the fruits of its labours. In the same way the second Changan was the capital of the Tang empire for three centuries, another powerful and stable national empire which inherited the united nation created by the Sui dynasty (AD 581–618), which, as we have seen, governed China for no more than a few decades. This remarkable and unparalleled repetition of history is summed up in the name of Changan, a city which seems to epitomise the splendour and mystery of these two dynasties which governed the entire Chinese world from the microcosmic capital aligned along the axes of heaven. This fact did not in any event pass unnoticed, for on two separate occasions the Japanese planned their own capital on the lines of Changan. The first of these was when they founded Nara at the beginning of the eighth century AD. This city rapidly rose to enduring fame, although its life as capital city was relatively short, not outlasting the eighth century AD, chiefly because of the excessive numbers of Buddhist monasteries inside the city boundaries, whose monks caused trouble by interfering in the government of the country. Compared with Changan's

Left: detail of a painting by Zhang Zeduan entitled 'Spring Festival on the Banks of the River' (Southern Song period, early part of the twelfth century AD). The painting is about 5 metres (16½ feet) in length, and provides a detailed account of life in the Song capital. Its animated scenes show us markets, houses, streets, the port, and a naval dockyard. In the middle of our illustration is the wooden bridge across the Bian river, which shows the high level reached at that period in the techniques of construction. This painting is in the Imperial Palace at Peking.

Below: detail of a painting entitled 'The Return to China of the Lady Wen' (early twelfth century, Southern Song period). The painting shows the triumphal return of this noble lady, who had been abducted by the Xiong nu. It gives a clear picture of the structure of the houses of the nobility at that period. The work is now in the Museum of Fine Art, Boston.

PAGODAS, TEMPLES, PALACES 149

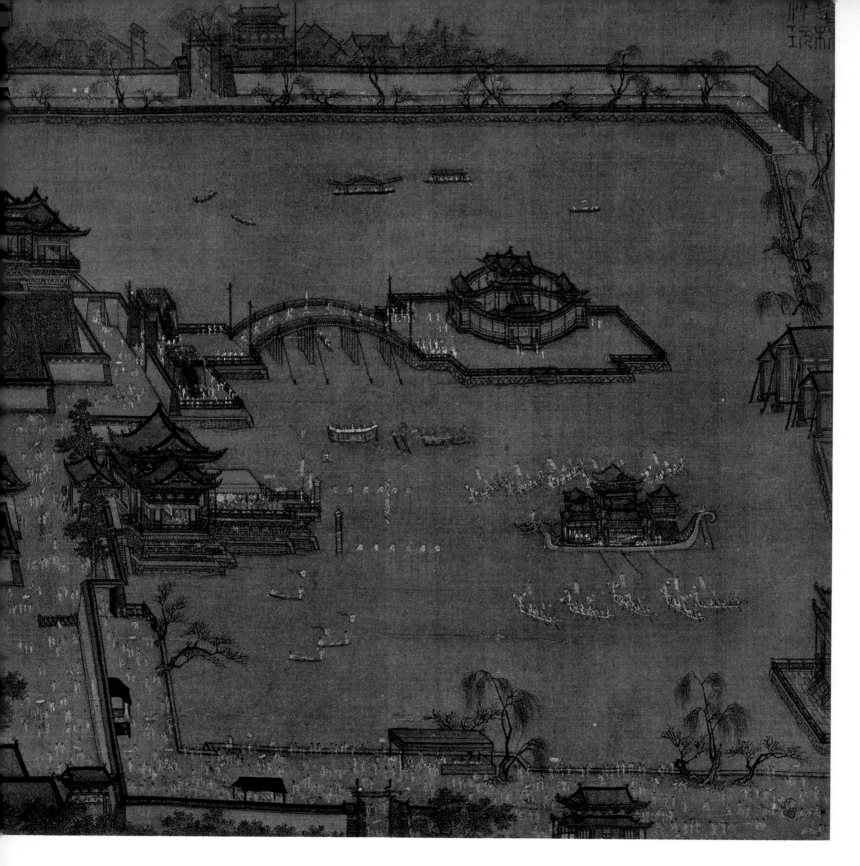

ordered division into quarters, Nara was planned somewhat chaotically, since the monastery enclosures were scattered here and there, breaking up the regularity of the pattern. Visitors to Nara today still go there to see the most interesting and ancient of Japan's Buddhist temples. The second capital was founded at the end of the eighth century, and adopted not only the plan, but even the name of Changan, being called Heyan Kyo, the 'city of peace'. Heyan Kyo enjoyed several centuries of fame and splendour, from the ninth to the twelfth centuries at least, and today, its name altered to Kyoto, is still one of the most famous and largest cities in Japan. The only difference between the Chinese cities and the Japanese cities modelled upon them lay in the fact that whilst the Japanese cities were never walled, the northern Chinese cities always had walls, the reason lying clearly in the particular historical circumstances and the danger of attack which threatened the latter. The city of Changan grew ever finer. The Tang's conquests in central Asia had reopened contact and given a fresh

Detail of a painting entitled 'Water Games on Lake Jinming', sometimes attributed to Zhang Zeduan; probably dating from the thirteenth century, Northern Song period. The scene is set on the lake of the Li Palace, which was the second residence of the Emperor, just to the west of Kaifeng. This painting is important because it illustrates the layout of gardens and palaces during the Song period. At the centre of the lake is a cross-shaped island connected by an arched bridge to the gate which leads to the palace; and on the island is a circular pavilion with open galleries.

A view of Suzhou, Jiangsu. Founded in the sixth century BC, Suzhou is one of the oldest cities in the Yangzi basin. Like the other cities of the region, it is traversed by a dense network of canals which make it possible to move goods by water between parts of the city.

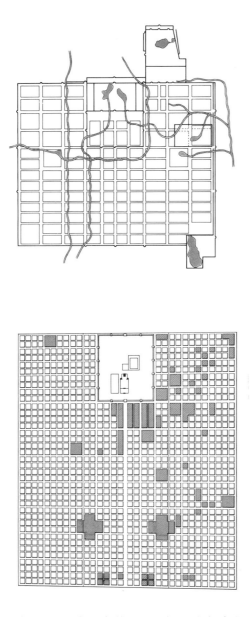

Top: street-plan of Changan, the capital of the Tang empire. This city was built by the Sui dynasty in the sixth century, at a short distance from the ruins of the splendid Changan of the Han, and following the same general plan. It was however under the Tang dynasty (AD 618–907) that the second city of Changan became a well-organised metropolis, humming with commercial activity.

Above: street-plan of Heyan Kyo, the Japanese capital founded in the eighth century AD on the model of the city of Changan.

Xian, Shânxi. Part of the wall which surrounded the ancient city of Changan (now Xian). The city was founded as the capital of the Sui dynasty, and was completed by the Tang dynasty under whom it became a famous centre of government. Changan was completely encircled by fortifications, which still surround the modern city of Xian. Outside the city walls runs a canal. Among the ancient cities of China, Xian is the only one that has retained this type of fortification – thanks in part to renovations carried out during the Ming dynasty. Inside the city, the Buddhist temples of the Tang period still survive today.

Ruicheng, Shânxi. The Yong le gong temple: wall-paintings in the Zhongyang dian, or Hall of Wang Zhongyang, who was the founder of the temple. The paintings date from the year AD 1368. The temple comprises three separate buildings, and is decorated internally with many paintings in an excellent state of preservation, which provide valuable information regarding Chinese life and Chinese costume during the Yuan period (AD 1271–1368). Some of the paintings show us the structure of contemporary buildings; others show us scenes of life indoors, as in the case of the detail reproduced here, which shows episodes from the story of Wang Zhongyang, the king on whose orders the temple was built.

CHANGAN REMEMBERED IN TWO SONGS

Farewell to Wei Wan on his departure for the capital

In the morning I hear a traveller
singing a song of farewell;
last night a light frost,
the first frost, came to this side of the river.
I cannot listen to the wild geese,
cannot listen to them in my sorrow.
Clouds and mountains stand watch
over the road you are to travel.
In the frontier city the pale dawn
makes its way through the chill of morning;
in the imperial gardens the sound of beaten
   clothes
widens out in the evening air.
Only in Changan
is life sweet,
while months and years continually
slip lightly away.

> Li Qi, a Tang poet,
> eighth century AD.

Always I think of you

Always I think of you
at Changan,
where the house-cricket of autumn chirps
from the golden stone of the well-head.
Here the brittle hoar-frost gleams coldly,
and the matting on the roof has a chilly colour.
The neglected lamp shines dully,
and nostalgia rends my heart.
I draw back the curtain and look out at the
   moon,
and sob into the empty void.
You too, fair flower of my heart,
have gone away into the clouds and the peaks.
Above is the dark-blue vault,
high in the heavens;
below is the running water,
running its broken course.
The sad mind takes flight
into the remote vastness of the sky.
The spirit of dreams cannot reach
the stony passes of the mountains.
Always I think of you,
And the depths of my soul are stirred.

> Li Bo, a Tang poet,
> eighth century AD.

impetus to the silk trade, and the long, safe roads linking China to Iran were filled with caravans and foreign embassies journeying to the great Chinese capital, so famed in legend, so rich, and with such sumptuous palaces for the reception of the embassies. The order of the buildings and businesslike efficiency of its inhabitants became proverbial.

In AD 634 a new and imposing residence was built alongside the largest building in the imperial palace, the Taiji or Great Peak. This was the Da ming gong, the Palace of Great Luminosity, which was followed in AD 714 by the Xingqing gong (Palace of Receptions and Audiences), surrounded by kiosks and pavilions, where banquets were given.

With the collapse of the Tang dynasty, Changan's period as capital city was for ever over. The political centre of gravity of the Chinese empire gravitated away from the east–west axis facing into Central Asia, to a north–south axis intended rather to create stronger ties between the destinies of the two great areas of China itself, the north and the south.

Today the city is known as Xian (Western Peace), and is the busy and populous capital of Shânxi province. Unique as Changan is, it established an archetype which was to be followed in subsequent capitals such as Peking, and so influenced their appearance.

These great cities were laid out in harmony with the dicta of astrology whenever possible, although in the case of Suzhou, with its canals between its houses so reminiscent of Venice, other circumstances proved decisive. Strangely, Marco Polo failed to perceive the similarity with his own home town, although he recorded that '. . . in this city there are a good six thousand stone bridges . . .'; he did not fail to mention its humming industries, however, saying of it, '. . . a noble city. . . . They have silk and live by trade and crafts, and they make many silken cloths, and are rich merchants . . .'

Suzhou, Jiangsi. Xi yuan, the Western Garden (AD 1869–1903 Qing Dynasty). The garden contains a temple known as Kaichuanglu, and a lake known as Fangsheng. Thanks to the light and graceful structure of its wooden balconies and concave roofs, the small pavilion illustrated above slips into the landscape without upsetting its balance, in a manner typical of Chinese gardens.

China at the Time of Marco Polo

THE VENETIAN traveller Marco Polo arrived in China with his father Nicolò Polo and his uncle Matteo Polo in 1275, at the age of twenty-one. This was a strange and unusual period in the history of Asia, and indeed in the history of the world – the period of the huge, short-lived, turbulent Mongol empire. Northern China was already in the hands of the Mongols. Southern China was still ruled by the Song dynasty, and had reached a high level of prosperity and culture. (Song painting and ceramics are highly esteemed by lovers of Chinese art.) Four years later, however, southern China (or 'Mangi', as Marco Polo calls it) also fell to the Mongols. Chinese history, as we have already seen, is characterised by a long series of dismemberments and reunifications of the national territory; and the Mongol conquest can, from one point of view, be regarded as a reunification in this sense. But it was a humiliating reunification, under the rule of an alien minority which had difficulty in administering the country because it failed to secure the cooperation or the complicity of the Chinese upper classes, and consequently had to entrust important posts to foreigners from other countries, such as Marco Polo himself. The Mongol dynasty was relatively short-lived, coming to an end in 1368.

During the brief period of Mongol supremacy, the warlike horsemen of the steppe exercised dominion over the tillers of the soil from the plains of eastern Europe to the Pacific Ocean, along the whole strip of pasture-land to the north of the Himalayas; they had absorbed the territory of many peoples more civilised than themselves, including Arabs, Turks, Iranians, and the inhabitants of the oases of central Asia; and they had invaded the countries of south-east Asia which lie to the south of China. According to some authorities, it was the existence of this sprawling empire, unique in history, that made possible the journeys of the Polo brothers and of Marco Polo himself, and various attempts to open up diplomatic relations between East and West, such as the missions to Mongolia of Johannes de Plano Carpini and William of Rubrouck. It also promoted a more general renewal of interest in the Western world regarding the countries of the East, and especially China. There is no doubt that the journeys of the Polo brothers were facilitated by the political situation. 'The Great Cane,' says Marco Polo, 'gave them two tables of gold, by which he did signify that they should pass freely through all his provinces and dominions, and that their charges should be borne, and to be honourably accompanied.' (*Travels*, chapter 4.) These were in effect passports, of a kind formerly issued by the Song emperors. The fact that they were made of gold indicated the high rank of the bearers.

There are over 150 manuscripts of *The Travels of Marco Polo*, in many different languages, including French, Latin, Italian and Venetian dialect. Little is known of Marco Polo, who does indeed seem to have been appointed by fate to reveal China to the Western world, except what can be gathered from the book; and he has far more to say about the things he sees than about himself. The Italian manuscript of the work in the Biblioteca Nazionale, Florence, is divided into 158 short chapters; but only the first thirteen, which form a prologue, deal with the reasons for the journey, the journey itself and the experiences of the travellers. The other chapters describe cities, countries, customs and historical events. This remarkable objectivity has caused some readers to doubt whether the journey ever took place at all. Among other things, critics point out that it is very strange that the Venetian never mentions the Chinese custom of drinking tea. This may however be explained by the fact that during his seventeen years in the service of the Great Cane (otherwise known as Qubilay or Kublai Khan, *qaghan* of the Mongols, and Emperor of China in the Yuan dynasty (as the Chinese historians call the period of Mongol domination), Marco Polo's position prevented him from getting deeply involved in Chinese culture or Chinese society. More recent examples have shown how difficult it is for a foreigner to achieve this at any time. He saw the Chinese, travelled among them, played a part in their government and made notes; but he may have had more social contact with the Mongols and with the other foreigners employed, like himself, in the administration.

Nicolò and Matteo Polo 'came to the city of the Great Cane, Lord of all the Tartars' by the route through the steppes, travelling from the Crimea to Bolghar on the Volga, through Bokhara and to the north of the mountain barriers to Karakoram. They may have gone on across the Great Wall to Peking. When they returned to Venice, many years later, they brought with them a message to the Pope from Qubilay, who was curious about Christianity because he had Nestorian Christians among his subjects. The Pope, however, had died, and they had to wait for the election of his successor before they could set out again with a reply for Qubilay. Nicolò's son Marco went with them. They were accompanied on the early part of their journey by two friars sent by Gregory X, the new Pope. But when they came to a town called Ghaza, as Marco Polo tells us, 'the Sultan of Babylon came into Armenia and did great hurt there, and for that cause, fearing to pass any further, the two friars tarried there, and wrote to the Great Cane, that they were come thither, and the cause wherefore they went not forward'. The Polos went on, following the well-known route of the Silk Road, although not without some initial hesitations and uncertainties. Starting from Ghiaza (otherwise known as Ayas or Laias), which was the eastern Mediterranean port of Lesser Armenia, they went on through Mesopotamia and Iran to Hormuz, where they wanted to take ship and continue their journey to China by sea. They changed their minds about this for some reason, and set off inland through Iran and across the mountains of Khorasan. From Herat they went on through Badakhshan and finally crossed the Pamir. 'Three days journey going forward, you

The said Nicolò and Matteo Polo, and Marco the son of Nicolò went on their journey, and came to a city called Bemeniphe [Kai ping fu], where the Great Cane was, but in the way they passed in great danger of their bodies, and saw many things, as shall hereafter be declared, and tarried in going between Ghiaza and Bemeniphe, a year and a half, by reason of great rivers, rain and cold in those countries: and when the Great Cane had knowledge that Nicolò and Matteo were returned, he sent to receive them, more than forty days' journey, and at their coming received them with great pleasure, and they kneeling down, making great reverence, he commanded them to arise up, demanding of them how they sped in their voyage, and what they had done with the pope, and after they had made their answer to all things, delivered to him the Friars' letters that remained in Ghiaza, and the oil they had taken out of the lamp that burned before the holy sepulchre of Jesus Christ, which he received with great pleasure, and put it up, and kept it in a secret place, with also the letters, and demanding of them, who Marco was, they answered, he was Nicolò's son, of the which the Great Cane was glad, and took him into his service, and gave orders to place him in his Court among his Lords and Gentlemen.

Marco Polo, *Travels*, end of Prologue.

shall go up an hill, upon the which is a river, and goodly fruitful pastures, that if you put in your cattle there, very lean, within ten days they will be fat. There be great plenty of wild beasts, and among them wild sheep, that some of them have their horns of four and some of seven, and some of ten spans long. And of these horns the herdsmen there do make dishes and spoons. In the valley of this mountain called *Pamir*, you shall travel ten days' journey, without coming to any town, or any grass, therefore it shall be needful, for the travellers that way, to carry provision with them, as well for themselves, as for their horses. There is great cold in that country, that the fire hath not the strength to seethe their victuals, as in other countries.' (Marco Polo, *Travels*, chapter 28.)

Descending from the Pamir into the Tarim basin, the three Venetians followed the northern branch of the Silk Road and went on into China. They reached the court of the Emperor Qubilay in May, 1275. The two brothers seemed to have engaged in trading, while Marco entered the service of the Mongols. He tells us that he was the governor of a Chinese city for three years, and that he took part in missions to Yunnan and Indo-China. Marco Polo provided the Emperor with reports on subject lands which he had never seen; he tells us that Qubilay 'loved to learn about the customs of the nations of the earth'. Such curiosity is quite foreign to the Chinese mind, and is an example of the difference of mentality that separated the Mongols from their subjects.

By the end of their long stay in China, the Polos must have been anxious to return to Europe; and the opportunity finally came in the form of another official mission. This time their task was to accompany a Mongol princess to the court of her future husband, the Ilkhan Argun, who was the Mongol ruler of Persia. They travelled by ship, taking a route via the southern China Sea, the Strait of Malacca, the Bay of Bengal and the west coast of India to Hormuz on the Persian Gulf. They were accompanied by a fleet of thirteen ocean-going junks, and the journey took fifteen months. Marco Polo had now travelled along both the two great commercial routes between East and West – the Silk Road across the continent of Asia, and the sea route (well-known to the Arabs) that passed through the Strait of Malacca.

In September 1298, three years after his return to Venice, Marco Polo was doing his duty as a good citizen of the Republic by fighting in the naval battle of Curzola against the Genoese. He was captured, and passed a year as a prisoner in Genoa. Among his fellow prisoners was the Pisan Rustichello, who had been captured at Meloria. Tradition tells us that Marco Polo dictated his memories of the marvels of China to Rustichello in prison; and that the book owes its Italian title of 'Il Milione' to the abundance of very large numbers that he quoted in it. Both these stories appear to be inaccurate. 'Million' is now thought to have been a traditional family nickname that other Polos had borne before Marco. And Luigi Foscolo Benedetto, who is the greatest authority on the many manuscripts of the *Travels*, has come to the conclusion that the work was originally written down in the strange mixture of French and Venetian that was used by the Latin conquerors of Constantinople after the fourth crusade; and that Marco Polo handed this rough draft over to his fellow-prisoner to be translated into a purer, although still Italianate, French, in the hope that this would invest it with a literary charm that would ensure its success with the noble audience of lords, emperors, kings and dukes, to whom Rustichello addresses his version.

The various versions of the book appeared under many different names, including *The Description of the World* (which may be the original title), *The Book of Marvels*, and *The Million* (which has become the generally accepted name in Italy). This is not the place for a full discussion of its importance and its fortunes. The name of Polo does not appear in the annals of the Yuan dynasty; but what he tells us about China is regularly confirmed by Oriental sources. The book is essentially truthful. For the peoples of Europe, the work marked the opening up of the hidden world of China, and gave rise to a myth, the cloudy mystery of which has not yet been fully dispersed by learned study. When Italian visitors go to China today, their hosts often refer to the name of the great Venetian traveller, out of politeness, on official occasions. The meeting between the eastern and

COAL, PEPPER AND PORCELAIN

And when they go from thence, for to go unto Cathay, they find a great mountain, where there is black stones, and they burn like wood, when they be well kindled they will keep a fire from one day to another, and they do burn of them in that country, though they have wood, but the wood is more dearer than are the stones.

... and at the end of these five days' journey, standeth a great and a fair city named Zaitun [not yet identified], which hath a good haven, and thither come many ships from the Indies, with many merchandises, and this is one of the best havens that is in the world, and there cometh ships unto it in such quantity, that for one ship that cometh unto Alexandria, there cometh 100 unto it. The Great Cane hath great custom for merchandises, in and out of that haven, for the ship that cometh thither payeth ten in the hundred for custom, and of precious stones and spices, and of any other kind of fine wares, they pay thirty in the hundred: and of pepper 44 of the hundred, so that the merchants in freight, tribute, and customs, pay the one half of their goods. In this country and city there is great abundance of victuals.

... and in this province is a city called Tiungiu [not yet identified] where they make the finest porcelain bowls in the world. Nothing like them is made anywhere else, and they are exported to all countries. And for a Venetian groat you may purchase three of the most beautiful and best ornamented bowls in the world.

Marco Polo, *Travels*, Chapters 62 and 105.

western extremes of the Eurasian land-mass was inevitable; and the name of Marco Polo, who both witnessed and described it, remains its symbol.

Western Influences in China

THE CULTURAL development of China, as is true of most great civilisations, was unique. Although the impact of foreign influences must never be ignored, such civilisations derive their character primarily from their original ability to invent organised patterns of life, of production and of expression which spring from the special genius of their people, from the way in which that people has come through its historical conflicts. The interplay of special national genius and national history produces that complex of language, customs, thought, artistic form, social organisation and methods of housing the population which we sum up under the single term of 'civilisation'.

Chinese civilisation was already mature and clearly defined when it first came into contact with another civilisation whose character was congenial with its own. This was Buddhism.

The second historic encounter of this kind was with the Jesuits, starting from the end of the sixteenth century. The most important figure is Father Matteo Ricci of Macerata (1552–1610). He is well known to the Chinese under the name of Li Mato. This encounter might have altered the history of China, and indeed of the world, far more deeply than the meeting with Buddhism. Behind the Jesuits stood all the civilised culture that had so far grown up in the Western world; and the Chinese wanted to acquire a practical knowledge of it. This important meeting of minds between East and West did not last for long. It continued for barely 150 years; and during the last fifty years it was restricted to personal contacts, which did not make any difference in the physiognomy of the two civilisations. The two systems remained mutually closed and impenetrable. Up to this time, the Chinese civilisation had led the world on the technological plane; but now it became hidebound by tradition and lost its power of innovation. About the same time, Europe was breaking free of the shackles of tradition which had held it back. Copernicus, Galileo and Newton laid the foundations of modern science. The Jesuits had gained much ground at the court of the Qing dynasty in the second half of the seventeenth century, especially with the Emperor Kangxi (1661–1722); but unfortunately they could not bring the message of European science to China, because that science had been rejected and condemned by the Church. Thus a great opportunity was lost to make an important contribution towards the development of China into a modern civilisation. Even so, it would have been valuable to continue and widen the dialogue with Peking that had been opened up by the praiseworthy efforts of the Jesuits. Unfortunately, however, other religious Orders arrived in China from the West, including the Franciscans, who began to quarrel with the Jesuits about ceremonial procedure (the so-called 'Question of the Rites'). The Pope himself intervened, sending delegations to China to involve the Emperor Kangxi himself in tiresome complaints. All this so exasperated the Chinese authorities that in the end they completely prohibited the teaching of the doctrines of Christianity and took up a hostile attitude towards the members of the various Orders. Officially speaking, the relationship between East and West was now severed. There remained, however, a personal relationship, based on respect, between the Emperor and some of the missionaries, who continued to frequent the court and to work for the Emperor Kangxi right up till the time of his death. They rendered the same service to the Emperor Yongzheng (1723–1735) in the same way, though he showed very little interest in their affairs, and also to the Emperor Qianlong (1736–1796), who was a good friend and generous patron to them. As a result of this fortunate development, various buildings were constructed in the European style in China, at the express orders of the Emperor himself.

There were in fact already some buildings of Western type in Peking,

Peking. Ruins of a Western-style building in the Yuan ming garden (AD 1747–1760). This is one of a group of five gardens which extend over a vast area to the north-west of Peking. The area also includes three hills – Wanjushan, Yuquanshan and Xiangshan. Yuan ming yuan is the largest of the five gardens. It contains an artificial hill and an artificial lake, according to the Chinese tradition of enriching and completing the natural beauty of a garden by the addition of the features which it lacks. The special character of this particular garden lies in the presence of Western-style buildings, in the rococo manner. For the planning and execution of this project, the Emperor Qianlong turned to the Jesuit fathers Castiglione, Moggi and Benoist. The building shown here was partly destroyed by British and French troops in AD 1860, and the ruins were further damaged in 1960.

where three Catholic churches had been built in the first half of the eighteenth century. Their Chinese names are Nan tang (Southern Church), Dong tang (Eastern Church) and Bei tang (Northern Church). Being purely religious buildings of no great beauty, they had no influence at any time on Chinese architecture. It may be remarked here that exactly the opposite had happened in France in the second half of the seventeenth century, after the appearance of two French volumes on Chinese subjects, both published at Amsterdam. The first, which came out in 1655, was the report of an embassy sent by the East India Company to the Chinese Emperor, and contained a picture of the Porcelain Tower at Nanking, accompanied by a description of that building. The other volume was edited by Athanasius Kircher and published in 1670; it was entitled *China monumentis illustrata*, and contained an accurate description of a nine-storey pagoda in Shandong. The accounts of these two buildings, both pagodas and both roofed with enamelled porcelain, made a great impression on the imagination of the French, so much so that Louis XIV ordered a *Trianon de Porcelain* for his gardens at Versailles in 1670. (Imitation porcelain had to be used for this building, because real porcelain was not produced in Europe until 1708.) Chinese art was considered in Europe to be a suitable subject for light-hearted imitation, while European art was not regarded in China as being worthy of attention at all, until the Emperor Qianlong took a fancy to it. The Jesuit Father Giuseppe Castiglione (1688–1766) had painted some pictures of baroque palaces, which caught the Emperor's eye, and led him to order the construction of some similar buildings in the imperial garden of *Yuan ming yuan* (the Garden of Perfect Splendour), which his grandfather Kangxi had started to lay out in 1709, to the north-west of the capital city. Giuseppe Castiglione had been sent to

Peking as an artist. He arrived in 1715, and later assumed the name of Lang Shinin, by which he is very well known in China, both as an artist of the traditional Chinese school whose work shows European influences, and as having introduced perspective of the kind used by Western artists into his pictures. He also made a Chinese translation of Andrea Pozzo's *Perspectiva Pictorum et Architectorum*, which was published in 1698 and was a book of fundamental importance for European artists in the eighteenth century. The Chinese translation was given the title of *Shi Xue*, or *Instruction in Seeing*. It cannot be described as a great success, because Chinese painters continued to take no notice of the rules of Western perspective. The only exceptions were Shen Yuan and Tang Dai, who did make use of perspective while painting a series of forty views of Yuang ming yuan in 1744. It seems, however, that they were working under the direct, personal supervision of Castiglione rather than following out the instructions contained in his book. The album containing these paintings is now in the Bibliothèque Nationale, Paris.

The Emperor had also seen pictures of European fountains, and these were added to his plans for a garden with European buildings. This seems to have been a complete novelty; for garden fountains had previously been unknown in China. The Garden of Perfect Splendour thus became the meeting-place of two different systems of embellishing the scenery of a park.

Friar Ferdinando Buonaventura Moggi was an architect from Florence, who lived and worked in Peking from 1721 until his death in 1761. Castiglione decided to entrust the buildings in the imperial garden to Moggi, who had already built the Dong tang church in Peking. For the construction of the fountains, he turned to the French Jesuit Michel Benoist (1715–1774), who was experienced in the art of hydraulics.

The new complex of buildings and fountains was constructed between 1747 and 1759, under the name of Xi Yang lou or European Palace. It was separated by a wall from the two neighbouring Chinese gardens (the Garden of Perfect Splendour and the Garden of Eternal Spring). The purpose of this separation was to keep a clear distinction between the two types of garden, which differed profoundly, not only in the style of the buildings, but also in their materials. The European buildings were of stone, with much use of marble; the Chinese buildings were mainly of wood and porcelain. The first phase of construction was completed in 1747, and comprised the Xie qi chu or Palace of Harmonious Delight and the Xu shin lou or Tower of Life-Giving Waters. Both the construction of the fountains and the patterns made by their waters are essentially baroque in style and inspiration, and architectural details such as columns, pilasters and capitals breathe the spirit of the Italian Renaissance, but otherwise the pavilion-shaped buildings and their roofs do not depart too far from Chinese tradition. The blending of styles produced an attractive effect, however, and the Emperor showed his satisfaction by ordering that the project should be continued. A gateway in the German baroque style was introduced into the north wall, and given the name of Hua yuan men or Flower Garden Gate. This opened into a maze-like garden, known by the names of Hua Yuan (Flower Garden) or Duo huang hua deng (Many Lanterns with Yellow Flowers). In front of the Xu shui lou a dual-purpose structure was erected, known as the Yang jiao long or Bird-Cage, which served both as an aviary and as a way into another part of the garden, with an elegant wrought-iron gate on one side and a monumental entrance of white marble, flanked with fountains and lawns, on the other.

The Fang wai guan or Belvedere was a small, two-storey palace, constructed of bricks, marble and building stone, with roofs of the Chinese type – another meeting-place for the styles of East and West. In front of the Belvedere stood the Wu zhu ting or Five Bamboo Pavilions, a group of purely Chinese buildings, connected to each other by a series of galleries. The Hai yan tang or Palace of Ocean Warmth was built to the east of the Belvedere; its outward appearance was that of a splendid one-storey villa with magnificent external stairways, but its contents were, quite simply, those of a water-tower. The horizontal lines of this building could be taken as reflecting either traditional Chinese architecture or the Renaissance style of Europe. The last building of the group stood a little further to the

THE EMPEROR AND MATTEO RICCI'S CLOCKS

The Fathers were taken as far as the second wall of the palace, and led into a courtyard, where the big clock had been put; a large crowd had assembled to see this sight.

The King sent one of his chamberlains to meet them; this was a eunuch of great wisdom, named Licino, who treated the Fathers with great friendship. He asked the Fathers various questions about their objects and intentions in giving this present to the King, and was very pleased to learn that they were not seeking any office, but were men of religion, interested only in serving God and living religiously, without wanting any of the things of this world. It was explained to him that these clocks enabled you to tell the time by day or by night, by the strokes of the bell or by the pointer which indicated the hours on the dial; that it would be necessary for him to appoint someone to learn how to keep the clocks in good order; and that it would take two or three days for him to learn everything that was necessary for this purpose. Licino went off to report all this to the King, who gave orders that four eunuch mathematicians from the Inner College (which has twenty or thirty members) should learn how to maintain and take care of the clocks, and that they should bring the clocks to him in his audience-chamber within three days. And so the Fathers spent the next three days and nights continually in the quarters of those mathematicians, teaching them about the clocks; they were treated with great respect, and the *Mathan* ordered his servants to pay all the expenses, to prevent them saying anything bad about him to the King. For word had gone abroad that he had received presents of great value from the Fathers, which was all untrue; but he had to spend several hundred scudos to get off without harm to himself. . . .

The four mathematicians studied the working of the clocks with great diligence, writing everything down in their script, because if they had forgotten anything it might well have cost them their lives. For this King is very cruel to them, and often causes them to be beaten to death with clubs, or killed in other ways, for very small offences. And the first thing they did was to convert into Chinese writing the names of all the wheels, shafts, pins and other parts of the clocks; and the Fathers gave them great help in finding various names for the parts that could be written down in Chinese. . . .

The three days were not fully up, when the King sent to ask why they had not yet taken him the clocks; and so they took the clocks in to him with great haste. The King was very pleased with everything, and rewarded the four eunuchs by raising them all one grade in the service, which is a method of increasing both their dignity and their income. The eunuchs were very pleased with this, and still more pleased that from then on two of their number were privileged to enter the King's presence every day to look after the small clock; for he wanted to have it always with him and took great pleasure in it. . . .

As for the larger clock, there was no suitable place in the inner palace where it could be installed at a sufficient height for the proper operation of its weights. And so the following year he sent it back to the Tribunal of Manufacturers and ordered that a wooden tower should be built for it, following a model supplied by the Fathers; it was an elegant and beautiful tower, with stairways, windows and balconies. He also ordered that a much larger bell should be cast for it; and he made it into a truly royal structure, with various ornaments, carvings and shutters, all gilded and painted with great
(continued on facing page)

skill, so that it cost him 1,300 ducats. And he gave orders that this tower should be placed in a garden outside the second wall of his palace, where he keeps other precious things and often goes to enjoy them. . . .

Matteo Ricci, *Commentaries*, AD 1583–1610.

Peking. Rigui, the sun-dial standing in front of the Taihe dian palace in the Imperial City (end of the seventeenth century). As in many other ancient civilisations, the first astronomical instrument to be invented in China was the gnomon – a simple pole planted vertically in the ground to measure the length of the shadows cast at various times by the sun. The gnomon was a first step towards the invention of the sun-dial. In Europe, the measurement of time was based on the sun-dial until the fourteenth century AD, whereas in China clepsydras and hydraulic clocks had been in use from a much earlier period.

Peking. Gu guanxiang tai, the old astronomical observatory (AD 1439–1442). Starting from the top left-hand corner of the photograph, we can see a celestial globe, a sextant, and (in the foreground) an armillary sphere or sphere of rings. This last instrument, which had been in use in China since the fourth century BC, reproduces the celestial sphere with its circles, and was used to determine the position of the heavenly bodies. In the invention of these and other astronomical instruments, the Chinese were about eleven centuries ahead of the West.

east. This was the Yuan ying yuan or View of Distant Lakes, which the Emperor used as a summer residence. Apart from some baroque decoration, its architecture was mainly in the traditional Chinese style.

When the garden and the buildings were completed, the spirit of baroque could be seen to triumph in the arches, in the marble facings of the fountains, and to a large extent in the architecture, where the broken lines, the lunettes, the pilasters and the exuberant decoration often nullify any attempt to avoid too wide a departure from Chinese taste, thanks to the grace of baroque line and the elegant fantasy of baroque form, seen within the framework of a wider organisation, which embraces streams, pools, trees, paths and open spaces. The works entitled *Great Fountains*, *View of the Fountain*, *Gate of Look-Out Hill* and *Eastern Gate of Look-Out Hill* all bear witness to the triumph of the baroque. To a somewhat lesser extent, the same is true of *Look-Out Hill* and *Perspective View to the East of the Lake*. The arches through which we see the carefully organised composition of the garden and its fountains lend a theatrical air to the whole picture.

The gardens of the Xi yang lou or European Palace must have been a fascinating example of the meeting of two cultures; but unfortunately they were completely ruined in 1860 by the English and French troops that invaded Peking. We cannot estimate what influence the European stylistic elements present in the palace might have exercised on Chinese artists if it

Peking, Gu gong (the Forbidden City). The courtyard between the Wu men and the Taihe men. The buildings date from AD 1899. The courtyard is crossed by five bridges with balustrades of white marble. Beyond the bridges is the Taihe gate, the entrance to the Taihe dian, or Pavilion of Supreme Harmony. The Forbidden City of Peking is the only surviving example of an imperial palace in China. Its construction was begun in AD 1404 on the orders of the Emperor Yong Le, and was completed in AD 1420. The rectangular walled space which surrounds it is oriented along the north–south axis, and is further surrounded by a canal. This area was enclosed within a larger rectangle of unfortified walls that delimited the Imperial City, which was reserved for the residences of state functionaries. There was much reshaping and rebuilding over the centuries, and many of the buildings date from the Qing period. The basic structure of the Forbidden City, however, remains unchanged.

had not been closed to all but the emperor and his intimates. All we know is that the experiment was an isolated one and that nothing is left of it today except a few ruins.

Peking

PEKING IS now one of the major cities in the world; it has eight million inhabitants, and is the capital of the most populous state on our planet. As with most other modern capitals, the Old City of Peking (which dates from the fifteenth century AD) occupies only a restricted area in the centre of the metropolis. Its actual measurements are, however, worth mentioning. The walled area, which includes the 'Tartar City' and the 'Chinese City' (we shall have more to say about these two names later), covers an irregular rectangle measuring 8.5 kilometres (5.3 miles) from north to south, and 6.5 to 8 kilometres (4 to 5 miles) from east to west. For purposes of comparison, it may be noted that the centre of Venice measures 1,300 metres by 800 metres (1,400 yards by 880 yards); that the north–south axis of the ancient city of Rome as defined by the Wall of Aurelian measures 4.8 kilometres (3 miles); and that the old city of Paris, from the Place de la

Bastille to the Place de la Concorde, measures less than 4 kilometres (2.5 miles).

The lay-out of Peking follows a geometrical pattern, in keeping with what has already been said about Chinese town-planning. The plan of the Old City is reminiscent of a nest of Chinese boxes. Working from the centre outwards, we come first of all to the rectangle of the imperial palace, traditionally known as Zi jin cheng or Purple Forbidden City, and surrounded by a strong wall. Around this first enclosure, a second walled rectangle formerly protected the 'Imperial City', but those walls no longer exist. The Gate of Heavenly Peace was originally the southern entry to the 'Imperial City'; it now opens on to the Tian an Men or Square of Heavenly Peace which is the centre of modern Peking and modern China. Outside the second rectangle was a third, known as the 'Inner City' (Nei cheng) or

Peking, Gu gong. Above is a photograph of the Taihe dian, the Pavilion of Supreme Harmony (AD 1695). It is the principal palace within the Forbidden City. It contains the great throne-room where the most important ceremonies took place, such as the celebration of the New Year and the issue of imperial edicts. The palace is approached by a stairway with balustrades of white marble. The stairway is built of wood, and is 63 metres (207 feet) in length and 35 metres (115 feet) in height. The double roof, weighty but well-proportioned, is covered with yellow tiles. Behind the Taihe dian two smaller pavilions stand on the north–south axis. These are the Zhonghe dian and the Baohe dian, which were used by the Emperor for ordinary audiences and routine business.

'Tartar City'. This third enclosure measures 6.5 kilometres (4 miles) from east to west and little less than 6 kilometres (3.75 miles) from north to south. There were plans to build a fourth, outer perimeter wall around the city, but this scheme was carried out only in part. A line of earthworks was built out from the southern section of the third wall to include an extra suburban area measuring 8 kilometres (5 miles) from east to west, and less than 3 kilometres (1.9 miles) from north to south, immediately to the south of the 'Tartar City'. The new enclosure was known as 'Wai cheng', or 'Outer City'; alternatively (and more traditionally) it was called the 'Chinese City'. The functional differences between the successive enclosures that we have described is indicated by their names. The 'Forbidden City' is the one at the centre, where the Emperor has his residence; the 'Imperial City' is the seat of the government of the empire; the 'Tartar City'

Peking, Gu gong. The throne-room in the Taihe dian (AD 1695). The furniture and decoration of this great hall are the last word in contemporary taste for sumptuous luxury. The great columns are entirely covered with gold leaf decorated with flowers and dragons. The throne – itself a masterpiece of elaborately carved and painted wood – stands on an inlaid and decorated wooden base. Behind it is a great screen with seven panels of gilded lac. On either side of the throne stand enamelled figures of cranes, the crane being a bird of great symbolical importance in Chinese mythology. Tall stands of carved wood support exquisite vases of porcelain.

THE ENVOY OF THE TSAR AT THE IMPERIAL PALACE

The Palace is an oblong Quadrangular Brick building, which is twice as long as broad, and the Roof covered with yellow glazed Tiles, on which were fixed Lions, Dragons and all sorts of Imagery. . . . The Ascent to the Hall was up several steps, and the farther part or entrance of it was provided with small open places or Windows, which were not glazed but peaked with paper. At the ends of this Hall were two Doors, the tops of which were adorned with a sort of carved work, somewhat like a crown, which was extraordinary well gilt. This building hath neither any room over it or arched Roof, but the height of the Room is to the very top of the Roof, which was composed of curious Panels, beautifully coloured, Japanned and finely gilded. . . .

The Throne is placed opposite to the Eastern Entrance, against the hind Wall, and is about three Fathom broad, and as many long; before it are two Ascents with six steps each, adorned with Rails and cast representations of Leaves very well gilt: on the right and left sides were also Rails of cast Imagery, which some report to be Gold, and others silver. . . . Exactly in the middle of this raised place is a Throne somewhat like an Altar, which opens with two Doors: and in it the Emperor's seat about an Ell high, covered with black Sables, on which he sat with his Legs across under him. This Monarch was then aged about 50 years, his Mien was very agreeable, he had large black Eyes, and his Nose was somewhat raised; he wore small black Mustachios, but had very little or no Beard on the lower part of his Face: he was very much pitted with the Small Pox, and of a middling Stature.

From *Travels Over Land from Muscovy to China*, 1706, by Evert Ysbrand Ides, the envoy of Tsar Peter the Great.

is the area inhabited mainly by the Manchu, the alien Tartar rulers of China during the last dynasty; the 'Chinese City', furthest towards the south, was so called to distinguish it from the Tartar City.

What we have just said obviously refers to the last couple of centuries of imperial China. Today the Forbidden City is a historic monument open to visitors, the walls of the Imperial City no longer exist, and modern Peking has extended far beyond its earlier limits.

In the old days, imperial edicts were issued at the Gate of Heavenly Peace, which was the southern gate of the Imperial City; the edicts were placed in a casket of gilded wood shaped like a phoenix, and lowered from a gallery running across the top of the gate to the high functionaries of state who were kneeling on the ground below. The edicts in their casket would then be placed on a wooden tray and taken to the Ministry of Ceremonies, to be copied and distributed throughout the empire. These edicts were officially known as 'imperial orders emanating from the Golden Phoenix'. After the fall of the empire, the space in front of the Gate of Heavenly Peace came to be used for public gatherings and popular demonstrations. A wider area in front of the Gate, where the ministerial enclave was situated, was later converted into the Square of Heavenly Peace, and became the political centre of the whole country.

But Peking as an important centre goes back far beyond the earliest of the successive rounds of planned city-building which have left the wonderful historical monuments described above. In the western part of the Outer City is the site of the ancient city of Ji, which had been the capital of an independent principality during the Time of the Warring States. During the Han period, Ji is mentioned by Sima Qian in his *Historical Memoirs* as 'a rich city with great plenty of fish, salt and chestnuts', and as 'the central market for products coming from the barbarian regions of the north and from Korea'. In the tenth century AD, the Kitan, who founded the Liao dynasty, enlarged the city and made it their second capital under the name of Nanjing (which means 'Southern Capital'). The Jürchen of the Jin dynasty built a still larger city on the same site, and called it Zhong du. This city was rectangular in shape and surrounded by a wall in accordance with Chinese tradition; it was destroyed by the Mongols when they conquered northern China. Next came Qubilay's capital, which Marco Polo describes under the name of 'Cambaluc', though its real name was Da du, which means 'Great Capital'. This was built on a site corresponding roughly to the later Inner City, though extending slightly further towards the north.

Old Peking as we see it today is essentially the city of the Ming. Zhu Yuanzhang, who liberated China from the Mongols and became the first Ming Emperor, set up his capital in the southern city Nanking. Da du (renamed Bei ping or Northern Peace), became the fief of one of his sons, who later succeeded to the throne. It was the new emperor, Yong le, who in AD 1403 transferred the capital back to northern China, where it remained for the rest of the Ming and Qing periods. Bei ping accordingly became Bei jing (Northern Capital), of which the Westernised form 'Peking' is a corruption.

The ground-plan of the Ming city of Peking was completed in AD 1524, when the 'Chinese City' was enclosed by a wall. From that time on, it remained practically unchanged until the end of the empire. The Temple of Heaven, the great rooms of the imperial palace, and certain other impressive buildings to be mentioned below, were faithfully reconstructed by the Qing. The architecture we see today is essentially the architecture of the Ming capital city. 'Peking', writes the sinologist Alexander Soper, 'is thus an epitome of the late architectural style, at least in its official version, which is a curious mixture of tradition and decadence.' The use of the word 'decadence' in this context has been criticised, but it can be defended if it is taken in the sense of imperfect adherence to tradition. This may arise from an attempt to accommodate elements from an earlier situation – as the Ming city of Peking accommodates elements from the city of Qubilay. The grid formed by the streets of the Ming Inner City lacks the logical and geometrical symmetry to be found in the town-plan of Changan. The imperial palace is neither at one end of the city (as at Changan) nor at its exact centre (which would be in keeping with the emperor's symbolical role as the hub of the universe). The geometrical centre of the Inner City of Peking is occupied by Coal Hill, an artificial mound constructed in an earlier period, which provides the Forbidden City with magical protection against evil influences coming from the north (which is regarded as the unlucky quarter by the Chinese). A more rewarding way of looking at Peking is to observe the way in which the city and its monuments reflect national tradition, following a system of construction and of the organisation of open spaces which is in harmony with Chinese culture. (It is especially difficult in China to draw a line between architecture and town-planning.)

A point of great importance here – a principle, in fact, and a constant factor – is the idea of the city as an *enclosure*. In Chinese, the same word means 'city' and 'wall'; the city is conceived as a walled city, a delimited space, an artificial world of civilisation opposed to the world of nature. The need for defence is obviously an important factor, but it is not the only one. For the Chinese, the essence of building is the delimitation, enclosure and walling off of appropriate functional spaces and setting them in relationship to each other. (In the West, on the other hand, building is thought of as primarily a process of covering, of providing a roof.) The quadrilateral of the Forbidden City is enclosed by strong walls, and is divided into smaller spaces, of varying size, importance and function.

In the second place, the plan is ideological – not to say doubly ideological. Geomantic considerations require that the street-plan should be rectangular and orientated to the four cardinal points, and that buildings should face towards the south (the city as a whole is conceived as facing towards the south in this sense). Politico-social considerations lead to the building up of a hierarchy with the emperor at its apex. The organisation of space expresses both the imperial function of guaranteeing stability and the elaborate ceremonials with which imperial orders are promulgated.

In the third place – and this is something complementary to the geomantic factor – we may note the tendency to arrange things around an axis. The north–south axis is the one most favoured. The central road which forms the main axis of Peking starts in the south near the Temple of Heaven and the Temple of Agriculture. (These two temples originally stood outside the city, but were included within its boundaries when the wall of the Chinese City was built.) From the temples it runs north through the gate of the Tartar City, through the Imperial City and into the Forbidden City, ending at a group of three ceremonial buildings called the Hall of Supreme Harmony, the Hall of Perfect Harmony and the Hall of the Preservation of Harmony. Behind these halls stand the three private palaces, and behind them the magical defence-work of Coal Hill. The axis principle found here is, however, subtly different from the axis principle of the baroque, which is concerned with visual effect. Building to an axis in China seems to be more of an intellectual exercise (expressing the principle of hierarchy). It is at the same time concerned with the practical problems of road traffic. It is *not* concerned with optical effects. On the visual plane, the line of the axis is broken by the successive city walls, by passing through a series of spaces that have been developed in very different styles; it is even interrupted by some of the most important buildings. The Gate of Supreme Harmony hides the three great ceremonial halls. In any case, the first of these halls is the largest, and blocks the view of the other two. The principle of the axis, in fact, is at odds with the principle of enclosing walls. In the particular case of Peking, it should be noted that the principal axis is not exactly in the middle of the city; the western side of the Imperial City, with its succession of lakes and gardens, is wider than the eastern side.

Finally we come to materials and colours. The walls that block the view and divide the spaces of the city into separate units are of masonry; they

Peking, Gu gong. The Zaojing, a highly decorated wooden ceiling in the Jiaotai dian. The building originally dates from AD 1561, but was extensively reconstructed in the Qing period. The ceiling shown here dates from AD 1655. It has been given the shape of a dome for purely decorative purposes, in keeping with a tradition described in the *Yingzao fa shi*, an architectural textbook written by Li Mingzhong in the Northern Song period. The most elaborate ceilings of all, with beams arranged in a spiral, date from the Ming period.

THE ENVOY OF THE TSAR AT DINNER WITH THE CHINESE EMPEROR

On the 12th of November the Viceroy sent some Mandarins to give me notice to appear with their Czarish Majesties' Credentials next Morning in the Castle; upon which I accordingly prepared myself. At eight in the Morning three principal Mandarins came to advise me that it was then a proper time to wait on the Emperor: besides their common Habit, they were also dressed in Robes, which were Embroidered some with Dragons, others with Lions, and a third sort with Tigers and Cranes on the Breast and Back worked with Gold Thread: they brought with them 50 Horses for my Retinue. . . .

Coming to the outer Gate of the Castle, there is a Pillar, with some characters engraven on it, where I was told I must alight, according to their Custom; so that I went on foot through five outer Courts to the Castle itself. I found a great number of Mandarins at the Court, all clothed in their richest Embroidered Robes, such as they wear in the Emperor's presence, who waited for me.

After we had mutually exchanged Compliments, the Emperor appeared on his Throne; upon which I delivered his Czarish Majesty's Credentials and after the usual Ceremonies and a short Speech, was conducted back.

On the 16th of the same Month, I was informed that I was invited to Eat before the Emperor: wherefore in the Morning, accompanied with the Mandarins thereto appointed, and the chief Gentlemen of my Retinue, I rode to Court. And in the sixth court, a great many Lords and Mandarins were standing in rows in their best Robes; and shortly after an order came down for us to appear above in the Palace. As soon as I entered, the Emperor mounted his exalted Throne, having near him some Persons who played very finely on the Fife, and a Life-Guard of twelve Men with Gilt Halberds without any sharp point to them, but adorned with Leopards' and Tigers' Tails. As soon as the King was seated, the Music ceased, and the Halberdiers seated themselves cross-legged on each side below the Throne. The Emperor's Table was furnished with cold Meats, Fruits and Sweetmeats, served up in Silver Dishes, and the whole covered with yellow Damask.

From *Travel Over Land from Muscovy to China*, 1706, by Evert Ysbrand Ides, the envoy of Tsar Peter the Great.

include high, strong defensive walls, and smaller walls separating courtyards or groups of buildings. The tops of the walls are generally protected by tiles. Also of masonry are the plinths or platforms on which the main buildings are constructed. The buildings themselves, however, are of wood; and from this point of view Chinese architecture can be regarded as an elaborate system of carpentry, in which functionalism is subordinated to expressive or decorative effects; it is also capable of producing work on a larger scale than might be expected. The front wall of the Hall of Supreme Harmony extends sideways for fifty-two metres (170 feet), which is exactly the width of the façade of St Mark's cathedral in Venice. Also of wood are the complementary structures that articulate, emphasise and lend visual harmony to the barrier walls – structures such as the galleries above the Gate of Heavenly Peace, and the corner pavilions associated with the walls of the Forbidden City. In an earlier chapter, we mentioned the visual importance and the dominating, weighty appearance of the roofs, which are invariably covered with terracotta tiles. Marble is the material employed for the screens and grilles used to mark the boundaries of certain areas (although they frequently offer only a symbolical barrier, which is no great obstacle to the view); and marble was also favoured for the bridges in the imperial palace and for processional stairways. This is a use of materials very different from that of Western architectural tradition. With the exception of marble, all materials were painted in colours different from their natural hue. Pleasure in the natural qualities of materials – the graininess of wood, the porous feel of terracotta, the harshness of stone – may be an important factor in Europe and Japan, but it is quite foreign to the traditions of Chinese architecture. The walls are painted red; bright colours, often including red and gold, are used for the woodwork; and the roof-tiles are enamelled. Artificiality of surface is a characteristic of Chinese architecture.

A contrast – perhaps a compensation – is provided by the Chinese garden. Space forbids us to do more than mention in passing the gardens around the lakes in the western part of the Imperial City, or the gardens of the nineteenth-century Summer Palace, outside the city walls. The Chinese garden is as different as it could be from the classical European garden, which is geometrically planned and architecturally structured. The Chinese garden is based on an artificial attempt to enhance nature, a system for the creation of an ideal landscape, an appreciation and reinforcement of natural beauty that has nothing to do with the imposition of a regular, geometrical pattern.

The Tian tan or Temple of Heaven exhibits a perfect articulation of space in relation to the requirements of ceremony and a complex web of symbolical motifs, together with an exquisite formal elegance. It consists of a complex of buildings constructed in the fifteenth and sixteenth centuries under the Ming dynasty. It was renovated, mainly by the Emperor Qianlong, in the eighteenth century. It is situated in a park which is nearly 7 kilometres (4½ miles) in circumference, immediately to the east of the southern entrance to the Chinese City. (The corresponding site to the west of the same entrance was formerly occupied by the Temple of Agriculture, which has now vanished; here the emperor used to perform the annual rite of ploughing the first furrow of the season.) The outer enclosure of the Temple of Heaven was square in shape, although the two northern corners were rounded; inside was a second wall with a similar ground-plan; the inner enclosure was divided in two by a transverse wall.

Passing through the west gate (which is the one through which the emperor used to make his ceremonial entrance), we enter the inner enclosure and come to the Palace of Abstinence or Zhai gong (where the emperor used to pause awhile to prepare himself for the ceremonies to follow). We then pass on to the central north–south axis along which the three principal buildings are sited. The southernmost of these buildings is the circular Altar or Huanqiu tan, built in 1530 and rebuilt in 1749. It is surrounded by two walls. The outer enclosure is square (symbolising the earth), and its wall is of red brick, crowned with blue tiles. In each of its four sides, corresponding to the four cardinal points, is a triple gate of marble. The inner enclosure is circular (symbolising the sky), and contains the actual altar, which consists of three superimposed circular terraces

Above: Peking. The Huangqiong yu, or Imperial Vault of Heaven (AD 1899). This temple forms part of the Altar of Heaven, a complex of buildings situated in the southern part of the Outer City of Peking. (The Outer City is an extension built to the south of the main fortified area in the Ming Period.) The Huangqiong yu was built to house a wooden tablet inscribed with a special prayer to the powers of Heaven; it is a small, circular, one-storeyed building. It stands on a circular base, surrounded by a balustrade of white marble.

Left: Peking, Gu gong. The photograph opposite shows the Jiaolou (seventeenth century). This is one of the four towers which mark the angles of the wall around the Forbidden City. The elaborate, three-tier roof, crowned by a cruciform structure, revives a feature of the architectural style of the Song period, which appears in certain paintings by the artist Li Si.

with decorative facings and balustrades; it has four marble staircases corresponding to the four points of the compass. The numbers and proportions of the architectural elements, the balustrades and the pavements are governed by the symbolical number nine and its multiples. The emperor used to visit this open-air altar at the winter solstice, to enter into communication with the powers of Heaven and submit a report to them on the events of the past year, in a document which he signed in a tent set up to the south of the square enclosure.

To the north of the altar is a circular wooden building with a conical, blue-tiled roof, known as the Huangqiong yu or Imperial Heavenly Vault. The 'Tables of Heaven' were normally kept in this building, and were taken across to the altar only on ceremonial occasions. The transverse wall mentioned earlier separates the two buildings just described from the Hall of Prayer for Good Harvest, or Qinian dian. This building was originally constructed in AD 1420, under the name of Hall of the Great Sacrifice, and was rebuilt in 1751. A noble and famous edifice, its design combines and transcends those of the other two buildings. A triple terrace of marble, with balustrades and staircases, supports a circular wooden structure, with three superimposed roofs, the top one being conical in shape and covered with blue tiles. The intricate wooden framework of the whole building is based on twenty-eight columns. Four of these are centrally situated and represent the four seasons; they are nearly 20 metres (65 feet) in height. The other twenty-four columns surround them in two circles of twelve columns each, symbolising the twelve months of the year and the

Peking, Tian tan. The illustration shows the Qinian dian, or Pavilion of the Good Harvest (AD 1896–1899). This is the principal building of the Altar of Heaven complex. It was here that the Ming and Qing Emperors came every spring to celebrate the rites necessary to ensure a good grain harvest. Circular in plan, with a three-tier roof, the original pavilion was constructed in AD 1540; some alterations were made in AD 1752. After being destroyed by fire, it was rebuilt, as closely as possible to the original design, in AD 1889. Only the colour of the roofs was changed; originally the top roof was blue, the middle roof yellow and the bottom roof green; but now they are all uniformly blue.

The Altar of Heaven complex comprises two pavilions – the Qinian dian and the Huangqiong yu – and the Altar itself, which consists of three concentric terraces with marble balustrades situated in the middle of a circular enclosure, which is enclosed in its turn by a walled square. In Chinese tradition, the circle represents the sky and the square represents the earth.

Peking, Tian tan. The illustration shows the Zaojing, the painted wooden ceiling of the Qinian dian (AD 1896–1899). In the buildings of the Altar of Heaven complex, the dimensions and quantities of the architectural elements have symbolical meanings. The circle, as has already been mentioned, represents the sky. The four columns that support the uppermost roof represent the four seasons, the twelve columns of the middle tier symbolise the months, and the twelve columns of the lowest tier the hours. These architectural symbols go back to the Han period, and find frequent expression in the structure of Chinese altars and temples.

twelve divisions (according to ancient Chinese practice) of the diurnal cycle. The Emperor visited the Qinian dian at the first full moon of the year, to render homage to Heaven and to offer sacrifice. To the east of the Hall of Prayer is a range of annexes – slaughterhouses, storehouses, cisterns and kitchens – for the preparation of offerings. An exquisite attention to detail is apparent everywhere – in the carving of the marble, the coloration of the woodwork, the corbelling of the roofs, and the arrangement of the tiles – but Chinese architecture finds its main expression in the interrelations of forms and the delimitation of spaces. It provides both a physical and a symbolical background for ritual ceremonies; it furnishes an analogy for the cosmic order at its point of contact with the order of humanity.

The architecture of the imperial palaces lacks the peaceful elegance and the wide, limpid proportional relationships of the Temple of Heaven. The style is solemn and magnificent, not to say breathtakingly sumptuous in certain interiors, which exemplify the 'treasures of the East' that used to excite the early connoisseurs of the exotic so much. There is, perhaps, something rather forbidding about the total effect.

The imperial palace of Peking is known as Zi jin cheng or 'Purple Forbidden City'. Purple is the colour associated with the Pole Star, and the word serves here to identify the royal residence with the centre of the universe. The enclosure in which it stands measures 960 by 750 metres (1,050 by 820 yards), and is surrounded by a ditch and by walls 10 metres (33 feet) in height. Each side of the rectangle has its own gate; and the Wu men or South Gate leads into a first courtyard which is traversed by the River of Gold Waters with its five marble bridges of delicately arched design, symbolising the five imperial virtues. On the far side of this courtyard is a wall containing the Gate of Supreme Harmony. The gateway of red masonry is crossed by wooden galleries and crowned by a tiled roof in the usual manner. The second courtyard is the ceremonial centre of the palace, and of the empire. It is surrounded by walls with galleries; this is where the storerooms were situated, which an eighteenth-century visitor from the West describes as full of ceramic and metal vases, hides and skins, jackets and coats made from the fur of fox, ermine and sable, precious stones, rare varieties of marble, pearls from Tartary, precious cabinets and caskets, bows, arrows, and other weapons captured from the enemy or offered by vassals. Two side gates lead into subsidiary axes parallel to the central one, each with its own series of pavilions and courtyards. (As the reader will have noticed, threefold repetition is a common pattern in Chinese cities.) In the middle of the courtyard is a balustraded triple terrace of marble, 7 metres or 23 feet in height, on which stands a row of pavilions, the middle one being smaller than the other two, so that the ground-plan of the terrace is shaped like a capital letter 'I'. Access to the terrace is provided by two parallel staircases separated by an inclined ramp carved with dragons. The central ramp was reserved for the use of the imperial palanquin. The three pavilions are of wood, with double roofs of enamelled tiles. Some of the roof-ridges are decorated with acroteria, while others have symbolical animals standing guard at the end of the roof-tree. The spacing of the columns that make up the frontal porticos of the pavilions is not uniform, but exhibits a rhythmical modulation with wider spacing at the centre and narrower intervals at the ends. The pavilions have highly significant names – the Hall of Supreme Harmony (Taihe dian), the Hall of Perfect Harmony (Zhonghe dian), and the Hall of the Preservation of Harmony (Baohe dian). These three superb throne-rooms were used for different purposes. The first was the scene of the most important ceremonies, such as the celebration for the winter solstice, the new year, the Emperor's birthday, the nomination of generals to military commands, and the announcement of the names of those who had earned promotion in the imperial examinations. The Hall of Perfect Harmony was used by the Emperor to prepare himself ritually to enter the Hall of Supreme Harmony, and for certain special ceremonies such as the ritual examination of the seed-corn. (A practical concern for agriculture is a constant factor.) The Hall of the Preservation of Harmony was used as a banqueting-room for ambassadors and vassals. On the far side of the court containing the three Halls, the Gate of Heavenly Purity leads through to a smaller walled courtyard. Here again there is a marble terrace on which stands a row of three pavilions. These buildings were used for different purposes at different times. The Palace of Heavenly Purity was originally the imperial bedchamber; it later became an audience hall. The Hall of Union was originally the throne-room of the empress. The Palace of Earthly Tranquillity was the residence of the empress during the Ming period. From this courtyard we pass on to the imperial garden, with its ancient trees, its bronze incense-burners, and its natural rocks placed on artificial pedestals. Finally we come to the Gate of Divine Pride, beyond which rises the mass of Coal Hill.

In the time of the Emperor Qianlong and his successors, the imperial seals were kept in the Hall of Union. The seals were engraved in splendid characters with the words *'wu wei'*. This is the Taoist rule of 'no action', or rather, according to the interpretation of Joseph Needham, abstention from any action contrary to nature. A political motto at loggerheads with history!

Peking, Beihai Park. The Forbidden City is surrounded by large open spaces, well planted with trees. To the west are the three artificial lakes called Nanhai, Zhunghai and Beihai, around which gardens have been developed in accordance with the traditional Chinese principle that the natural scene should be completed and fulfilled by the addition of any elements that may be lacking, so as to create a microcosm of natural perfection. In the background stands the White Pagoda or Bai Ta, which was built in 1651.

Overleaf, page 182: Peking, Yihe yuan. The Foxiang gu, or Temple of the Ten Thousand Buddhas (1888). From the height of this imposing four-storeyed pagoda, the visitor looks down on the Kunming lake; in the distance are the Dragon King island, connected with the shore by a bridge with seventeen arches, and the Duobao ta pagoda, covered with tiles of various colours. The Foxiang gu is octagonal in shape and is about 50 metres (165 feet) in height.

Appendices

Chronological Table

5000 BC Beginning of the Neolithic period in China, represented by the Yangshao culture in the western part of the northern plain and by the Longshan culture in Shandong.

Chinese tradition records an Age of the Five Emperors or Age of the Five Sages, during which succession was not hereditary. These leaders must be regarded as culture-heroes. The last of the five was the Sage Yu, the Regulator of the Waters; and he was succeeded by his son, who founded the Xia dynasty.

2205–1766 BC Traditional dates of the Xia dynasty, made up of seventeen reigns.

1523 BC Traditional date of the beginning of the Shang dynasty. Use of bones for divination. Casting in bronze. The realm included Shandong, Shanxi and Hebei; also Shânxi and Henan.

1400–1200 BC The period in which the ideographic script is thought to have made its appearance, in the archaic style known from inscriptions on bones used for divination.

1122 BC Traditional date of the end of the Shang dynasty (which may more probably have taken place in 1100 BC).

1028 BC Wu, Duke of Zhou, conquers the Shang king Zhouxin, assumes the title of king and founds the Zhou dynasty. The kingdom is divided into fiefs which are allocated to the relations of the new king; though one fief, comprising the territory of Song, is ruled by the heirs of the Shang dynasty. (Confucius later claimed descent from the princes of Song.)

841 BC The dethronement of a weak king is followed by the *Gung He* regency. (*'Gung He'* means 'Public Harmony'.) From this date onwards Chinese history is systematically recorded in annals.

771 BC The kingdom of Zhou is invaded by two probably nomadic and certainly barbarous tribes, the Rong and the Di. The Zhou capital city, near Xian, is destroyed. A new capital is founded at Luoyang in Henan. This marks the beginning of the period of the Eastern Zhou, which continues, in name at least, until 221 BC.

722–481 BC The Chun Qiu period, which takes its name from the *Annals of Spring and Autumn*, a chronicle of the state of Lu, wrongly attributed to Confucius.

551–479 BC Traditional dates of the life of Kong fu zi (Confucius).

513 BC Earliest known mention of an object made of cast-iron.

480–390 (approx.) BC Life of Mo Ti.

453–221 BC The Time of the Warring States; some authorities regard this period as starting in 403 BC. The boundaries of the Chinese world were widened to take in the state of Chu in the middle of the Yangzi valley, the state of Wu along the lower course of the Yangzi, and the state of Yue on the south-east coast.

370–334 BC Life of Meng zi (Mencius).

325 BC The rulers of all the larger Chinese states have now assumed the title of *'wang'* or king, which they had usurped from the King of Zhou, whose rule is now confined to his capital city of Luoyang.

THIRD CENTURY BC The *Dao de jing*, the fundamental text of Taoism, was written during this period.

234 BC Death of Han Fei, the thinker whose ideas are basic to the 'School of Law'.

221 BC Zheng, the ruler of Qin, having unified China by defeating and annexing all the other 'Warring States', assumes the title of shi Huang di, or First Emperor. The Qin system of administration, inspired by the teachings of the School of Law, is extended to the whole Chinese world. A Great Wall is built to protect the northern frontier against the incursions of the Xiong nu.

213 BC The Burning of the Books.

210–202 BC Shi Huang di dies on an expedition to the east coast in search of the Islands of the Immortals (210 BC). The Qin dynasty comes to an end in 206 BC, among plots, assassinations, rebellions and civil wars. The only victor to emerge from this struggle is Liu Bang, formerly a village headman, who founds the Han dynasty in 202 BC.

202 BC–AD 9 Empire of the Early Han or Western Han.

154 BC Suppression of the rebellion of the 'Seven Kingdoms' in the eastern provinces. The independence of local potentates was subsequently reduced by the establishment of the principle that when one of them died his estates must be divided up equally between his sons – a useful measure for the centralisation of power.

181–47 BC The Emperor Wu. This is the first great period of Chinese imperial expansion, which followed the lines laid down by the First Emperor Qin. The Kingdom of Nan Yue, comprising the province of

Canton and part of northern Vietnam, was conquered in 111 BC. The conquest of the kingdom of Yue (Fujian) followed in 110 BC, and that of northern Korea in 108 BC. After Zhang Qian's journey into central Asia in 139–126 BC revealed the possibility of trade with the Western world and of useful alliances against the nomadic tribes, a series of great victorious offensives against the Xiong nu in 124–121 BC ensures the establishment and maintenance of the caravan route through Kashgar, opening up communications with India, Persia and the frontiers of the Roman world. Some important economic measures are put into effect on the advice of the merchant Song hungyang. They include the establishment of a monopoly for coining money, state control of iron, and the setting up of provincial granaries to keep the price of corn stable. It is accepted that Confucianism provides the ideological basis for society and for the state.

28 BC Beginning of systematic record of sun-spots.

AD 2 First known census. It shows a population of 57,671,400 persons in 12,366,470 families.

AD 9 The Wang family had long been in a privileged position, since it was the custom of Han emperors to marry Wang women. Wang Mang, the head of the Wang family, now deposed the emperor and took his place.

AD 9–23 Xin dynasty, otherwise known as the usurpation of Wang Mang.

AD 23–25 The Xin dynasty is overthrown by popular uprisings and by rebellions of the Han nobility, who had been reduced to the rank of private citizens. The Han dynasty is restored by Liu Xiu, a member of a collateral branch, who transfers the capital from Changan to Luoyang.

AD 25–220 Empire of the Later Han or Eastern Han.

AD 65 First mention of a Buddhist community in the Chinese world, at Pengcheng in Jiangsu.

AD 73 The general Ban Chao is sent to re-establish Chinese control in central Asia, which had been lost during the usurpation of Wang Mang. In thirty years of campaigning, Ban Chao reaches the shores of the Caspian Sea.

AD 126–144 Tired of the intrigues for power of the families related to the imperial house, the Emperor Han Shun begins to entrust the administration to the eunuchs, who prove to be intelligent but corrupt.

AD 139 Death of the poet, mathematician and astronomer Zhing Heng, who invented the first seismograph.

AD 148 Arrival at Luoyang of the Parthian monk An Shigao, the first translator into Chinese of Indian Buddhist texts.

AD 167–168 Death of the Emperor Han Huan di, and succession of Han Ling di at the age of twelve. The Empress mother becomes regent, and turns to the men of letters to curb the excessive power of the eunuchs. The eunuchs accuse the men of letters of conspiracy; their association is proscribed, and vast purges follow.

AD 184 The misgovernment of the provinces causes the great rebellion of the Yellow Turbans, under the leadership of Zhang Zhue. The armies raised to put the rebellion down prove to be uncontrollable.

AD 189–220 The death of the Emperor Ling di without any immediate heir is followed by fighting over the succession. The eunuchs are massacred. Luoyang is sacked. Civil war leads to the fall of the Han and the division of China into three kingdoms.

AD 220–280 The Three Kingdoms: the kingdom of Wei (AD 220–265), the kingdom of Shu Han (AD 221–263), and the kingdom of Wu (AD 222–280).

AD 263 The kingdom of Wei absorbs Shu Han.

AD 265 Sima Qian dethrones the King of Wei and founds the Jin (Zin) dynasty.

AD 280 The Jin dynasty conquers Wu, completing the reunification of China.

AD 265–316 Dynasty of the Western Jin (Zin) at Luoyang. Civil strife, indiscipline among the barbarian mercenaries, and the sacking of the capital city of Luoyang in AD 311, together with the general state of increasing anarchy and poverty, cause heavy emigration towards the south. The Western Jin dynasty is finally overwhelmed by the rebellion of barbarians with a veneer of Chinese civilisation, but finds a new lease of life at Nanking under the leadership of Sima Rui.

AD 284 An embassy from the Roman empire visits Nanking, the southern capital city.

AD 304–439 The Sixteen Kingdoms of the Five Barbarians (in northern China).

AD 317–589 The southern dynasties at Nanking: the Eastern Jin (Zin) (AD 317–420), the Song (AD 420–479), the Qi (AD 479–502), the Liang (AD 502–557) and the Chen (AD 557–589).

AD 386   Foundation of the empire of the Toba (or Northern Wei).

AD 412   The Chinese Buddhist monk Fa Xian, returning from his journey to India, Sri Lanka and Sumatra, lands in Shandong.

AD 439–535   Northern China unified under the empire of the Northern Wei, otherwise known as the empire of the Toba or Tabgatch, who were one of the three Xianbei tribes. (The years from AD 440–589 are known to Chinese historians as the Nan Bei or 'Period of the Northern and Southern Empires': the north being ruled by the Wei and their successors, who were barbarians with a veneer of Chinese culture, and the south by the succession of dynasties reigning in Nanking.)

AD 534–557   Empire of the Eastern Wei (part of the Northern Wei empire, which had split up).

AD 535–556   Empire of the Western Wei at Changan (another part of the former empire of the Northern Wei).

AD 556–581   Empire of the Northern Zhou, replacing the Western Wei.

AD 557–577   Empire of the Northern Qi, who replace the Eastern Wei, and are then conquered by the Northern Zhou.

AD 581–618   The Sui empire. The general Yang Jian usurps power at Changan in AD 581 from the Zhou; he goes on to conquer southern China, entering Nanking in AD 589. This puts an end to a period of division which began in the third century with the Three Kingdoms.

AD 604–618   Reign of the Emperor Yang di, the second and last of the Sui. For traditional Chinese historians, he is the archetypal example of a bad emperor.

AD 618   Li Yuan (later the Emperor Gao Zu), the general in charge of the defence of the realm against the nomads in Shanxi, rebels against the government at the instigation of his son Li Shi-min (later the Emperor Taizong). Li Yuan takes Changan and founds the Tang dynasty.

AD 618–907   The Tang empire.

AD 626–649   The Emperor Taizong, whose reign represents the first stage of a great expansion in Chinese power. The threat posed by the Turks (who had become the major power of the steppes) is eliminated. The caravan routes of central Asia are opened up (AD 630). The oases of Transoxiana pass under Chinese control. Spheres of influence are set up beyond the Pamir, at Samarkand, Bukhara and Tashkent. An expeditionary force is sent to the kingdom of Magadha in India to influence the succession to the throne in the interests of China (AD 648). Later the rule of the Tang is extended to Manchuria (AD 660) and Korea. At the height of the power of the Tang dynasty, seventh-century China dominates Asia from Korea to Iran, from the valley of the Ili to the centre of Vietnam.

AD 629–644   Journey to India of the Chinese Buddhist monk Xuan Zang.

AD 643   A Byzantine embassy arrives at Changan.

AD 654–705   Wu Zhao (later the Empress Wu) was the concubine of the Emperor Taizong (AD 626–649) and his successor the Emperor Gaozong (AD 649–683). She received the official title of Empress in AD 655, and became the de facto ruler of China after the death of Gaozong in AD 683. In AD 684 she deposed his legitimate heir, and put to death various members of the imperial family and hundreds of nobles. In AD 690 she usurped the imperial title, and ruled as sole monarch till AD 705. This was the first case in Chinese history of rule by a Dowager Empress. Among the instruments of her authority were a civil service selected by examination (a method systematically introduced in AD 669), and the Buddhist clergy with their wide political and economic powers.

AD 661–708   Events in Persia: Peroz, the last of the Sassanid kings of Persia is attacked by the Arabs and asks China for help (AD 661). He is temporarily restored to his throne with Chinese military assistance (AD 662) but is again driven out in AD 674 and takes refuge in Changan. He makes a final attempt to reconquer Persia and returns to Changan to die in AD 708.

AD 712–756   Reign of the Emperor Xuan Zong (Ming Huang). This is considered the high point of the Tang dynasty and of the first civilisation of China.

AD 751   The Arabs defeat a Chinese army near Alma Ata on the River Talas.

AD 755–763   An Lushan, the commander of the army on the northern frontier, rebels and occupies Luoyang and Changan. Other dramatic developments follow: Shi Shimin takes over command of the rebellious army; and the Emperor Su Zong reconquers the capital, not without great difficulty, with the help of Tibetans and Uighurs. These disturbances cause a breakdown of the defensive system on the frontiers of the empire. The difficulty of putting down the revolts puts increased independence in the hands of the Jiedushi, or commanders of military regions. With the help of their troops, these officials begin to usurp the power of the central government over the provinces.

AD 875 (approx.)   Estimated date of a Buddhist sutra found at Dunhuang, which is the first example of a book produced by wood engraving.

AD 868–884   The 'travelling rebellion' of Huang Chao. The army stationed on the frontier between Nanzhao (Yunnan) and Annam (which was then a Chinese province) having mutinied, Huang Chao takes command and ravages southern China. After thirteen years of devastating raids, he captures Changan in AD 880, driving out the imperial court. After this rebellion, the last years of the Tang dynasty pass in a state of anarchy.

AD 907   Zhu Quanzhong founds the Liang dynasty at Kaifeng. This is the beginning of another period of division – the Five Dynasties and the Ten Kingdoms.

AD 907–960   The Five Dynasties and the Ten Kingdoms. There is a sequence of short-lived dynasties at Kaifeng: the Later Liang (AD 907–923); the Later Tang (AD 923–936); the Later Jin (AD 936–946); the Later Han (AD 947–950); and the Later Zhou (AD 951–960). At the same time the rest of the empire is divided into the Ten Kingdoms, which coincide closely with the military regions of the Tang dynasty.

AD 946–1125   A barbarian empire with a veneer of Chinese civilisation is set up by the Liao (Kitan) along the north-west frontier. (The Kitan are Tartars who have expelled the Turks from the north-eastern regions; and their chieftain now assumes the title of Emperor and extends his authority inside the Great Wall. At a later stage, the Kitan make their capital at Peking, which thus becomes the seat of an imperial dynasty for the first time.)

AD 960   Zhao Guangyin, a general in the service of the Zhou dynasty, is proclaimed emperor at Kaifeng, and takes the name of Song Tai Zu. He extends his power to the southern states by peaceful means.

AD 960–1127   Empire of the Northern Song at Kaifeng. This is a period of relative national unity, following the fragmentation dating from the end of the Tang dynasty. Chinese sovereignty does not, however, extend to the Liao empire (Hebi and Shanxi), the Xia empire in north-west Mongolia, Vietnam or Korea.

AD 990 (approx.)   A geomantic text mentions the magnetic compass.

AD 1017–1073   Life of the philosopher Zhou Tunyi.

AD 1038–1227   Empire of the Western Xia (Tanguti) on the north-western frontier.

AD 1041–1048   The first attempts at printing with moveable type.

AD 1067–1085   Innovators versus Conservatives. The Innovator Wang Anshi is entrusted with the government in AD 1067, and new laws are introduced in the fiscal, administrative and military fields. Wang Anshi is removed from power in AD 1076. His opponent, the historian Sima Guang rises to power, and the new laws are abrogated in AD 1085.

AD 1100–1126   Reign of Hui Zong, the last emperor of the Northern Song, a generous patron of the arts and a great painter in his own right. After the invasion of the Jin and the fall of Kaifeng, he ends his life as a prisoner.

AD 1115–1234   Empire of the Jin or Tungusi (another barbarian race who have adopted Chinese culture), along the north-eastern frontier. In AD 1126 the Jin conquer northern China; the Song retreat to the south.

AD 1116   A Chinese text describes the liquid-mounted magnetic compass and gives a value for magnetic declination.

AD 1126   As the Jin invaders press on, a new Song Emperor from a collateral branch of the family leads the dynasty in its retreat to the south. The Jin reach Hangzhou.

AD 1127–1279   Empire of the Southern Song at Hangzhou.

AD 1129–1200   Life of Zhu Xi, originator of the philosophy known as 'Neo-Confucianism'.

AD 1131   The commander of the Song army, General Yofei, forces the Jin back to the other side of the Yangzi. While he prepares to conquer northern China, however, he falls victim to a conspiracy organised by the Prime Minister Cai Jing. The frontier is established along the northern watershed of the Yangzi valley.

AD 1210   Jinghiz Khan begins his attack on China, invading the Jin empire in the northern part of the country. Capture of Peking.

AD 1224   Jinghiz Khan attacks the empire of the Xia – a barbarian dynasty who have adopted Chinese culture. Terrible destruction by the Mongols causes heavy emigration towards the south.

AD 1235   The Mongols attack the Song empire in southern China.

AD 1263   Qubilay (Kublai Khan) succeeds to the Mongol throne, and transfers his capital from Karakoram to Peking, which is rebuilt.

AD 1271–1368   The Yuan dynasty. Having absorbed the empire of the Xia in AD 1227 and the empire of the Jin in AD 1234, the Mongols adopt the dynastic name of Yuan in AD 1271. In the years from AD 1276–1279, they occupy the empire of the Southern Song, which completes their control of the whole of China.

AD 1275–1291   Marco Polo in the service of Qubilay, as one of the many foreigners in the Mongol adminstration.

AD 1276   Forty-one years after the first Mongol assault, the Southern Song lose their capital city of Hangzhou.

AD 1279   The last Southern Song Emperor dies when his fleet is destroyed off the south China coast.

AD 1281   Unsuccessful attempt by the Mongols to invade Japan. The Chinese-Korean invasion fleet is destroyed by a storm – the Divine Wind or kamikaze.

AD 1300 (approx.)   Death of Wang Shifu, a Peking dramatist, the author of Xixiangji. The first flowering of the Chinese theatre takes place during the Yuan period.

AD 1348–1368   Togan Timour, the last of the Yuan emperors, progressively loses control of the empire, as twenty years of anti-Mongol rebellion take their toll.

AD 1356   Zhu Yuanzhang (later Emperor Hong Wu, the founder of the Ming dynasty) occupies Nanking and makes it his capital.

AD 1368–1644   Ming empire.

AD 1369   The Ming armies take Karakoram, the ancient capital of Jinghiz Khan.

FIFTEENTH CENTURY AD   The Ming repair, rebuild and extend the Great Wall.

AD 1402–1424   Reign of the Emperor Yong Le. Compilation of the first Chinese encyclopaedia.

AD 1405–1433   The Emperor Yong Le entrusts Zheng He, a Moslem from Yunnan, with the command of a series of naval expeditions. Fleets of large, specially-built ships sweep the seas of south-east Asia and the Indian Ocean, reaching the Red Sea and the coasts of east Africa. This aggressive naval policy is however abandoned when a minor comes to the throne and the power of the eunuchs is increased.

AD 1421   The decision is taken to transfer the capital from Nanking to Peking.

AD 1505–1520   Reign of the Emperor Zheng De. Increase in the power of the eunuchs, which is always associated with bribery and corruption, especially in the appointment of administrative officers for the provinces.

AD 1514   First appearance of Portuguese navigators on the coasts of Guangdong.

AD 1522   Chinese ports closed to the Portuguese as the result of their acts of violence and their rivalry with Arab merchants. At about the same time, the Ming begin to make use of cannon previously bought from the Portuguese.

SIXTEENTH CENTURY AD   *Jin Ping Mei*, an early Chinese novel, is probably the work of a civil servant living in the second half of the century. Some critics regard the work as a satire. The Chinese novel comes into existence and develops rapidly during the Ming period.

AD 1552   St Francis Xavier, the first Christian missionary to set out for China, dies on an island in the estuary of the Pearl River, without having set foot on the Chinese mainland.

AD 1575   Arrival of the first Christian missionaries at Canton.

AD 1592–1598   War against Japan in defence of the Chinese vassal-state of Korea, which had been invaded by Hideyoshi.

AD 1598   Father Matteo Ricci obtains permission to go to Peking, where he stays until his death in AD 1610.

AD 1610   Nurhachu, the leader of the Manchu, declares his independence of China and proclaims himself emperor, founding the Qing dynasty.

AD 1627   Beginning of a period of major military rebellions and peasant uprisings which mark the decline and fall of the Ming dynasty.

AD 1636   The missionary Adam Schall in charge of the cannon foundry at Peking.

AD 1644   The rebel Li Zicheng takes Peking. The last Ming Emperor hangs himself in the gardens of the imperial palace. Wu Sangui, the commander of the frontier army, refuses to recognise the usurper Li Zicheng, and offers the throne to the Manchu. In the following years, Wu Sangui leads a series of campaigns against the supporters of the Ming in the south, and so consolidates the Manchu dynasty (this is known as the 'Ming-Qing' period).

AD 1644–1911   The empire of the Qing (Manchu). The ruling Manchu minority adopts the language and culture of China, but follows a policy of rigorous racial separation.

AD 1661–1722   The long reign of the Emperor Kangxi. Using cannon produced with the help of the Jesuit missionaries, Kangxi puts down the rebellion led by Wu Sangui, and repels a Russian attempt to invade northern Manchuria. He also imposes Chinese rule on Mongolia and central Asia (Xinjiang), and conquers Tibet. Chinese sovereignty is extended to Korea, Annam, Burma and Thailand.

AD 1673   Rebellion of Wu Sangui and secession of the southern provinces. Control over the south is not restored until the death of Wu Sangui in AD 1678.

AD 1685–1686   The armies of the Qing besiege the Russian fortress of Albazin.

AD 1689   Treaty of Nerchinsk between the Russian and Chinese empires.

AD 1697   The Qing occupy Outer Mongolia.

AD 1705–1706   First attempt of the Qing empire to occupy Lhasa in Tibet.

AD 1723–1735   Reign of the Emperor Yongzheng.

AD 1736–1796   Reign of the Emperor Qianlong.

AD 1751   The Qing empire finally establishes control in Tibet.

AD 1758–1759   Rebellion of the peoples of the Tarim basin and reconquest of the area by the Chinese.

AD 1762   A census is taken and records a population of 200 million inhabitants.

AD 1763   Death of the author Cao Xueqin, who leaves his novel *The Dream of the Red Chamber* uncompleted.

AD 1774   Rebellion of the White Lotus sect. The last years of the Emperor Qianlong's reign are marked by a number of similar rebellions, which are symptomatic of the bad economic and social conditions in the empire. The increase in population has caused a rise in the price of land and the formation of a class of landless peasants.

AD 1791–1792   The last expansionist venture of the Qing empire is a military expedition against Nepal, which comes near to exhausting the resources of the state.

AD 1793   British embassy to Peking, led by Lord Macartney.

AD 1796   Abdication of Qianlong, who has been Emperor for sixty years, and does not want his reign to be longer than that of his grandfather, the great Kangxi. He is succeeded by his son Jia Qing.

AD 1799   After the death of Qianlong, his minister He Shen is arrested by the new emperor, Jia Qing, who confiscates the vast fortune accumu-lated by the minister during his long period of power. This proves to be a sum equivalent to £80 million at nineteenth-century values. This scandal unmasks the corruption of the administraon.

AD 1830   A census is held and records a population of 394,780,000 inhabitants.

AD 1840   The 'Opium War' between Britain and China.

AD 1842   The Treaty of Nanking marks the end of the Opium War. Hong Kong is ceded to Britain, and the following Chinese ports are opened up to foreign trade: Canton, Shanghai, Amoy, Fuzhou and Ningpo. Beginning of the system of 'Concessions' with extraterritorial jurisdiction, which lasts a century.

AD 1850   Beginning of the Taiping rebellion. Its leader claims to be the adoptive younger brother of Jesus Christ, and to be directly inspired by God.

AD 1853   The Taiping gain control of Guangxi and march north to take Nanking, which they make their 'Heavenly Capital'.

AD 1858   The Treaty of Aigun gives Russia all the territory to the east of the Ussuri.

AD 1858–1860   France and Britain make war on China.

AD 1860   French and British troops sack Peking and destroy the Summer Palace.

AD 1861   Death of the Emperor Xianfeng at a hunting-lodge in Mongolia, where he had taken refuge at the time of the Franco-British attack on Peking. Ci Xi, a former concubine of the Emperor who had been raised to the rank of Imperial Consort, managed to seize power in the capital, and put the members of the Council of Regency to death. She remained in power as Dowager Empress until her death in 1908.

AD 1864   The imperial troops besiege and capture Nanking, and the leaders of the Taiping commit suicide. This is the end of the Taiping War.

AD 1868   The first Chinese steamships.

AD 1872   Chinese students are sent to the countries of the Western world for the first time.

AD 1879   Yan Fu, a naval officer, returns to China after a period of study in Britain, and begins to translate Western books about politics and sociology into Chinese.

AD 1883–1885   Franco-Chinese war, as a result of which China loses her sovereignty over Indo-China.

AD 1894–1895   War between China and Japan, ending in the Treaty of Shimonoseki, by which the victorious Japanese take Taiwan and the Pescadores Islands.

AD 1898   The Hundred Days Reform. A series of decrees aimed at the modernisation of the country, drafted by reformers supported by the Emperor Guang Xu, lead to a *coup d'état* by the Dowager Empress Ci Xi, who secures the support of Yuan Shikai, the commander of the new modernised army. The reformer Tan Sitong is executed.

1900–1901   The Boxer Rebellion. The embassies at Peking are besieged, and an international military expedition is sent against the Chinese capital.

1911   The revolution. The garrison of Hankou mutinies, and disaffection spreads. The army proclaims a republic. The Regent turns for help to Yuan Shikai, who immediately claims absolute military and civil powers.

1912   Sun Yatsen is proclaimed President of the Chinese Republic on January 1st. Abdication of the Qing. Sun Yatsen renounces the presidency, which passes to Yuan Shikai.

1913   Parliamentary elections. The Revolutionary Republican Party or Guomindang (Kuomintang) easily defeats the followers of Yuan Shikai, who is nevertheless in a strong position because of his control of the army, and succeeds in getting himself elected President with full powers by the same parliament, which is dissolved soon afterwards.

1914–1916   Yuan Shikai tries to found a new dynasty, but the revolt of the army in the south and the pressures exerted by his own generals in the north induce him to resign the presidency. He dies in June 1916.

1916–1927   'The Time of the War-Lords'. Power passes into the hands of the military governors of provinces.

1919   'The Movement of the Fourth of May'. This movement begins with a demonstration of protest at Peking University against the clauses of the Treaty of Versailles which grant the former German Concessions to Japan, ignoring the claims of China.

1921   Foundation of the Chinese Communist Party at Shanghai.

1925   Death of Sun Yatsen in March. 'The Movement of the Thirtieth of May'. The measures taken by the police of the International Concession of Shanghai to repress a demonstration by students and workers cause a widespread movement of hostility towards foreigners and boycott of foreign goods.

1926   The Nationalist government of Canton begins its 'Northward March' to crush the war-lords. The commander of the Nationalist forces is Jiang Jieshi (Chiang Kaishek). Wuhan falls to the Nationalists, who move their government there.

1927   Communist uprising at Shanghai, led by Zhou Enlai. The Nationalist army takes Nanking. Jiang Jieshi lands at Shanghai, destroys the Communist administration and massacres its supporters. He then proclaims the constitution of a new Nationalist government with its capital at Nanking, breaking with the Nationalist government at Wuhan. On August 8th a brigade of the Nationalist army at Nanchang commanded by Zhu Di mutinies and proclaims itself the 'Red Army'.

1928   Yan Xishan, war-lord of Shanxi, joins the Nationalists and takes Peking. The Red Army attacks some southern cities but is repulsed; it then regroups at Jingangshan. Meeting at Jingangshan of Zhu Di and Mao Zedong, and setting up of the first 'Red Base'.

1931 The 'Red Base' on the frontier between Jiangxi and Hunan is proclaimed to be the 'Chinese Soviet Republic' (Ruijin, November). The Japanese have had a presence in Manchuria for some time, based on rights acquired from the Russians after the Russo-Japanese War of 1904–1905; they now occupy the whole region and proclaim it to be an independent state with the name of Manchukuo. The head of the new state is Buyi, the deposed Chinese emperor.

1933 In the name of Manchukuo, the Japanese occupy the Chinese province of Jehol (the western part of Inner Mongolia).

1934 Buyi becomes Emperor of Manchukuo (Manchuria) which is now a satellite state of Japan.

1934–1935 The Long March. Under the pressure of the 'campaigns of extermination' launched by Jiang Jieshi 100,000 Communist soldiers leave Jiangxi in October 1934, and set out on a journey of about 10,000 kilometres (6,250 miles), under the leadership of Mao Zedong and Zhu Di. They finally arrive, with their numbers reduced to 30,000 men, at Yenan in Shânxi, Mao Zedong emerges as head of the Communist party.

1936 The 'Xian Incident'. Jiang Jieshi goes to Xian to direct the 'campaign of extermination' against the Communists, and is isolated in the spa of Tangshan by his colleague General Zhang Xueliang, and forced to accept an agreement with the Communists for the defence of the country from the Japanese. (The agreement is negotiated with Zhou Enlai.)

1937 The 'Marco Polo Bridge Incident' on July 7th marks the beginning of a general offensive by the Japanese, which leads to the occupation of Peking, Tianjin, Shanghai, and Nanking. The war with Japan, and the occupation of more and more extensive areas of China by the Japanese, continue until the surrender of Japan at the end of the Second World War.

1938 To slow up the advance of the Japanese, the Chinese open breaches in the banks of the Yellow River, which deviates from its normal course and finds its way to the sea to the south of the Shandong peninsula. The Japanese occupy Hankou and Canton, while the government of Jiang Jieshi retires to Chongqing.

1940 Wang Qingwei sets up a Japanese-controlled Chinese government at Nanking.

1942 The Western Powers negotiate with the Chinese government the abrogation of all the rights, privileges and concessions granted to them following the Opium War.

1945 Agreement concluded at Chongqing on October 10th between the Guomindang government of Jiang Jieshi and the Chinese Communist Party.

1946 Beginning of the civil war between the forces of the Guomindang and those of the Communists. The Guomindang achieve some initial successes.

1948 At the end of the year, the Guomindang troops are defeated by the Army of Popular Liberation at the decisive battle of Huai Hai in the valley of the Huai river.

1949 The Chinese People's Republic is proclaimed at Peking on October 1st. The Nationalist government takes refuge in Taiwan.

1950 Mao Zedong (who has never been abroad before) visits Moscow. The Soviet Union signs a treaty with China. Intervention of China in the Korean War.

1951 The Chinese army occupies Tibet, thus re-establishing the control over this country lost by China in 1911.

1953 Beginning of the first Five Year Plan for the industrialisation of China.

1955–1956 Introduction of the system of co-operative farms.

1957 The policy of 'Let a Hundred Flowers Blossom'.

1958 Beginning of the 'Great Leap Forward'. Extension to the entire country of the system of popular communes.

1960 The Soviet Union withdraws its technicians from China and ends economic aid.

1962 War between China and India on the Himalayan frontier.

1966 Beginning of the 'Great Proletarian Cultural Revolution'. One million Red Guards assemble in Peking. Among the public figures disgraced are Liu Shaoqi, Deng Xiaoping and Peng Jen.

1968 The Army takes control of the administration. Thousands of Red Guards are sent to distant provinces.

1969 The Ninth Congress of the Chinese Communist Party declares that the Cultural Revolution has reached its triumphant conclusion and acclaims Lin Biao as 'Mao's closest comrade in arms'. Incidents between Chinese and Soviet troops on the Ussuri river.

1970 In September, Lin Biao disappears from political life. A few months later it is announced that he has died in an aeroplane accident in Mongolia, while on the run after an unsuccessful plot to assassinate Mao Zedong.

1971 In October, the Chinese People's Republic enters the United Nations, and takes over the Security Council seat previously held by the Nationalist government in Taiwan.

1972 Visit to China by Richard Nixon, President of the United States.

1976 Death of Zhou Enlai. Death of Mao Zedong in September. Hua Guofeng, already Prime Minister, is also elected Chairman of the Chinese Communist Party in October. Arrest of Mao's widow, Jiang Qing and her supporters. Campaign against the 'Gang of Four'.

1977 Return to public life of Deng Xiaoping, who becomes a Deputy Prime Minister in July.

1979 In the middle of February, Chinese troops invade the northern provinces of Vietnam. They withdraw a few weeks later.

1980 Posthumous rehabilitation of Liu Shaoqi. Hua Guofeng resigns as Prime Minister, but remains Chairman of the Chinese Communist Party. He is succeeded as Prime Minister by Zhao Zyiang. Seven Deputy Prime Ministers lose office, including Deng Xiaoping.

1981 The trial of the Gang of Four ends with the condemnation to death of Jiang Qing and Zhang Chunquao, and a sentence to penal servitude for Wang Hongwen. These sentences are however suspended for two years. In June, Hu Yaobang is elected Chairman of the Chinese Communist Party; Hua Gofeng is demoted to Vice-Chairman.

The Pin Yin and Wade-Giles Transcription Systems

A Table of Equivalents

For the transcription of Chinese names we have used the Chinese system known as 'pin yin', which has now been generally adopted in China itself and in all the countries of the Western world. The problem remains a difficult one, however, and we have thought it best to provide this comparative table of the pin yin and the older Wade-Giles system. The basis of the Wade-Giles system is to give English values to consonants and groups of consonants and Italian values to vowels.

PIN YIN	WADE-GILES	PIN YIN	WADE-GILES	PIN YIN	WADE-GILES
a	a	dang	tang	heng	hêng
ai	ai	dao	tao	hong	hung
an	an	de	tê	hou	hou
ang	ang	deng	têng	hu	hu
ao	ao	di	ti	hua	hua
ba	pa	dian	tien	huai	huai
bai	pai	diao	tiao	huan	huan
ban	pan	die	tieh	huang	huang
bang	pang	ding	ting	hui	hui
bao	pao	diu	tiu	hun	hun
bei	pei	dong	tung	huo	huo
ben	pên	dou	tou	ji	chi
beng	pêng	du	tu	jia	chia
bi	pi	duan	tuan	jian	chien
bian	pien	dui	tui	jiang	chiang
biao	piao	dun	tun	jiao	chiao
bie	pieh	duo	to	jie	chieh
bin	pin	e	ê	jin	chin
bing	ping	ê	eh	jing	ching
bo	po	ei	ei	jiong	chiung
bu	pu	en	ên	jiu	chiu
ca	ts'a	eng	êng	ju	chü
cai	ts'ai	er	êrh	juan	chüan
can	ts'an	fa	fa	jue	chüeh, chüo
cang	ts'ang	fan	fan	jun	chün
cao	ts'ao	fang	fang	ka	k'a
ce	ts'ê	fei	fei	kai	k'ai
cen	ts'ên	fen	fên	kan	k'an
ceng	ts'êng	feng	fêng	kang	k'ang
cha	ch'a	fo	fo	kao	k'ao
chai	ch'ai	fou	fou	ke	k'ê, k'o
chan	ch'an	fu	fu	ken	k'ên
chang	ch'ang	ga	ka	keng	k'êng
chao	ch'ao	gai	kai	kong	k'ung
che	ch'ê	gan	kan	kou	k'ou
chen	ch'ên	gang	kang	ku	k'u
cheng	ch'êng	gao	kao	kua	k'ua
chi	ch'ih	ge	kê, ko	kuai	k'uai
chong	ch'ung	gei	kei	kuan	k'uan
chou	ch'ou	gen	kên	kuang	k'uang
chu	ch'u	geng	kêng	kui	k'ui
chua	ch'ua	gong	kung	kun	k'un
chuai	ch'uai	gou	kou	kuo	k'uo
chuan	ch'uan	gu	ku	la	la
chuang	ch'uang	gua	kua	lai	lai
chui	ch'ui	guai	kuai	lan	lan
chun	ch'un	guan	kuan	lang	lang
chuo	ch'o	guang	kuang	lao	lao
ci	tz'ŭ(ts'ŭ)	gui	kui	le	lê, lo
cong	ts'ung	gun	kun	lei	lei
cou	ts'ou	guo	kuo	leng	lêng
cu	ts'u	ha	ha	li	li
cuan	ts'uan	hai	hai	lia	lia
cui	ts'ui	han	han	lian	lien
cun	ts'un	hang	hang	liang	liang
cuo	ts'o	hao	hao	liao	liao
da	ta	he	hê, ho	lie	lieh
dai	tai	hei	hei	lin	lin
dan	tan	hen	hên	ling	ling

PIN YIN	WADE-GILES	PIN YIN	WADE-GILES	PIN YIN	WADE-GILES
liu	liu	qiang	ch'iang	tui	t'ui
long	lung	qiao	ch'iao	tun	t'un
lou	lou	qie	ch'ieh	tuo	t'o
lu	lu	qin	ch'in	wa	wa
lü	lü	qing	ch'ing	wai	wai
luan	luan	qiong	ch'iung	wan	wan
lüe	lüeh	qiu	ch'iu	wang	wang
	lüo	qu	ch'ü	wei	wei
	lio	quan	ch'üan	wen	wên
lun	lun	que	ch'üeh	weng	wêng
luo	luo		ch'üo	wo	wo
ma	ma	qun	ch'ün	wu	wu
mai	mai	ran	jan	xi	hsi
man	man	rang	jang	xia	hsia
mang	mang	rao	jao	xian	hsien
mao	mao	re	jê	xiang	hsiang
me	me	ren	jên	xiao	hsiao
mei	mei	reng	jêng	xie	hsieh
men	mên	ri	jih	xin	hsin
meng	mêng	rong	jung	xing	hsing
mi	mi	rou	jou	xiong	hsiung
mian	mien	ru	ju	xiu	hsiu
miao	miao	ruan	juan	xu	hsü
mie	mieh	rui	jui	xuan	hsüan
min	min	run	jun	xue	hsüeh, hsüo
ming	ming	ruo	jo	xun	hsün
miu	miu	sa	sa	ya	ya
mo	mo	sai	sai	yan	yen
mou	mou	san	san	yang	yang
mu	mu	sang	sang	yao	yao
na	na	sao	sao	ye	yeh
nai	nai	se	sê	yi	yi
nan	nan	sen	sên	yin	yin
nang	nang	seng	sêng	ying	ying
nao	nao	sha	sha	yo	yo
ne	nê	shai	shai	yong	yung
nei	nei	shan	shan	you	yu
nen	nên	shân	shen	yu	yü
neng	nêng	shang	shang	yuan	yüen
ni	ni	shao	shao	yue	yüeh
nian	nien	she	shê	yun	yün
niang	niang	shei	shei	za	tsa
niao	niao	shen	shên	zai	tsai
nie	nieh	sheng	shêng	zan	tsan
nin	nin	shi	shih	zang	tsang
ning	ning	shou	shou	zao	tsao
niu	niu	shu	shu	ze	tsê
nong	nung	shua	shua	zei	tsei
nou	nou	shuai	shuai	zen	tsên
nu	nu	shuan	shuan	zeng	tsêng
nü	nü	shuang	shuang	zha	cha
nuan	nuan	shui	shui	zhai	chai
nüe	nüeh	shun	shun	zhan	chan
	nüo	shuo	sho	zhang	chang
	nio	si	sŭ, szŭ, ssŭ	zhao	chao
nuo	no	song	sung	zhe	chê
o	o	sou	sou	zhei	chei
ou	ou	su	su	zhen	chên
pa	p'a	suan	suan	zheng	chêng
pai	p'ai	sui	sui	zhi	chih
pan	p'an	sun	sun	zhong	chung
pang	p'ang	suo	so	zhou	chou
pao	p'ao	ta	t'a	zhu	chu
pei	p'ei	tai	t'ai	zhua	chua
pen	p'ên	tan	t'an	zhuai	chuai
peng	p'êng	tang	t'ang	zhuan	chuan
pi	p'i	tao	t'ao	zhuang	chuang
pian	p'ien	te	t'ê	zhui	chui
piao	p'iao	teng	t'êng	zhun	chun
pie	p'ieh	ti	t'i	zhuo	cho
pin	p'in	tian	t'ien	zi	tzŭ(tsŭ)
ping	p'ing	tiao	t'iao	zong	tsung
po	p'o	tie	t'ieh	zou	tsou
pou	p'ou	ting	t'ing	zu	tsu
pu	p'u	tong	t'ung	zuan	tsuan
qi	ch'i	tou	t'ou	zui	tsui
qia	ch'ia	tu	t'u	zun	tsun
qian	ch'ien	tuan	t'uan	zuo	tso

Bibliography

WORKS OF GENERAL INTEREST

Granet M. *La Civilisation Chinoise*, Paris, 1929
Grousset R. *Histoire de la Chine*, Paris, 1947
Eberhard W. *Chinas Geschichte*, Berne, 1948
Creel H. G. *Studies in Early Chinese Culture*, 1948
Tsui Chi. *Histoire de la Chine et de la Civilisation Chinoise*, Paris, 1949
Fitzgerald C. P. *China, a Short Cultural History*, London, 1954
Watson W. *China before the Han Dynasty*, New York, 1961
Corradini P. *La Cina*, Turin, 1969
Gernet J. *Le monde chinois*, Paris, 1972
The Cambridge History of China, Cambridge, 1979
Elisseeff D. and V. *La Civilisation de la Chine classique*, Paris, 1979

WORKS OF SPECIALIST INTEREST

Stein A. *The Thousand Buddhas: Ancient Buddhist Paintings from the Cave Temples of Tun-Huang on the Western Frontier of China*, London, 1921
Ashton L. *An Introduction to the Study of Chinese Sculpture*, London, 1924
Siren O. *Les Palais Impériaux de Pékin* (3 vols), Paris, 1926
Bagchi P. C. *Le canon buddhique en Chine*, Paris–Calcutta, 1927–1938
Siren O. *L'Architecture* (IV), Paris–Brussels, 1930
Boerschmann E. *Die Baukunst und Religiöse Kultur der Chinesen: Pagoden*, Berlin and Leipzig, 1931
Malone C. B. *History of the Peking Summer Palaces under the Ch'ing Dynasty*, Urbana, 1934
Kelling R. *Das Chinesische Wohnhaus*, Tokyo, 1935
Inn H., and Schao Chang Lu. *Chinese Houses and Gardens*, Honolulu, 1940
Boerschmann E. 'Pagoden im nördlichen China unter fremden Dynastien', in *Der Orient in Deutsche Forschung*, Leipzig, 1944, pp. 182–204
Silcock A. *Introduction to Chinese Art and History*, London, 1947
Ashton L., and Gray B. *Chinese Art*, London, 1947
Bachhofer L. *A Short History of Chinese Art*, London, 1947
Binyon L. *The Flight of the Dragon*, London, 1948
Fung Yu Lan. *A Short History of Chinese Philosophy*, Princeton, 1948
Siren O. *Gardens of China*, New York, 1949
Creel H. G. *Confucius, the Man and the Myth*, New York, 1949
Yang Lien-cheng. *Topics in Chinese History*, Cambridge, 1950
Grousset R. *La Chine et son art*, Paris, 1951
Buhot J. *Arts de la Chine*, Paris, 1951
Needham J. *Science and Civilisation in China*, Cambridge, 1954 (series of 7 volumes in course of publication)
Davidson J. L. *The Lotus Sutra in Chinese Art, a Study in Buddhist Art to the Year 1000*, New Haven, 1955
Sickman L., and Soper A. *The Art and Architecture of China*, Harmondsworth, 1956
Siren O. *Chinese Painting* (7 vols), New York, 1956–7
Willets W. *Chinese Art*, Harmondsworth, 1958
Gray B. *Buddhist Cave Paintings at Tun-Huang*, London, 1959
 Asčepkov E. A. *Architektura Kitaya, očerki*, Moscow, 1959
Cheng Te-k'un. *Archaeology in China*, Cambridge, 1959
Watson W. *Ancient Chinese Bronzes*, Rutland, 1962
Boyd A. *Chinese Architecture and Town Planning*, London, 1962
Boyd A. 'Chinese Architecture' in *World Architecture*, London, 1963
Wu N. I. *Chinese and Indian Architecture*, New York, 1963
Pirazzoli M., and T'serstevens. *Chine*, Fribourg, 1970
Takeshima T. *The Study of the Ying tsao fa shih, Chinese Book of Architectural Technique*, Tokyo, 1970
Maspero H. *Le Taoïsme et les religions chinoises*, Paris, 1971
Segalen V. *Chine, la grande statuaire*, Paris, 1972
Corradini P. *Confucio e il Confucianismo*, Fossano, 1973
Pisu R. *Qui Pechino*, Milan, 1976
Meyer J. F. *Peking as a Sacred City*, Taipei, 1976
Cheng F. *Mille ans de peinture chinoise*, Paris, 1980
Bussagli M. *Architettura orientale II*, Milan, 1981

Extracts from Chinese literature and from the memoirs of travellers and missionaries have been drawn (with the kind permission of authors and publishers where applicable) from the following works: G. Bertuccioli, *La letteratura cinese*, Sansoni Accademia, Florence–Milan, 1968; *Anthology of Chinese Literature* edited by Cyril Birch, New York, 1965, and Harmondsworth, 1967; H. A. Giles, *A History of Chinese Literature*, London, 1901, and Rutland and Tokyo, 1973; *Le trecento poesie T'ang* edited by M. Benedikter, Turin, 1961; P. Pasquale d'Elia, *Fonti Ricciani*, I; *Relazione delle cose più notabili scritte negli anni 1619, 1620, 1621 dalla Cina*; Matteo Ricci, *Commentari della Cina, 1583–1610*; Evert Ysbrand Ides, *Travels Over Land from Muscovy to China*, London, 1706. The quotations from Marco Polo's *Travels* are taken from the Elizabethan translation of John Frampton (1579), using the edition published in London in 1937.

The drawings on pages 84, 128, 129, 130 and 134 are taken from *Chinese Art* by W. Willets, London, 1958. The map on pages 60–61 was produced with the help of the Geographical Institute of the University of Genoa.

The illustration on page 22 has been reproduced by kind permission of the British Museum, London. The illustration on page 30 has been reproduced by kind permission of the Metropolitan Museum of Art, New York, and of the Cultural Relics Bureau, Peking (Photograph: Seth Joël).

Index of Names